Class Conflict in Chinese Socialism

STUDIES OF THE EAST ASIAN INSTITUTE
COLUMBIA UNIVERSITY

CLASS CONFLICT IN CHINESE SOCIALISM

RICHARD CURT KRAUS

New York   Columbia University Press   *1981*

Library of Congress Cataloging in Publication Data

Kraus, Richard Curt.
Class conflict in Chinese socialism.

(Studies of the East Asian Institute)
Includes bibliographical references and
index.
1. Social classes—China. 2. Social
conflict. 3. Social structure. 4. Communism—
China. I. Title. II. Series.
HN740.Z9S63 305.5'0951 81-7754
ISBN 0-231-05182-4   AACR2

Printed in the United States of America

Columbia University Press
New York   Guildford, Surrey

*Clothbound editions of Columbia University Press books are Smyth-sewn
and printed on permanent and durable acid-free paper.*

The East Asian Institute of Columbia University

The East Asian Institute of Columbia University was established in 1949 to prepare graduate students for careers dealing with East Asia, and to aid research and publication on East Asia during the modern period. The faculty of the Institute are grateful to the Ford Foundation and the Rockefeller Foundation for their financial assistance.

The Studies of the East Asian Institute were inaugurated in 1962 to bring to a wider public the results of significant new research on modern and contemporary East Asia.

Contents

Preface

In the course of its protracted struggle for power, the Chinese Communist Party developed a deep concern for social inequality, elaborating both programs and institutions to mobilize the support of the impoverished and oppressed against the wealthy classes which provided support for its enemies. This book explores the fate of this revolutionary commitment to class struggle in the generation since the establishment of the People's Republic of China in 1949.

Within socialist China, the interpretation of class conflict has been a question of bitter, sometimes violent controversy. Neither the Marxist classics nor the prior experience of the Soviet Union have provided decisive answers to such fundamental questions as when recently dispossessed ruling classes could be said no longer to exist; the nature of the relationship of workers, peasants, and intellectuals to the new socialist state; and how the officials of this state are related to the rest of society. The practical ramifications of such issues are so clearly important that their discussion has never been detached and academic, but rather has been embedded within serious political and social struggles over what kind of society China should be. To put the matter sharply, class analysis in China is an aspect of the class conflict it is intended to comprehend.

As an example, consider the awkward new assessment by the Communist Party of its former Chairman, Mao Zedong. In the view of his successors, who seek to borrow Mao's prestige while sanitizing his ideas, among the late Chairman's most bothersome errors was that he saw conflict among classes where it (and they) did not exist. From this class analysis, Mao concluded that an old revolutionary ought to advocate a radical program to limit the sources of privilege and to consolidate the material benefits available to the working masses. A contrary analysis, at one time entertained by Mao and still advanced by Deng Xiaoping and his circle, is that class conflict, save for a few noisy echoes, was put on its way out of China with the creation of socialist institutions in 1956. If indeed state control of productive assets assures a minor role for class conflict, then Mao's radical activism rested upon a false basis, and needlessly disrupted a society which already had settled the class issue.

I am keenly aware that my analysis does not always capture the subtlety of Chinese discussions of the question of class. Nor does my academic prose adequately represent either the grandeur or the sordidness of the struggles which I describe. Failures of insight and style, as well as any factual errors which may remain in the text, are my own, and should not be attributed to the institutions and individuals whose assistance I have enjoyed. These include Columbia University's East Asian Institute and Research Institute on International Change; the Universities Service Centre of Hong Kong; and the Department of Sociology, Center for Asian Studies, and Graduate College of the University of Illinois. Too many individuals have generously shared their experiences with me to be named here, but I am deeply grateful for information and suggestions offered by friends and colleagues from both China and the West. Among those who have read and commented upon various portions of this study are Thomas Bernstein, Steven Butts, Randall Edwards, Joel Glassman, Steven Levine, Patrick Maddox, Roberta Martin, Andrew Nathan, Michel Oksenberg, William Parish, James Reardon-Anderson, Susan Shirk, Dorothy Solinger, Anne Thurston, and Martin King Whyte.

I have rendered Chinese names and phrases in *pinyin* romanization throughout this book, except in those cases where I quote English-language publications which have used the older Wade-Giles romanization system.

Richard Curt Kraus

July 1981

Class Conflict in Chinese Socialism

CHAPTER ONE

Introduction: The Problem of Class in Socialist China

In 1965 in Beijing, Mao Zedong discussed the fate of revolutions with the visiting French Minister of Culture, AndreMalraux. According to Malraux, his host remarked that "Humanity left to its own devices does not necessarily reestablish capitalism . . . but it does reestablish inequality. The forces tending toward the creation of new classes are powerful." [1] Mao might have made his point still more forcefully: even when humanity has not been left to its own devices—and it has not been in China—inequality persists.

Although Chinese socialism has not eradicated inequality, it has altered the forms which it assumes. The most fundamental such alteration has been the restriction of private property, a success of the revolution which gives rise to an apparent paradox in contemporary Chinese society. Leaders of the Chinese Communist Party have frequently characterized their society as one rent by large-scale struggle among classes; yet the property relationships that underlie a conventional Marxist conception of class were essentially destroyed nearly three decades ago, as China socialized its economy. How, then, is one to make sense of the continued use of such terms as "bourgeois" and "landlord" in a society where such classes certainly cannot exist as we know them from capitalist experience?

One approach is to presume, as many students of China tacitly do, that the language of class in fact does not make much sense, that it serves primarily as a cloak for self-interest, or that its meaning is so abstruse that it can only arouse pedantic curiosity. [2] Such a view is encouraged by the vagueness of much discussion of class in the Chinese press, where concrete references to social structure are often lacking.

It is dubious, however, that a vocabulary employed so extensively as has been the language of class in China can be merely rhetorical in nature. This language, derived from the Marxist tradition but modified in its new context, became the principal medium for political discourse in the People's Republic. Political discussion is often far removed from social analysis, a phenomenon no doubt as true in China as in any other country. But where alternative terminologies are so often considered illegitimate, the language of class must serve as the vehicle for discussions of more serious significance.

Much of the difficulty in grasping the Chinese concept of class stems from the tumult within the society it is intended to analyze. Revolution, then rapid industrialization have compressed a broad range of radical social changes within a single generation. The problem is not that class is without meaning, but that it has come to bear multiple connotations, as competing forces in a rapidly changing society have endeavored to utilize the concept to buttress their own interests. The search for the meaning of class, then, must be made alongside an examination of the changes which have been made in China's social structure. Changing Chinese approaches to the class system of the People's Republic are themselves elements in the social conflict which they prescribe, illuminate, and obscure. Little progress in extending our comprehension either of Chinese social tensions or of systematic self-representations by the Chinese of their society is possible without appreciating the complex interaction of theories of class with the practice of social inequality in which these theories are embedded.

Thus our search must have three foci. It must perforce deal with the character of class relationships in socialist society, and with the adaptation of Marxist social theory to Chinese conditions. The combination of these two themes gives rise to a third: Mao Zedong's role as critic of inequality since liberation. In this introductory chapter, I will sketch the issues which these themes entail.

Class Conflict in a Socialist Society

Underlying this study is the assumption that the class analyses made by the Chinese of their own society warrant respectful attention. Since the founding of the People's Republic, outsiders have considered its society and politics through various classificatory schemes. The Chinese people have been broken down into elites and masses, divided into mobilizers and mobilized, and assigned to occupational groups and factions. They have been examined as modernizers, revolutionaries, totalitarians, bureaucrats, and as inheritors of ancient dynastic tradition. Although many of these approaches have enabled observers to organize information about contemporary China in an illuminating manner, there has been surprisingly little interest in understanding China in terms employed by the Chinese themselves. I do not claim that the Party's class theories offer a magic key which can unlock all the mysteries of social conflict in the People's Republic. I do argue that it seems prudent to add to our present arsenal of conceptual tools some of those which have been widely used by the subjects of our investigations.

It is easy to understand why this is not common practice. Liberal scholars, unaccustomed (and disinclined) to analyze their own societies in class terms, have turned to other concepts when they approach China. Marxists, who might be expected to be more comfortable with class-based interpretations, face other problems. Some have uncritically accepted official Chinese perspectives, forgetting that these are colored by the social conflicts which they describe. A more serious obstacle is the Marxist fixation upon private property, the absence of which poses serious difficulties for analysts used to asking who *owns* the means of production. Thus there is a need to recognize both that socialist classes must involve social relationships more complex than simple property ownership, and that Chinese interpretations may provide important clues, if not final answers, to the issue of class in the People's Republic.

It is easier to describe broadly the changes in China's class structure since liberation than to offer a simple formula for understanding class conflict in socialist society. The classes which were dominant before the revolution had based their power upon private property, which was severely restricted in what the Chinese call the "socialist transformation" of 1955–1956. In the countryside, land reform had earlier destroyed the foundation of the old landlord class; the subsequent collectivization of agriculture removed the possibility of the rise of a new group of landlords. Similarly, the socialization of private industry and commerce drastically constricted the economic basis of China's urban bourgeoisie. These reforms were reinforced by the sudden termination of Western imperialist influence, which had been supportive of the former ruling classes.

But as the old propertied classes were weakened, socialization and aggressive economic expansion contributed to the rise of other social groups. Socialist China's still embryonic social structure is characterized by a proud new status for a growing industrial proletariat, an obvious beneficiary of policies intended to raise China from poverty. However, 80 percent of the population is still peasant. Agricultural collectivization has altered the context in which peasants live and work, and while their economic position is still not high, both the rural emphasis in Chinese developmental strategy and the peasant contribution to the Communist victory have increased the peasantry's prominence in national affairs.

Much more controversial is the position of bureaucrats in the new social structure. The displacement of the old ruling classes has raised the autonomy and influence of bureaucrats, but their character as a social group remains ill-defined. From an organization of militant activists, leading revolution at the mass level, the Chinese Communist Party after liberation became a body of full-time salaried administrators, working within formal bureaucratic structures. This trend was intensified by the civil service scheme which was introduced to accompany the economic reforms of socialist transformation.[3] While tendencies toward the development of a clearly defined consciousness as a social group have no doubt been impeded by the lowly origin of many of China's new bureaucrats, the great fear of Maoists has been that these cadres will become a new elite group, pursuing its own narrow interests at the expense of workers and peasants, and amassing privileges to bequeath to its children.

Anxiety about the possible emergence of a powerful bureaucratic class is perhaps easily understandable in China, where the landed upper class of former dynasties organized its domination over the rest of society through an elaborately graded state bureaucracy. Entrance to this civil service was secured by successful participation in a national examination system which was only abolished in 1905—within the lifetimes of the leaders of the Communist revolution. Centuries of familiarity with bureaucratic hierarchy so colored Chinese cultural orientations toward social interaction that even popular conceptions of hell are filled with ranked officials and their red tape. Little wonder that contemporary revolutionaries entertain profound suspicions toward developments within the bureaucracy.

China's social structure is thus still a fluid one—both because the dust of revolution has not yet settled and because of the grand scale of economic construction which has been undertaken since liberation. Yet within this turbulence, the bureaucrats possess significant advantages which may well facilitate their consolidation as a new dominant class. Most obvious is the prior destruction of landed and business classes, which removed the two groups most typically at odds with bureaucratic power. Equally important, however, is the central role of the political apparatus in China's drive for industrialization, which adds collective control over the means of production to the powers of a group that has already destroyed its chief rivals.

To be sure, there have been vigorous efforts in China to prevent the rise of a new and privileged bureaucratic class. One approach has stressed ideological appeals, such as the cultivation of a "serve the people" mentality, consciously drawing upon egalitarian aspects of China's revolutionary heritage. Structural innovations have also been introduced, including both insitutions which force bureaucrats to share the life-styles and work experiences of ordinary citizens and repeated campaigns to open the bureaucracy to people of humble birth. However, the persistence of these efforts suggests less that a potential bureaucratic class has been dispersed than that its formation is viewed by many as a continuing threat. Although a single generation is too brief a period for the consolidation of a new class structure, in the years since 1949, China's bureaucrats have hesitantly emerged as a distinctive social group, gradually discovering their common interests and identity.

The rude statistics available in the West sustain such an impressionistic account of China's changing social structure. The number of industrial proprietors declined from 222,800 in 1952 to 132,000 in 1955, the eve of socialization.[4] The industrial work force increased from 3,004,000 in 1949 to 9,008,000 in 1957.[5] But the rate of growth for bureaucrats was more rapid still. The Guomindang government employed about 2,000,000 state functionaries in 1948; by 1958 there were almost 8,000,000 state cadres in China.[6] For the city of Shanghai, where total employment between 1949 and 1957 increased by 1.2 percent per year, workers and staff in factories grew by 5.8 percent annually, while health and government workers increased at an annual rate of 16 percent.[7]

From another perspective, bureaucrats controlled less than 10 percent of China's gross national product before 1949; by 1972 this figure had risen to 30 percent.[8] This change reflects the intensity of the Communist's attack upon private property, which today has a very limited role in the economy. Three levels of ownership are distinguished in China: state ownership (by the whole people), collective ownership (by units of producers, such as production brigades or handicraft cooperatives), and individual private ownership. The relative importance of each of these in 1973 was as follows:[9]

	State	Collective	Private
Industry (value of industrial output)	86%	14%	0%
Agriculture (share of production)	1–9%	over 90%	1–9%
Commerce (share of retail sales)	92.5%	7.3%	0.2%

Private ownership had disappeared in industry, formed a minute share of commercial activity, and was significant only in the private plots of peasants (which were in fact owned by the collective and assigned temporarily to peasant families).

None of these data, however, will support the bald assertion that the People's Republic is clearly dominated today by a new class of bureaucrats. A more ambiguous assessment may be of greater heuristic value: the bureaucrats are a class in formation, one historical possibility embedded in China's present which may be realized in succeeding generations.

I do not intend to suggest that the Chinese revolution overthrew one set of ruling classes merely to supplant them with a new one, that the revolution was not worth its enormous costs of violence and suffering. To the contrary, the broad range of social reforms introduced in the People's Republic have made possible better lives for the mass of the Chinese population and a new respect for China as a nation. The achievements of the Chinese revolution certainly have not been those of the bureaucrats alone, but their central place in organizing social change evokes admiration for their administrative skill and sense of public service. Although China's officials will be described in sometimes negative language in the pages below, I have no desire to portray them as the simple villains of a drama in which their collective role has often revealed a heroic aspect.[10]

Nonetheless, the structure of conflict in China has been altered, with the former dominance of propertied classes replaced by competition among groups within a bureaucratized society. In such a context it is not surprising that bureaucrats, who collectively control the use of China's productive assets, often prevail. What is worthy of greater attention is the fact that the emergence of a bureaucratic class has been resisted most strenuously by some of its own members.

The situation is one of great ambiguity: do socialist bureaucrats form a class, and if so, on what basis?[11] These are not simply the questions of external analysis, but are issues of intense political debate within China as well. There, the Party has endeavored to apply its own Marxist tradition of class analysis to the problem. But the fit has not been a neat one; many of the Party's intellectual assumptions were undermined by socialist transformation—most notably the practice of distinguishing class membership according to individual property ownership. The effort to fashion new answers to the problem of class has itself been caught up in the conflicts under analysis. The stakes have been high, as the power to define classes carries vital implications for the allocation of scarce resources among competing groups in the society.

Central to the argument which follows is the proposition that there have been two broad types of class conflict in China since liberation. The first has been a struggle among economic groups identifiable by the classically Marxist test of the ownership of the means of production. Class conflict organized around the axis of private property was particularly fierce in the early years of the People's Republic; since the socialist reforms of 1956, this conflict has become one between *former* owners and nonowners, and has been transferred largely (but not exclusively) from the economic realm to the level of ideological and institutional influence.

The second type of class conflict reflects the new social organization introduced by the reforms of the Communist Party, with a diminished place for market mechanisms and a vastly increased significance for bureaucratized social relationships. Here, conflicts of material interest have divided people in ways not directly tied to individual ownership of private property. Although inequalities grounded in the new class tensions of socialist society have increasingly superseded those arising from the former private property system, the persistence of vestiges of the latter has obscured recognition of the former.

The Sinification of Marxism

Since the Chinese Communist Party has consciously applied to Chinese society an analysis drawn from the Marxist tradition, a study of the changing significance of class must also be a detailed examination of the sinification of Marxism. Beyond the pioneering works of Meisner, Schram, and Schwartz,[12] this process is perhaps more talked about than studied. It is perhaps time to move beyond the correct but no longer exciting proposition that the Chinese Communists are nationalists as well as Marxists, and look closely at what happens to a central concept of Marx when it is applied in a Chinese context. Two issues are of special interest: voluntarism and the persistence of class conflict after the socialization of private property.

The conventional wisdom concerning the Chinese adaptation of Marxism holds that Marx's original economic determinism has been altered by a strong emphasis upon consciousness, or revolutionary will, which can overcome "objective" economic conditions. This voluntarism is often treated "as a Leninist sin: thou shall not give the forces of history a push,"[13] which has been carried to new lengths of heterodoxy by the Chinese Communist Party. But recent scholarship on Marx has exposed as false the conception of Marx as a theorist of the one-way effects of economic base upon superstructure. Instead, Marx saw base and superstructure as dialectically interrelated in a subtly changing unity.[14] This recognition has only begun to enter the study of Chinese ideology.[15]

It is nonetheless true that political movements calling themselves Marxist have differed in their interpretations of Marx's theory, some (including Marx's own German Social Democrats) reading Marx as the rigid determinist who has become the liberal stereotype.[16] Chinese Marxism has devoted greater attention to superstructural issues, from the Party's long-established tradition of raising consciousness through political study to the mass mobilization of the Great Leap Forward. It is important to remember, however, that the realm of superstructure in Marxist theory encompasses not only *ideas,* as Western students of China have long appreciated, but also *institutions,* which too often have been ignored. Above all, Chinese Marxism has followed Lenin in its concern for the state as the central institution by which coercion is organized in society, and in which are embedded many of the mysteries of class conflict. The issue, then, is not one of Chinese turning Marxism into a voluntaristic theory, but rather the specific ways in which Marx's analysis of superstructural phenomena have been received in China.

Voluntarism's mark on the Party's class theory before liberation was an insistence that persons could overcome the ideology of the class of their social origin.[17] More concretely, formal economic criteria for class membership were sometimes supplemented by political standards. To a considerable extent, this practice was a function of the small number of proletarians in the Communist movement. To insist upon firm working-class credentials in a peasant society would have been to deny the possibility of a mass revolutionary party.[18]

Since the relationship of individuals to the means of production formed the basis for the Party's earlier class differentiation, has the socialization of private property reinforced the voluntarist heritage? After socialist transformation, Mao and other leaders so often stressed the primacy of politics—which must be "in command" because it was "the lifeline of all economic work"—that class took on an increasingly obvious political color. This trend reinforced earlier Party traditions of criticism, self-criticism, and the reform of mistaken ideas through participation in a larger consciousness.[19] The problem of a political conception of class was that its standards could only be loosely defined, thus encouraging the casual use of class analysis to stigmatize any political rival. As we will see in later chapters, an extremely politicized class analysis encouraged much persecution of individuals during the Cultural Revolution.

Yet there has been a strikingly different concurrent development in Chinese class theory since socialist transformation: a reluctance to allow modification of the presocialist class designations of former class enemies. Indeed, there have been strong tendencies to regard the former relationship to the means of production as inheritable, so that the children of old landlords, rich peasants, and capitalists have at times been treated as a caste within Chinese society. The fact that one cannot simply proclaim that a bad class background has been willed away suggests that voluntarism in Chinese Marxism has important limits.

The Party thus has entertained contradictory notions—that class position can be changed with heightened consciousness, and that class is a question of heritage. Their interplay has been an issue only because of another hallmark of Chinese Marxism: the notion that class conflict continues after socialization of the means of production. At one time Stalin had argued that class contradictions sharpened after socialism, but Stalin had also argued against what he called "petty bourgeois equality-mongering" as the range of inequalities in Soviet society was systematically extended. To the contrary, the Chinese theory of socialist class conflict has been associated with radical initiatives to end special privileges and to spread the benefits of the revolution more evenly throughout Chinese society. This approach was all the more noteworthy because it appeared at a time (the early 1960s) when Soviet doctrine moved furthest away from admitting the existence of class conflict, arguing that the Soviet Union had become a harmonious "state of the whole people."

But it has not been easy for Chinese Marxists to elaborate the notion that class contradictions exist between leaders and ordinary citizens in socialist society. Willingness to grapple with these new contradictions has required intellectual boldness, but the risks of political conflict have tempered that boldness with caution. Fear of providing Chinese and Soviet critics with ammunition for accusations of heresy certainly made Maoists reluctant to jettison the older Marxist fixation upon private property relationships. And the equally well-established Marxist inclination to regard bureaucrats as the servants of some other class muddied comprehension of the new contradiction. Ascendant classes often base their claims to privilege in universalistic language, thereby denying the existence of the class differences which they enjoy. The traditional Marxist treatment of bureaucrats has permitted Chinese cadres to do the same, presenting themselves simply as the vanguard of the proletariat. It is easy to understand the appeal of this aspect of Marxism to many postrevolutionary officials.

Maoist interpretations of the changes in China's social structure have assumed the language of past class analyses, with new connotations attached to old and familiar terms. Innovations in the theory of class have been presented as venerable Leninist tradition, with elaborate citations from Marxist classics to mask the new as the old. Bureaucratic resistance to such novelty has meant that the forms taken by the Maoist class theory have been influenced strongly by calculations of the political movement. This suggests that the broader process by which Marxism has been turned from a foreign into a native Chinese theory must be understood in terms of the conflicts in which it has been used as a weapon.

Mao Zedong as Critic of Socialist Inequality

The tentative appearance of a new bureaucratic class and the adaptation of Marxism to resist this trend are linked through the third focus of this study, Mao Zedong's role as a theorist of class in socialist society. Mao's stature as a revolutionary strategist and as a political leader in the People's Republic have both long been recognized. Less fully appreciated, however, is Mao's activity as social thinker since liberation.

The growth of bureaucratic power and privilege presented Mao with one of his greatest intellectual and political challenges (the two are impossible to separate in this man's career), no less significant than the preliberation task of adapting Marxism to the needs of rural revolution. No ruling Communist Party has ever come to grips with this problem, and thus Mao's efforts, often made against the wishes of old revolutionary comrades, are especially noteworthy. Now that Mao is dead, it is appropriate to review the evolution of his thoughts on class conflict in socialist China, both to comprehend his major theoretical interest after liberation and to understand more clearly some of the issues which underlie the social conflict which has followed his death.[20] This task is especially timely now, when the continuing relevance of Mao's radical heritage is being challenged by his political successors in Beijing, as well as by many Westerners interested in Chinese affairs. While the former undoubtedly will use Mao's memory in accord with their immediate political needs, perhaps I may persuade some of the latter to pause before judging his ideas now merely to be curios from China's recent but quite dead past.

Mao's relationship to China's bureaucrats was complex. One can easily compile a long series of antibureaucratic statements by Mao, whose denunciations of red tape, pomposity, and formalism began early in the revolution and continued until his death.[21] Despite the consistency of Mao's distaste for bureaucratic ways, one cannot fairly portray him merely as the adversary of the bureaucrats. For Mao was not only the enemy of bureaucratic abuse, he was also China's leading cadre for over a quarter of a century. As such, Mao was the patron of the industrious official, the innovator of the organizational techniques which continue to govern the bureaucracy after his death. If Mao was clearly identified with opposition to bureaucratic faults, he was no less obviously associated with the proud successes of a social group which he helped to fashion.

Mao was not necessarily schizophrenic to feel alternate pride and contempt for the cadres he led. For Mao sought to nurture a dedicated band of leaders, closely bound in life-style and emotion to the populace of China. Speaking in 1937 on "The Question of Cadres," Mao demanded:

> They must be cadres and leaders versed in Marxism-Leninism, politically far-sighted, competent in work, full of the spirit of self-sacrifice, capable of tackling problems on their own, steadfast in the midst of difficulties and loyal and devoted in serving the nation, the class and the Party. . . . Such cadres and leaders must be free from selfishness, from individualistic heroism, ostentation, sloth, passivity, and sectarian arrogance, and they must be selfless national and class heroes. . . .[22]

Mao set high standards for cadre behavior, and the gradual change of antibureaucratic sentiment into "class" analysis was rooted in his disappointment with many cadres after the victory of the revolution.

The critical year for this study is not 1949, when Communist power was established throughout China, but 1956, when socialist institutions were introduced on a wide scale. In that year of socialist transformation, China's leaders were united in an optimistic assessment of class conflict in their country. China had succeeded in overthrowing the old ruling classes, in casting out the imperialist powers, in rebuilding a war-ravaged economy, in establishing an institutional basis for socialist construction, and in apparently forging a new unity among the Chinese people. All these factors contributed to a hopeful mood in which large-scale social conflict seemed less prominent than at any time in the Party's memory. This mood was strongly reinforced by the rising influence of the Soviet Union, whose Communist Party argued that antagonistic class conflict did not arise under socialism.[23] In the course of the revolution, the Party in China had developed an elaborate analysis of classes, including a system by which the class of each individual was identified and recorded. In the optimistic year of 1956, it seemed as if class were simply a matter of these leftover presocialist designations, the significance of which had already been gravely undermined as private property ceased to be an adequate guide to primary social divisions in the populace.

The notion that the class issue had been largely resolved by the introduction of socialism contained a fundamental assumption about the Chinese revolution: the struggle had ended with liberation, land reform, and socialist transformation, when the former exploiters were relegated to inferior positions with respect to those whom they had formerly oppressed. Justice had been done, and the world had been righted. This was and is a static view of the revolution, in which the major political task of the present is to prevent a capitalist-feudal restoration in which the former exploiters and their children might usurp the fruits of victory from the worker-peasant masses.

Mao Zedong shared this deep concern toward the defeated enemy, but ultimately was unwilling to accept a conception of class in which the revolution was something to be preserved rather than continued. Even in 1956, when Mao shared with other leaders the feeling that class conflict was diminishing in China, he was busy applying his theory of contradictions to socialist society. Less remarkable for its originality than for the consistency with which Mao applied it, the theory of contradictions presumes that progress results from the dialectical resolution of social tensions, and that political leadership can identify and tap key points of friction in society, thus serving as midwife to the birth of new social forms.[24]

From the early days of Mao's participation in the revolution he had visualized these social tensions through the principal medium of a property-linked concept of class, in the tradition of Marx and Lenin. When socialist transformation weakened the foundations of that concept, Mao maintained his commitment to a broader vision of social conflict in his celebrated speech, "On the Correct Handling of Contradictions Among the People." In this speech, class categories played a much diminished role in the Chairman's analysis, but the dialectical unwinding of social tensions remained constant.[25]

This outlook, dynamic as well as dialectical, could not long coexist comfortably with a notion of class which had become frozen in time, a relic of the revolution. But Mao's sensitivity to contradictions did not generate mere armchair speculation about the character of class in socialist China. Instead, his rethinking of class was shaped by the exigencies of political struggle.

Three particular episodes were critical in leading him to elaborate a new conception of class conflict.[26] Harsh criticism of the Party by the former bourgeoisie during the Hundred Flowers Movement in early 1957 convinced him that the influence of the former exploiting classes did not end with socialization, that class conflict was a long-term phenomenon. Equally harsh criticism within the Party of Mao's economic policies, especially the radical mass mobilization of the Great Leap Forward in 1958, persuaded him that even veteran Party leaders with exemplary class backgrounds could oppose socialism. And Soviet mockery of efforts to discover a distinctively Chinese road to socialism convinced Mao and his colleagues that revisionism could come to power in a socialist state. If the Soviet leadership could oppose revolutionary policies, could not also China's? For the first time it appeared that there was a serious possibility that the Chinese revolution might be overturned from within.

Thus, after a decade of Communist rule, Mao found his policies under both internal and external attack. Analytically, the property-bound theory of class conflict which the Party had used to secure victory was insufficient to explain these events. On the defensive in politics, and in need of a theory by which to relate this political struggle to China's changing social structure, Mao's response was to reconsider the nature of class conflict in socialism.

A major aspect of Mao's program for regaining power lost after the Great Leap Forward was to utilize in a highly conscious manner the old appeals of class conflict which had served so well in the years before liberation. During the civil war class struggle had unified diverse Communists beneath Mao's banner, a process which Mao hoped to recapture. But it was not to be so simple, for the intervening changes made by the Communist Party in the organization of society meant that the old appeals to class had to be refashioned for use in a new environment. This procedure was approached cautiously but with increasing determination as Mao discovered that many of his former allies had become adversaries who now seemed to the Chairman uninterested in continuing the revolution which they had once waged together.

The first phase of the Maoist reanalysis of class had begun with the recognition that the old class enemies still were not resigned to socialism, from which Mao concluded that socialism was characterized by the persistence of class conflict. A second and more controversial phase contained the notion that the success of the revolution was imperiled not only by former exploiting classes, but also by a new kind of class enemy, one specific to socialism: a group of fat and contented bureaucrats, happy to enjoy the privileges of the society which they administered. These were the "revisionists," "new bourgeois elements," and "capitalist roaders" who were the chief targets of Maoist criticism.

As Mao and his associates searched for ways by which this new and unpropertied "bourgeoisie" might be identified, attention was shifted away from the old system of property based class designations. The new standard chosen was political behavior. The central question was no longer to what class one belonged in a narrow, juridical sense, but rather what class was served by one's conduct.

Implicit in this new approach to class was a more dynamic orientation toward a continuing revolutionary process. The fundamental division of society, Mao recognized, was now centered around the socialist institutions which had been created after liberation. As old classes were defeated, new class enemies emerged from the ranks of the victors. Liberation was not enough; inequality and injustice persisted, and further efforts at redistribution were necessary to prevent a revisionist abortion of the revolution.

A central theoretical issue became the relationship between the old class contradictions and the new ones. Mao's analysis suggested that the persistence, in socialist society, of superstructural remnants of bourgeois influence helped lead cadres, workers, and peasants into the arms of the old exploiters. An important aspect of the new theory of class, then, became the notion of "cultural revolution": transformation of the economic base alone was insufficient; only when China possessed truly proletarian culture and institutions could its socialism be secure. In the early 1960s this corollary of the new theory of class was manifest in a series of campaigns to study contemporary heroes who had resisted the bourgeois influences in their environment. In 1966, however, a more explicit kind of Cultural Revolution was initiated, backed by more forceful measures than emulation campaigns.

But Mao's adversaries within the Party discovered that they

could deflect criticism by interpreting class conflict one-sidedly in terms of past property relationships, directing attention away from the behavioral component of the new analysis. In this way, persons of good class designation were said to possess a "natural redness" early in the Cultural Revolution, as cadres under fire protected themselves by attacking former landlords, capitalists, and their children.

The Cultural Revolution overcame much resistance to Maoist social reforms. At the same time, anti-Maoist cadres were deprived of the ideological weapon of "natural redness." Maoists successfully insisted that when the two standards of behavior and class designation were at odds, greater weight must be placed upon behavior. In practice, however, persons from unsavory class backgrounds continued to be the objects of special political attention, frequently serving as scapegoats for conservative officials.

From the experience of the Cultural Revolution, Mao and his colleagues learned that the reestablishment of a doctrine of class struggle was not in itself sufficient to inhibit the rise of a new bureaucratic class intent on pursuing elitist policies. Class conflict in socialist China was an ambiguous weapon, one which could be used by conservatives to legitimize the status quo as easily as by radicals to inspire new revolutionary efforts. But it was only in the course of political conflict that Mao discovered the conservative connotation which might be attached to his emerging reanalysis of class.

Perhaps because of disappointments with the results of the Cultural Revolution, Mao initiated a third phase in his reanalysis of class shortly before his death. The first phase had focused attention on the old class contradictions of property, while the second phase added to these a concern for a new kind of class opposition. This most recent, most tentative, and most radical step in the refurbishing of the concept of class conflict was an effort to isolate more accurately the social basis of the "new bourgeoisie," with diminished attention to the capitalists and landlords of yesterday.

A campaign to study the dictatorship of the proletariat in 1975 and the Antirightist Campaign in 1976 provided the occasion for Maoists to argue in public for the first time that new exploiting groups found their strength precisely in the institutional structures which the revolution had established in order to remake society. For built into the social organization of the People's Republic of China were structural inequalities introduced before liberation but perpetuated unavoidably in socialist society. The "bourgeois right" to inequality found its ultimate expression in the state apparatus through which that right was enforced, and although inequality had to be restricted if China was to advance toward communism, the new bourgeoisie would prefer to extend it. Although this final Maoist interpretation of class was expressed in language which was sometimes arcane, its logic was revolutionary: the workers and peasants who constituted the majority of the population were in a relationship of class conflict with the bureaucrats who formulated policies affecting their lives. In 1976, the year of his death, Mao was quoted as saying of China's cadres:

> With the socialist revolution they themselves come under fire. At the time of the cooperative transformation of agriculture there were people in the Party who opposed it, and when it comes to criticizing bourgeois right, they resent it. You are making the socialist revolution, and yet don't know where the bourgeoisie is. It is right in the Communist Party—those in power taking the capitalist road. The capitalist-roaders are still on the capitalist road.[27]

The notion that Marx's theory of class provides an inadequate basis for understanding patterns of inequality in socialist society was certainly not new with Mao Zedong. Even within the Marxist tradition there have been others who have analyzed the rise of bureaucratic groups within socialist society in class terms—one thinks immediately of Trotsky and of Milovan Djilas as Mao's precursors. What makes the Maoist effort distinctive is not that it is a better analysis (although in some respects it is), but that it was the product of a Marxist in power. Earlier Marxist attempts to achieve a class-oriented critique of socialism have been offered by defeated politicians, arguing from resentful impuissance. It is the political strength which undergirded the Maoist perspective that gives this analysis special interest. Rather than observe the transfiguration of Marxist class theory into a device for legitimizing the new socialist order, Mao refashioned the concept of class into a tool with which to contest the accretion of privilege by a new class of dominant bureaucrats.

As a theoretical enterprise, this final Maoist effort added needed rigor to the search for the source of class tensions in socialist China. But as a practical political measure, the approach could not help alienating many of the officials whose interests it sought to identify and limit. Soon after Mao's death in 1976, those of his associates who were most closely associated with the propagation of this theory (the so-called "Gang of Four") were purged and accused of distorting the Chairman's understanding of class. Since Mao's death, the discussion of class conflict has followed a course much less menacing to those who occupy favored positions in the new social hierarchy of China.

At the end of 1955, as socialist institutions were being introduced into China, Mao likened the event to "discovering a new continent."[28] As Mao attempted to chart this continent, however, he discovered that there were many among his Party comrades who did not wish all its features to be revealed. If socialism is a new continent, it is a land-mass still in formation, and Mao's theory demanded constant attention to keep it in touch with the changing social structure it needed to analyze. For the classes in socialist China were not sharply delineated, and "new bourgeois elements" were discovered through ongoing political struggle, not through dispassionate reflection. The novelty of both the situation and the analysis means that the Maoist revival of class cannot be dismissed as a mere romantic effort to recapture the great revolution. It was a new endeavor, designed to cope with the tensions presented by a distinctively socialist society.[29]

The Communist Party's analysis of the classes of Chinese society was the basis for a broad series of structural reforms which ultimately rendered that analysis obsolete. But social change proved more rapid than the Party's ability to update its analysis, and in directions which weakened its enthusiasm for doing so.[30]

The first generation of socialist China has been a troublesome time for dispassionate social analysis. In such an atmosphere, social theories have been political weapons, and the definition of social categories, which amuses academic sociologists in the West, has become at once the medium and the object of class conflict. For if a particular way of viewing social structure is apt to tilt future perceptions and encourage certain consequences over others, social categories cannot be said to be neutral or indifferent. In the People's Republic, alternative conceptions of class have been used to promote conflicting visions of what China is and should become; the conflict over class conflict is thus a subtle one, in which contrasting images have been backed by social forces competing to control the definition of China's social reality.

CHAPTER TWO

Two Models of Social Stratification

Taking the socialist transformation of 1955–1956 as a dividing point, two phases in China's changing postliberation class structure may be distinguished. In the first of these, the property-based classes against which the Communist Party had waged revolution were still active, although progressively restricted until the institution of socialist reforms undermined their material bases. The workers and peasants upon whose support the Party depended could similarly be distinguished by their varied relationships to the means of production. The second phase, which has continued from 1956 through the present, has been characterized by a restructuring of social relationships on a new and more bureaucratic foundation, following the collapse of landlord and capitalist authority. Although this process is far from complete, distinctions of political (rather than economic) power have increasingly become the axis around which social groups may be identified. The bureaucrats ascendant after 1956 may be viewed as a presumptive leading class, still not fully self-conscious of its social position but separated in power and life-style from the worker and peasant majority of the population.

Associated with these two patterns of class relationships have been two important official economic hierarchies: a stratification by class category, established in the years prior to socialization, and a stratification by occupational rank which has taken form since socialist transformation. These two models of stratification are abstractions, and cannot capture the rich complexity of social inequality in the People's Republic. Nonetheless, it is necessary to consider these two models of stratification in some detail in order to disentangle the web of class conflict in socialist China. In the process, it is important to make a sharp distinction between class and stratification.

Stratification by Class Designation

One lesson of the Communist Party's protracted revolutionary struggle was a sensitivity to the shifting contradictions among the classes of Chinese society. From the outset, the Party's interest in class analysis was strategic, not academic. Mao's 1926 essay, the "Analysis of the Classes in Chinese Society," opens with the questions which Maoist class analysis has pursued ever since: "Who are our enemies? Who are our friends?"[1] In order to reach someday the classless society of Marx's communist future, the Party first had to specify the class relationships of the present. Only in this way could potential popular support be identified and mobilized, the enemy classes be isolated, and the wavering intermediate classes be won over to the side of revolution. The Party's early position as a minority under sustained attack by numerically superior opponents dictated a concern for class analysis in order to maximize its potential support. By the time of liberation, the Party had developed a sophisticated understanding of fluctuating configurations of class alignment as it skillfully worked its way through United Front politics against a series of successfully vanquished enemies.[2]

By the time of liberation in 1949, the abstraction of class had acquired a special concreteness as the Party implemented a series of broad social reforms. As an adjunct to policies such as land reform, in which it was necessary to identify those persons who should receive benefits and those who should lose them, the Party found it necessary to specify the class membership of individual Chinese. Building upon earlier rural policies, the Party applied a complex system of over sixty class designations[3] in a series of sometimes violent campaigns (see the appendix).

These class designations ranged from categories which were clearly bad, such as capitalist and landlord, through the intermediate designations of petty bourgeoisie and middle peasant, to the workers and poor peasants in whose name the revolution had been made. In the period in which the designations were assigned, they provided a basis for consensus within the Party about the meaning of class: a person's class was a matter of record, the officially determined class designation. Prior to liberation, in areas under Communist control, detailed investigations were carried out in order to identify each person's class membership.

The definition of class which the Party employed is Lenin's:

> Classes are large groups of people which differ from each other by the place they occupy in a historically determined system of social production, by their relation (in most cases fixed and formulated in law) to the means of production, by their role in the social organization of labor, and, consequently, by the dimensions and mode of acquiring the share of social wealth of which they dispose. Classes are groups of people one of which can appropriate the labor of another owing to the different places they occupy in a definite system of social economy.[4]

The class categories associated with this Marxist conception had been derived from the experience of nineteenth-century Europe, and there was a problem in fitting them to a society which was neither capitalist nor industrial. From a European perspective, Chinese Marxists had a surfeit of peasants in their Party, and some way had to be found by the Chinese to explain how these peasants could be the leading force in a revolutionary Marxist movement.

One solution was to incorporate political and attitudinal considerations into the calculation of class position, a trend which complemented the Party's traditions of distinguishing class standpoint from class origin, and of emphasizing rectification and thought reform as ways in which persons can acquire ideologies not characteristic of their class of origin. The intellectual problem of how to accommodate revolutionaries of nonproletarian origin (and counterrevolutionaries from the working class) is symbolized by the figure of Marx. If Marx was not somehow a proletarian, how could Marxism be a revolutionary theory? The same point applied to many of the Party's leaders, including the rich peasant's son, Mao Zedong.[5]

This development was also a response to the difficulty of making specific those social relationships which Marx had considered to be abstract in nature. A Russian revolutionary had earlier addressed this problem:

> In an analysis of the "abstract type" of society, i.e., any social form in its purest state, we are dealing almost exclusively with its basic classes; but when we take up the concrete reality, we of course find

ourselves faced with the motley picture with all its social-economic types and relations.[6]

But the voluntarist strain in Chinese class identification should not be overemphasized.[7] As the Party faced China's motley picture of social-economic types, it relied upon the relationship to the means of production as the basic test for class membership. And as the territory under Communist administration expanded in the years immediately prior to liberation, the Party began a systematic classification of the populace into property-based class categories, a process which was not completed until the early 1950s.[8]

Ordinary Chinese were unfamiliar with Marxist terminology, and even many cadres had but a rudimentary grasp of the language of class analysis. Thus after liberation many articles appeared in the Chinese press which described the structure of Chinese society in Marxist categories, enumerating the various classes so that all persons might comprehend the significance of their new class designations.[9]

Although such articles were part of a larger effort to acquaint Chinese with Marxism-Leninism, discussions of class often seemed to be linked to Chinese society in a particularly concrete way. Mao's 1926 "Analysis of the Classes in Chinese Society" was reprinted, along with many commentaries on how to study this opening work in the new first volume of Mao's selected writings.[10] One of the commentators summed up the mood of the time with the blunt observation that discussing classes with reference to foreign books instead of Chinese characteristics was worth less than dog shit.[11]

For purposes of discussion, the system of class designations may be divided into sets, according to the different types of economy, or modes of production, which characterized preliberation China. By far the most important of these are what the Chinese called the "semifeudal" class relationships of the countryside and the capitalist relations of urban centers.

Since the revolution led by the Communist Party was based in the rural areas, the semifeudal set of class designations was more elaborate than others. The differentiation of rural classes was complex, both because of the wide range of social relationships which they encompassed and because of the Party's extended experience with them, which heightened sensitivity to rather subtle distinctions in class position. The most basic rural class designations were generally names of strata within classes, including hired agricultural laborer, poor peasant, middle peasant, well-to-do middle pleasant, rich peasant, and landlord. The varieties of landlord are particularly impressive, including enlightened, bankrupt, tyrannical, reactionary, hidden, and overseas Chinese landlords.

Rural class designations were fixed in the course of land reform.[12] Before land could be confiscated and redistributed on a more equitable basis, local cadres had to determine from whom it should be taken and to whom it should be given. Land reform was thus the primary goal, to which the identification of class membership was ancillary. It is doubtful that the participants in this campaign could have imagined the long-range significance of the designations, but such knowledge could not have made the conflict over land reform any more severe.

Because the issues at stake were so great—one's livelihood and relations with fellow villagers—and because of Party's desire to employ the land reform campaign to mobilize the peasantry in the Communist cause, the process of designating class membership became a rather formal one. Outside work teams were sent to villages to lead land reform; to assist them in the differentiation of classes, the Party published a guide with definitions of the various categories.[13]

These definitions were often quite specific, with such details as the proportion of income derived from exploitation which distinguished rich peasants from well-to-do middle peasants, or the number of years of exploitation which were necessary to warrant classification as a landlord. To these definitions were added even more precise explanations and illustrations to assist cadres and the masses in their decisions. These were particularly important in resolving ambiguous cases, such as landlords who had married poor peasants or members of the Red Army who had rich peasant families. The standards required calculation of labor and of exploitation in order to put flesh on Lenin's definition of class, although considerations of political stance (as in the case of revolutionary soldiers with rich peasant fathers) were also incorporated into them.

The land reform campaign was often violent, as it concentrated ancient social tensions into an officially sanctioned form of class conflict. And although there was public discussion of the standards being applied, and opportunities for appeal of contested decisions, there were numerous cases of local abuse of the central guidelines.[14] Sometimes this resulted from the intrusion of personal grudges and favoritism into class determination, but there was also a frequent tendency to locate mechanically an assumed 10 percent quota of landlords and rich peasants.[15]

Since land reform took place in successive areas of China only after their liberation, the determination of class designations was accomplished far earlier and probably more thoroughly in North China, where liberation preceded the establishment of the People's Republic, than in the South, where land reform was not completed until the early 1950s. By that time, rural Chinese had been made keenly aware of their own class designations as well as those of their neighbors.

A different set of categories was employed for the classification of urban residents, one which reflected the Party's perception of the cities as centers of capitalist rather than feudal social relationships. The fundamental categories ranged from worker, through the various strata of the petty bourgeoisie—including such diverse types as peddlers, small shopowners, independent handicraftsmen, and those engaged in the liberal professions—to the bourgeoisie, among whom could be distinguished compradore, industrial, and commercial capitalists.

Surprisingly little is known about the ways in which these urban class designations were applied to individuals. In fact, it is striking that I have found nowhere a written account of this process, and that among Chinese emigrants in Hong Kong I met no one who was capable of providing a coherent description of it. The image which rather haltingly emerges is one in which urban residents of the early 1950s were asked to specify their own class membership, either through their work units or their neighborhood administrations. These self-reported class designations were then apparently examined for accuracy by the Party, and that was the end of it. The fixing of urban class designations was not a central aspect of a major political campaign.[16]

It seems probable that class relationships were more evident in the capitalist cities than in the countryside, and the profusion of articles on class analysis may have meant that most urban residents knew to what class they belonged. But it is also likely that the absence of issues so compelling as those raised by land reform, coupled with the almost casual manner of linking individuals to class designations, may have resulted in urban Chinese being less well-versed in class categories and their political significance than their rural counterparts.

Although the vast majority of the population was included in these urban and rural sets of class designations, in some areas neither a capitalist nor a semifeudal conception of class relationships was appropriate. The Party's compulsion for classification thus resulted in still other sets of class categories.

Many of the areas inhabited by China's national minorities, for instance, were perceived as representing still different stages of historical-economic development. The case of Tibet may serve as an example.[17] As with the rest of rural China before liberation, Tibetan society was characterized as semifeudal. But this was not because of capitalist intrusions into a feudal society; rather it stemmed from the lingering remnants of Tibet's prefeudal slave society. Tibetan class categories thus include a great mass of slaves and peasant serfs, and both religious and secular feudal lords, who formed 5 percent of the population.

Still other sets of class categories existed for groups engaged in various distinctive forms of economic enterprise. The fishing people of South China, for instance, have never been fully integrated into the peasant economy of their landbound neighbors. The peculiarity of their pre-collective social structure is reflected in the categories which the Party employed to describe it. The major designations include fishing worker, small boatowner, boatowner, and fishstall-owner—which suggest the special process of production in the fishing community.[18]

The system of class designations encouraged the perception of a China divided into hierarchies of related classes, with each individual occupying a niche determined by position in the production process. The catalog of possible designations had to be broad enough to encompass the entire range of Marxist historical stages, from slave society through feudalism and capitalism, all of which the Party maintained existed in China at the time of liberation.[19]

A few of the designations, however, are not unique to any one class hierarchy. These include some of the best and worst of possible categories: revolutionary cadre and revolutionary soldier were determined by service in the Communist cause, while a negative classification such as "military officer for an illegitimate authority" was designed to identify those who had worked for the Guomindang, regardless of social origin. Similarly, there were some feudal elements present in urban areas, and capitalist categories in the countryside, as neither of the leading modes of production formed an isolated system.

By the end of the great classification, in theory each person could be located in an appropriate slot in this complex system of class designations, although in fact some individuals were not classified. We know that entire villages were omitted, and it seems likely that some non-Han Chinese, who were often isolated from political currents affecting the majority ethnic group, may also have avoided individual class identification.[20] The profusion of class categories necessary to accommodate the whole range of social relationships was perforce rather unwieldy. Since errors in its application in the countryside have been acknowledged, it is perhaps likely that greater mistakes were made in urban centers, where procedures for classification were less well developed.[21]

Class and Stratification

In order to comprehend this vast pigeonholing of the Chinese populace, one must refer to Karl Marx, whose theories the Party worked so systematically to apply. Gaining access to Marx's concept of class is no easy task, however, as he used the notion in a variety of contexts, never stopping to define it in uncertain terms. "Relationship to the means of production" and "position in the production process," phrases commonly employed as shorthand indicators of what Marx meant by class, fail to convey much sense of how he employed it. Many have commented, with some surprise, upon the lack of precision with which Marx treated this central idea in his social theory. One author attributes it to Marx's desire to refine class further before offering a systematic exposition.[22] Another suggests that Marx sacrificed conceptual precision to his primary goal of explaining the structure and dynamics of bourgeois society.[23] And a third argues that "discrepant uses of the term 'class' were probably the less important for Marx because, according to his theory, further social development would render them obsolete."[24]

Whatever Marx's reasons, his theory of class has been a subject of considerable controversy among both academic commentators and practicing revolutionaries. But if it is impossible to define rigorously what Marx "really" meant by class, much can be learned by considering what Marx's class is not. It is certain that Marx never understood class to be what twentieth-century Western social science calls "social stratification." By this I mean the hierarchical ranking of individuals according to some single standard (income, wealth, prestige, and power are the most commonly used), or according to some composite set of criteria. Marx's use of class can be distinguished from social stratification in several ways.[25]

Unlike social stratification, which typically deals with the relative placement of individuals on a scale of individuals, class is an abstraction for understanding the characteristics of groups within total societies. The ranking of individuals according to income or wealth may describe the distribution of benefits in society, but when such an enterprise is not bound up with a theory of how groups are related to production, it says nothing about class.

Unlike social stratification, which is essentially a static concept, class is embedded in history, is dynamic, and is centered upon the question of change. For Marx, "the theory of class was not a theory of a cross section of society arrested in time, in particular not a theory of social stratification, but a tool for the explanation of changes in total societies."[26] Social stratification is like a photograph—perhaps accurate and suggestive of relationships—but class is like a movie, in which each frame is perceived within the context of what has passed before and what may follow. Class attempts to capture a process which includes unstable relationships, a far more ambitious project than the more limited possibilities of social stratification.

Unlike social stratification, which may be applied in any social context, class is historically specific. The capitalist class system is not applicable to all times and places in the way that one might compare hierarchies of prestige or power from disparate nations. Instead, a nation's class relationships are peculiar to its own historically rooted mode of production.

Social stratification may describe relations of harmony as readily as hierarchies torn by dissension, but Marx's class cannot be detached from social conflict. Whereas social stratification looks at steps on a ladder, classes are defined by their opposition within a system. This conflict generates class consciousness and political organization, two important markers of a class's existence.

Social stratification is inclusive of all members of society. Marx's class concept is an exclusive one, admitting only those groups which meet its criteria. Indeed, in Marx's analysis of capitalist society, only proletariat and bourgeoisie are pure classes. For other groups, class is a matter of degree:

> the absence of one criterion may be offset by a higher degree of another characteristic, just as in the evaluation of a work of art a lower level of artistic technique may be offset, for instance, by originality of idea or power of expression. A work of art can be a work of art to a greater or lesser degree, just as a social class may be a class to a greater degree.[27]

This variability in what constitutes a class is nowhere clearer than in Marx's famous characterization of the French peasantry as isolated and self-sufficient.

> In so far as millions of families live under economic conditions of existence that separate their mode of life, their interests and their culture from those of the other classes, and put them in hostile opposition to the latter, they form a class. In so far as there is merely a local inter-connection among these small-holding peasants, and the identity of their interests begets no community, no national bond and no political organization among them, they do not form a class.[28]

With this distinction sharply drawn, it becomes apparent that the Chinese Communist Party, in the process of applying Marx's class analysis to Chinese society, subtly transformed class into stratification. Although class designations were intended to make concrete the abstractions of Marxist theory, in application they unavoidably assumed the character of a hierarchy of social stratification.

This change was perhaps unavoidable. Mao's early conception of the purpose behind class analysis—to distinguish enemies from friends—is not different from Marx's. In fact, one student of Marx asserts that " 'Who is the enemy' is a question that can be asked whenever Marx uses 'class.' "[29] But when Marx inquired about the enemy, a different sort of response was possible than when the same question was posed by the Chinese Communist Party. I do not mean to dismiss Marx as a mere armchair theorist in noting that certain changes took place in his theory as the Chinese applied it because the Party was engaged in a protracted civil war, rather than an historical analysis. The detached, historically informed insight of Marx was not replicable as the Party was forced to determine which groups could be relied upon in a life-and-death revolutionary struggle. For the Party, the task of discovering enemies possessed an immediacy which Marx, sitting in the British Museum, did not face.

In the course of the revolution, enemy and friend became concrete individuals, interacting within local communities, rather than grand social groups with shifting boundaries contending over the fates of total societies. A tendency to reify class reached its ultimate point in the assignment of class designations in the thousands of villages throughout China.

E. P. Thompson observes that

> the notion of class entails the notion of historical relationship. Like any other relationship, it is a fluency which evades analysis if we attempt to stop it dead at any moment and anatomise its structure. The finest-meshed sociological net cannot give us a pure specimen of class, any more than it can give one of deference or love.[30]

This fluency was halted as the Party used its analytical concept as an operational one. The choice was not willful, nor is it helpfully viewed as a betrayal of Marx by a Party acting in his name. On the contrary, it is difficult to imagine what alternative the Party had to identifying individual class membership.[31] In what other manner could land be reapportioned and the revolutionary alliance be consolidated? Facing a problem which Marx had never confronted, in the effort to be true to their Marxist convictions the Chinese enacted a precision of class identification which Marx was unlikely ever to have imagined.

In the West, students of human inequality typically have employed either the concept of class or the concept of social stratification, but seldom both. The rejection of class, which has been strongest in the United States, has often held that class may have been useful for the analysis of early industrial Europe, but is simply too blunt a tool to apply to advanced industrial societies.[32] The critique of social stratification, frequently European in origin or orientation, has insisted that attention to minute hierarchical gradations within a population obscures broader currents of social conflict, that stratification is an inherently conservative conception of inequality.[33]

In this debate social scientists have too often forgotten that the choice need not be an exclusive one. Class and stratification cap-

ture different aspects of social reality, and may be not only com-
plementary but mutually necessary. Rodolfo Stavenhagen argues
that class structures give rise to distinctive stratification orders, as
dominant classes influence hierarchies of social rank in the same
manner that they imprint their interests upon other superstructural phenomena, such as religion, ideology, and politics. If this
is so, an important question is the effect upon social stratification
of a change in the class system with which it is associated. Stavenhagen's response is suggestive:

> As with all phenomena of the social superstructure, stratification sys-
> tems acquire an inertia of their own which acts to maintain them,
> although the conditions that gave rise to them may have changed.
> As class relationships are modified by the dynamics of class opposi-
> tion, conflict and struggle, stratification systems tend to turn into
> "fossils" of the class relations on which they were originally based.
> For that reason they may cease to correspond to existing class rela-
> tionships and may even enter into contradiction with them, particu-
> larly in the case of revolutionary changes in the class structure.[34]

One example of a stratification order which has been turned into
a sociological fossil is the persistence of aristocratic distinctions in
Europe well after capitalist industrialization had undermined their
basis in the power of a land-owning ruling class. Another example
is the system of class designations in China.

In this perspective, the property-based class relations of preliberation China underlay the stratification of class designations by
which the Communists ranked the population as they consolidated their power. But the success of the revolution brought on
the destruction of the property system of which the class designations were an artifact. The new system of class relationships
associated with the introduction of socialism to Chinese society is
still embryonic, tentative, and obscure. Less obscure, however, is
a new and bureaucratically oriented stratification by which
Chinese are increasingly identified. As consideration of a prominent social hierarchy may illuminate the new class relationships
upon which it rests, I will now turn to China's new social stratification of occupational rank.

Stratification by Occupational Rank

After a prolonged period of foreign invasion, civil war, and revolution, China cannot be said to have had a clearly defined social "structure," a word which suggests a certain permanence and regularity. The Communist Party, just beginning to turn itself from a guerrilla organization into a more routinized and bureaucratic one, played a central role in the postliberation reorganization of society. As if unconsciously acknowledging that the stratification of class designations had been outmoded by the socialist transformation of 1956, the Party advanced a new system of social stratification by which to categorize the population. Perhaps because of bureaucrats' concern for order and rationality in the planning of China's industrialization, individual Chinese have since been ranked within an elaborate system of work-grades, denoting with clarity each employee's position in a hierarchy of job-related rewards and privileges (see the appendix).

Among the most striking aspects of Chinese work-grades is their universality: almost everyone is given some sort of job ranking. These ranks indicate income levels, prestige, and authority. Income differentiation, far from having no place in Chinese socialism, is actually more highly structured than in the United States. Large sections of the American work force are not included in any systematic schedule of wages or salaries—farmers, operators of small businesses, physicians, and corporation executives at once come to mind—and even most scheduled personnel do not participate in very formal job hierarchies, apart from civil service and military employees. Furthermore, there are significant non-salary income sources in the United States which make the chaotic multiplicity of salary schedules inadequate as an index of income.

China is far from placing all of its work force on a single scale, but it does seem to approximate this more than most societies.[35] The number of work-grade hierarchies is small, and they are often compatible. Moreover, unlike in the United States, the role of salary supplements is limited.[36]

The stratification of occupational ranks may be divided into horizontal groupings, which I shall call "sectors," much as the stratification of class designations may be divided horizontally into several modes of production. A sector[37] refers to a set of occupations related by shared participation in economic activity of a special type. Unlike class, which stresses a common position in the production process (as among capitalists, no matter how their funds may be invested), sector calls attention to shared experience at all levels of the occupational hierarchy within a single functional realm. The industrial sector thus includes all persons whose livelihood is associated with factories, regardless of occupational rank.

Sector is not a theoretically derived conception, and is encountered in diverse formulations. One with a long history in the Party is the triad of worker-peasant-soldier *(gongnongbing)*. Here horizontal distinctions of either occupational rank or class designation are not at issue, but rather the functional role played by all peasants, workers, and soldiers within Chinese society. A more inclusive set of sectors, used by Mao and thus often found in the Chinese press, is a grouping of seven: industry, agriculture, commerce, education, the military, government, and the Party *(gong, nong, shang, xue, bing, zheng, dang)*.[38] After socialist transformation, the Party increasingly divided its own work along functional lines, recognizing several systems *(xitong)*, such as finance and trade, rural affairs, and political-legal work.[39] These systems coincided roughly with sectors, whose prominence they enhanced.

In the years of revolutionary struggle, the cadres of the Communist movement were without a well-defined hierarchy of ranks.[40] Remuneration for work done followed the "supply system," in which cadres were provided with life's necessities in a rather egalitarian manner, with only three differentiated grades by which cadres were issued housing, food, etc. This procedure was maintained for several years after liberation, only to be replaced in the national wage reform which accompanied socialist transformation.

The formal hierarchy of civil service ranks which was introduced along with socialization reflected the strong Soviet influence then present in China. Each state cadre was assigned to one of 30 grades *(jibie)*, with grade 1 for the Chairman and Vice-Chairman of the state, and grade 26 for the lowliest cadre. Ranks 27 through 30 were reserved for janitorial and other service personnel.

The cadre ranking system contains a mechanism to compensate for regional disparities in the cost of living; it also contains a far less egalitarian distribution of income than did the supply system. Barnett's investigation of a single ministry concluded that the minister received a salary nine times greater than that of the lowest ranking cadre. But the system is important for providing markers of status and power as well as income differentiation.

Rank is known within an organization, and is even evident outside through such manifestations as distinctions in dress, deport-
ment, or access to automobiles. And the civil service scheme obviously provides a ladder for bureaucratic promotions.[41]

Military bureaucrats, the cadres of the People's Liberation
Army, are graded by a comparable system. The egalitarian relationships of the revolutionary Red Army were undermined by the
establishment of a system of officer ranks (replete with fancy
Soviet-style uniforms) in 1955. The well-known abolition of
ranks in 1965 did away with gold braid and honorific titles, but it
certainly did not imply the elimination of graded distinctions of
authority and income within the armed forces. This system is
closely coordinated with the grades of civilian cadres.[42] Thus
while a senior captain *(dawei)* was equivalent to a grade 17 civilian
cadre (e.g., a county-level administrator), the bureaucratic position now held by that former captain *(yingzhang,* or battalion
commander) is still calibrated with the same civilian rank. Residents of China say that military grade distinctions, like those of
civilian cadres, are often highly visible. Thus one can recognize
personnel at the battalion level and below by their padded jackets
(mianao), which set them apart from their overcoated superiors.

Another important cluster of work-grades introduced by the
wage reform includes industrial workers.[43] Following Soviet
practice, most state-owned enterprises divide their workers according to skill and experience into a hierarchy of eight (but
sometimes fewer) grades. A typical ratio between the highest and
lowest wages is three to one, although this may be misleading,
insofar as workers might take as their reference point the higher
salaries of the cadres who manage the factories. Very important
distinctions exist among permanent workers, who receive pension
and health-care benefits, and temporary workers, who do not.
Contract workers, employed seasonally and drawn from agriculture, may not be graded in this system at all. Given the egalitarian
tone of Maoist politics, it is striking that the work-grade hierarchy, like the cadre work-grades, has remained unchanged in its
basic structure up to the present, including throughout the turbulent years of the Cultural Revolution. Reasons for this durability will be taken up in a later chapter, but it suggests that workers
have had ample time to become accustomed to a clear hierarchy
of positions by which they may gauge their relative standing.

Additional formal job-ranking schemes abound. There are 25

grades of educational administrators, 12 ranks of professors.[44] Engineers are divided into 8 levels, and technicians may attain 5 possible ranks.[45] Writers, actors, and opera singers are graded as state cadres, and even the inmates of labor reeducation camps are sorted into grades for wages.[46]

Far less rigorously stratified into a hierarchy of occupational ranks are China's peasants. Agriculture is predominantly a collective rather than a state undertaking. The only fully socialist part of the agricultural sector consists of state farms, often located in underdeveloped frontier regions, whose workers presumably receive wages according to standardized work-grades. For the vast majority of peasants who work within the commune system, however, remuneration takes the form of shares of the collective production. But even here there have been strong tendencies to divide peasants into quasi-bureaucratic ranks.[47] While there is enormous local variation in rural incentive policies, the shares of output earned by most peasants are determined by some system of classification into ranks *(dengji)*. The most widespread technique in the 1960s was the *Dazhai* model, in which peasants placed themselves in several grades through mutual evaluation. Ten or twelve grades were typical, with the strongest, most highly skilled, and politically most conscious peasants being assigned the first few grades, the lowest positions going to the elderly, the infirm, and the very young. These grades were reviewed periodically (annually, or often at each harvest), and provided a way of determining how much the work-points earned by a peasant would be worth at the division of the agricultural surplus.

Like cadre or worker stratification, the peasant ranks are typically known within the production unit, and offer a basis for identification, although other forms of social distinction are more likely to be popularly recognized. In part, this is because the peasant ranks do not form a hierarchy for career promotion, as a peasant typically attains the highest grade in early maturity, when productivity is highest. Drops in grade follow the decline in strength which accompanies increasing age, unless the peasant possesses such superior agricultural knowledge that a high grade may be retained. Decreasing rank, however, need not mean a declining income, if the unit's productivity increases at a rapid enough rate to raise the value of each work-point to offset the loss.

The agricultural sector is an important but only partial exception to the development of a persuasive and surprisingly stable stratification of occupational rank in socialist China. The significance of this social hierarchy is strongly colored, however, by the stratification of class designations which antedates it.

The Interaction of the Two Stratifications

The interrelationship of these two models of social stratification forms an important aspect of the context within which the transformation of China's class structure is taking shape. The political implications of their coexistence will be addressed in subsequent chapters. Here I will consider the connection between them in a preliminary manner: by asking what each stratification measures, by discussing the extent to which they intersect, and by evaluating briefly their links to changes in class relationships.

It should be clear that these are not the only stratifications of the Chinese populace: informal notions of relative wisdom, beauty, and occupational prestige are found in China as in any society. Class designation and occupational rank assume special weight because they are both (at least superficially) economic stratifications, and because they are both officially sanctioned.

The class designation system (which I will also call the property model of stratification) represents the Party's effort to capture economic relationships at a time when private property was still a primary element in the determination of social position. Even if the Party perhaps overemphasized property's impact, and even if it was sometimes sloppy in identifying individual social rank, the hierarchy of class designations nonetheless is rooted in a social structure in which propertied classes were a leading force. In socialist China, these designations must represent something else; they serve as an index to former relationships to the means of production, as historical markers to a social world which no longer exists.

Since 1956, the stratification of occupational rank (or the socialist model of stratification) has become a better index to current economic position. Its parallel ladders of neatly graded steps have emerged from the social reorganization which has been led by the Communist bureaucracy. As work-grades have usurped the economic aspects of the class designations, the property model has increasingly become a measure of political status, of social honor.

Another obvious distinction between the two models is locational. As the child of land reform, the property model is more elaborately drawn, and was more systematically applied in rural China than in urban areas. The opposite is true of the socialist model, which has had a greater impact in the cities, home of bureaucrats and industrial workers. The continuing dominance of collective rather than state enterprise in the countryside has deterred the extension of work-grade stratification there.

But the relationship between property and socialist models of stratification is more complex than this, for although the old class system was overthrown, the stratification hierarchy derived from it was not. Work-grades may have supplanted class designations as a current guide to the economic position of individual Chinese, but class designations have persisted as an officially structured memory of former social relationships. The superimposition of work-grades upon class designations has meant that individuals have been identified by two distinct scales of official social position. And because these scales measure different qualities, a person's position in one stratification may not accord with location as measured by the other.

The impact of such status discontinuity has not been constant. Interest in class (regardless of its meaning) has varied over time, and attention to class designations has varied with it. As public discussion of class has risen and fallen, the salience of work-grades has first diminished, then increased. The rhythm of political campaigns has also affected the relative significance of the two stratifications models: at the height of most mass movements, class designations have been vital indicators of political security and anxiety. One young emigrant summed up a feeling no doubt common to the minority with bad class designations in the Cultural Revolution: "If your class designation is good, you can do anything you please; if your designation is bad, then you must endure a lifetime of bitterness."

The cross-cutting of the two stratifications is not random in its impact, but rather affects the sectors of the work-grade system differentially. This can be illustrated in a diagram where the horizontal categories are sectors and the vertical ones are groups of related class designations. The industrial and military sectors have fewer personnel with bad class designations than the commercial and educational sectors, both of which employ many persons of dubious class origin, primarily petty bourgeoisie. The Party's re-

Possible Class Designations in Seven Sectors

	industry	military	party	government	agriculture	commerce	education	
worker	x	x	x	x				
poor peasant, lower-middle peasant	x	x	x	x	x			
petty bourgeois, well-to-do middle peasant			x	x	x	x	x	
rich peasant, capitalist, landlord					x	x	x	

NOTE: Data on the actual distribution of class designations among sectors are not available. Chinese press accounts of problems of class consciousness in different sectors sustain the image presented above, however. Class designations are collapsed into four groups on the basis of recurring Party estimates of their relative reliability and revolutionary commitment. An x in a cell indicates that a relatively large number of persons with those class designations are apt to be employed within that sector. I have not attempted to estimate the relative magnitude of these numbers, although one can easily imagine that the largest number of worker designations are to be found in the industrial sector, for instance, or that most rich peasants are in agriculture (see chapter 6 for a discussion of class designations of those born after liberation).

sponse to this differentiation of sectors has been twofold: first to make the commercial and educational sectors special targets in campaigns which stress class struggle, and second, to shore up these weak sectors through transfusions of personnel with good class designations (as in campaigns to transfer military personnel and poor and lower-middle peasants to commercial work).

How is this tension between two stratification models related to the ongoing changes in China's class relationships? The opposition of class and stratification which I have sketched suggests that the work-grade model might be seen as a device by which bureaucrats have attempted to shape society in their own image. As a new and still poorly consolidated class, however, these bureaucrats are ambiguously perceived by others in Chinese society. Certainly the parameters of China's bureaucratic class are cast in deeper shadow than the stratification order that has flourished under its influence. And it is this socialist model of inequality which has been the focus for the postliberation restratification which aroused Maoist anxieties. Accordingly, the Maoist reanalysis of class in China shifted from a preoccupation with the old and familiar inequality of property to the new and still poorly understood distinctions of a more bureaucratized society.

The durability of class designations must be understood in terms of their usefulness to many groups in contemporary China. As economic inequalities of property have been supplanted by the new inequalities of occupational rank, many cadres have found class designations useful as a way of reducing popular consciousness of this change. Poor and lower-middle peasants, in particular, can find pride in class designations which accord them a status more lofty than their actual material position. Each of the stratifications dulls sensitivity to the inequalities represented by the other scale. The only group which has an unambiguous interest in dealing solely with the new socialist stratification model consists of those associated with the former propertied classes, who seek redress of their low status. Even radical cadres, alarmed at the development of bureaucratic privilege, might pause before attacking a stratification order by which they fare well.

Thus the competing claims of the two models have formed the background for Maoist theorizing about inequality in socialist society. The relationship between the two has been a prolonged process by which residues of the Party's presocialist class analysis have become attached to new social tensions. That bureaucrats would prefer focusing attention upon the property model, while ex-capitalists and landlords and their children would prefer the socialist model, is an irony of the revolution, the consequences of which have yet fully to be resolved.

CHAPTER THREE

Socialist Transformation and the Displacement of Class

In the midst of liberation, land reform, and the consolidation of Communist power in the cities, there was considerable curiosity about the socialism which the Party promised. Slogans such as "The Soviet Union's today is China's tomorrow" offered only vague clues about the Party's plans for Chinese society. Pressed by ordinary peasants, some cadres responded that "socialism is electric lights and telephones," or that socialism would mean the end of cooking: when guests came, all that would be necessary was to place a chicken into a machine and out would come a prepared meal.[1]

The Party's leaders were conscious of both the promise and the potential difficulties of socialization—that it could not resolve all China's problems overnight, and that it might bring new tensions in a society still healing the wounds of civil war. Many cadres were thus prepared to introduce socialism in a series of deliberate stages. Mao and his supporters pushed instead for a more radical pace, ridiculing gradualist cadres as "tottering along like a woman with bound feet and constantly complaining, 'You're going too fast!'"[2] Mao's urgency rested upon a conviction that socialist reforms were the best way to increase production at a rapid rate, concern that a delay in the introduction of these reforms would permit the emergence of new landlords and capitalists, and anxiety that the Party would lag behind activist elements in the population.

Mao prevailed, and the speed of the socialist transformation of 1955–1956 astonished many Party members. In July of 1955, only 14.2 percent of peasant families were members of cooperatives.

By May 1956, this had changed to 91.2 percent.[3] Following this initiative in agriculture, the socialization of private industry and commerce was even more rapid, so that private property played only a limited role in Chinese society after 1956.[4]

The Party quickly recognized the rapid conclusion of socialist transformation as a major victory in which the social bases of the former ruling classes had been destroyed. But an unanticipated consequence of this success was the negation of the Party's elaborate class analysis. It was no longer possible to discern a legal relationship between individual Chinese and the means of production, and the class theory upon which the Party had based its revolution was not easily applicable to a suddenly socialist society. Socialist transformation had made the property model of stratification obsolete, as it established the institutions upon which the socialist model was to be built. In 1956 and 1957 the Party made the uneasy discovery that social reforms had subverted its theory of class.

Confusion about Class

The great classification of the Chinese populace after liberation had made both cadres and ordinary citizens sensitive to the language of class analysis. But after liberation, some people presumed that the defeat of the Guomindang meant that the social basis for counterrevolution had been destroyed. "The enemy has been overthrown" was a way of thinking which the Party felt interfered with the recognition of continuing political problems.[5] It continued to emphasize class analysis, but there is evidence that by the middle of the decade many Chinese did not regard class as a key concept. The Party's *Study* magazine found it necessary to point out that "there is no one on earth who is not a member of a class."[6] The Director of the Central Committee's Rural Work Department complained of young people who ignored questions of class policy.[7] And Hua Guofeng, then a local cadre in Hunan, criticized other local leaders for failing to perceive class changes in the countryside.[8] The sudden success of socialist transformation did not quiet such doubts about class, but rather intensified them.

Class conflict certainly did not seem to be a central issue at the Party's Eighth National Congress, which met in September of 1956. The last such meeting had been in 1945, when the Communists were still a rebel force. Within a decade the Party had gained national political power and begun a broad series of social reforms, accomplishments which no doubt contributed to the buoyant mood of the Congress. The imperialists had been driven from China's shores, and landlords and capitalists had been tamed at home. A massive program of industrialization had begun with Soviet advice, making China's economic prospects brighter than at any time in a century. A civil service reform was under way as well, transforming old guerrilla fighters into modern administrators. And all these achievements were reinforced by the socialization of agriculture and industry.

To be sure, class was not forgotten at this meeting. No one believed that the Party's recent success in circumscribing the role of private property meant that a classless society had been fashioned overnight. The Party's own tradition of considering class standpoint as separate from actual economic position was too strong to permit such a naïve assumption. Yet class conflict seemed to many cadres a concern more appropriate to a past era of revolution than to a new age of socialist construction.

This consensus within the Party leadership was expressed in the most important speech of the Congress, the Political Report delivered by Liu Shaoqi. Liu enumerated the classes which had been completely or basically destroyed, or which were in the process of transformation: bureaucrat-compradore bourgeoisie, landlords, rich peasants, and national bourgeoisie, all the main objects of China's socialist revolution.[9] Because of this, argued Liu, the victory of socialism in China was basically assured, and the major social contradiction was no longer between workers and capitalists.

A resolution adopted by the Congress identified the new primary contradiction as one "between the advanced socialist system and the backward social productive forces."[10] The Party's chief task was not to wage a continuing class struggle but to administer the industrialization effort so as to bring the productive forces into harmony with the new institutions of socialist China.

Beyond the Party's evident success in revolution, there were other grounds for a sanguine attitude toward class conflict. Planned industrialization had markedly expanded the ranks of the working class, thus strengthening the social foundation for the proletarian hegemony which the Party sought to foster.[11] The example of the Soviet Union, clearly a model for Chinese socialist construction, also contributed to the new confidence that class tensions were lessening. Chinese analysts of Soviet society agreed that class conflict had diminished there, as it would similarly diminish in China.[12] Stalin had for a time insisted that class contradictions grew more intense in socialist society, but in an important commentary on Khrushchev's 1956 criticism of Stalin, a *People's Daily* editorial argued that "after the elimination of classes, the class struggle should not continue to be stressed as though it were being intensified, as was done by Stalin, with the result that the healthy development of socialist democracy was hampered."[13]

This image of a Party responding in unity to socialist transformation by lessening its concern for class conflict is sharply at odds with the Party's subsequent version of these events. During the Cultural Revolution, Mao Zedong was presented as the constant defender of the centrality of class conflict against Liu Shaoqi and other revisionist leaders who in this period were alleged to have proposed a "theory of the dying out of class struggle." The inaccuracy of this retrospective view can be demonstrated by reviewing Mao's own comments on class in the mid-1950s.

On the eve of socialization, Mao's speeches and articles insisted upon the need to maintain vigilence against the recently defeated class enemies, and to continue the method of class analysis.[14] This is, of course, consonant with other contemporary appeals to maintain an interest in class. But as socialism became less an ambition than a reality, Mao's attention to class slackened as much as any other leader's. The Chairman's important speech of April 25, 1956 "On the Ten Great Relationships" discusses the ten leading contradictions within Chinese society: heavy industry versus light industry and agriculture, coastal industry versus interior industry, economic construction versus defense construction, state versus units of production versus individual producers, central authorities versus local authorities, Han versus minority Chinese, Party members versus non-Party Chinese, revolution versus counter-revolution, right versus wrong, and China versus other countries. There is no class terminology, even in the discussion of counter-revolutionaries.[15]

Mao's brief remarks to the Eighth Party Congress in September contained no reference to class struggle, and indeed, when a decade later his comrade Kang Sheng referred to the discussion of the extinction of classes in Liu Shaoqi's Political Report, Mao rejected the opportunity to claim retroactive wisdom about the persistence of class conflict: "We read the report, it was passed at the general meeting. Liu and Deng alone cannot be held responsible." [16] Finally, the December 1956 *People's Daily* editorial (quoted above) which criticized Stalin for overemphasizing class struggle was later revealed to have been written by Mao.

It is impossible, then, to sustain the argument that there were sharp disagreements within the Party leadership about the place of class in China through the end of 1956. Mao did not then claim that class conflict was a fundamental characteristic of socialist society, and his Cultural Revolution adversaries did not assert that class conflict had completely disappeared. Instead, there was imprecisely defined consensus that class would decline in significance as socialist institutions replaced private property.

Contradictions Among the People

This consensus seemed to vanish in the following year. A superficial reading of documents from the turbulent Hundred Flowers Campaign suggests that the Party's leaders had developed contradictory opinions about class. Thus in Mao's celebrated speech "On the Correct Handling of Contradictions Among the People," given in February 1957, a remarkably different note is sounded:

> The class struggle is by no means over. The class struggle between the proletariat and the bourgeoisie, the class struggle between the different political forces, and the class struggle in the ideological field between the proletariat and the bourgeoisie will continue to be long and tortuous and at times will even become very acute. The proletariat seeks to transform the world according to its own world outlook, and so does the bourgeoisie. In this respect, the question of which will win out, socialism or capitalism, is still not really settled. [17]

Contrast this with Liu Shaoqi's talk in April of 1957 to a group of cadres in Shanghai:

> Now, enemies inside the country have been basically eliminated, the landlord class has been wiped out long ago, the bourgeoisie has also been basically eliminated, and the counterrevolutionaries too have been in the main wiped out. That is why we say that the class

struggle between the main classes inside the country has been in the main concluded.[18]

This sort of juxtaposition of statements on class by Mao and by his Cultural Revolution opponents was common a decade later.[19] Although it suggests that serious disagreements existed immediately after the completion of socialist transformation, the impression of a theoretical conflict about class in 1957 is false. The issue is complicated by the fact that Mao's February contradictions speech was not published until June, and then in an admittedly revised version. Here it is necessary to pause and consider the Hundred Flowers Movement and its implications for class conflict.[20]

The Party's optimistic assessment in 1956 that the old exploiting classes had been tamed provoked a greater willingness to utilize the skills of the former bourgeoisie, and especially its intellectuals, in China's industrialization. Zhou Enlai argued that "the overwhelming majority of the intellectuals have become government workers in the service of socialism and are already part of the working class."[21] On this assumption that the connections between the intellectuals and their predominantly bourgeois social origins had been weakened, Zhou advised greater attention to the material needs and working conditions of intellectuals.

Yet another use to which the former bourgeoisie could be put was to release its critical powers, to invite its active participation in political affairs in order to broaden the socialist democracy which Stalin had damaged in the Soviet Union. Mao in particular was taken with this notion; as he analyzed the events in Hungary in 1956, he concluded that the Hungarian Communist Party had invited popular resistance by ignoring public opinion. The death of Stalin had also encouraged Chinese leaders to think about developing a more distinctively Chinese variety of socialism, early hints of which can be seen clearly in Mao's speech "On the Ten Great Relationships," where many aspects of the Soviet model are explicitly criticized.

Mao argued that the Party should break with Soviet practice and act upon the new unity of the Chinese people to encourage a healthy dose of political criticism in order to keep the bureaucracy responsible to popular sentiment. Under the slogan, "Let a Hundred Flowers Bloom, Let a Hundred Schools Contend," extensive criticism of China's cadres was offered through the spring of 1957 by students, intellectuals, and businessmen.[22] But Mao's plan was not well received by all the Party's leaders. It was rumored that some leading cadres had walked out of the room when Mao had demonstrated his support for the Hundred Flowers in his Contradictions speech of February 1957, and that 80 percent of high-ranking cadres had disapproved of its content.[23] While this report is little more than gossip, Roderick MacFarquhar argues persuasively that Liu Shaoqi and Peng Zhen (leader of the Beijing Party organization) attempted to protect cadres against what might turn into a major rectification movement.

As is well known, the blooming of the hundred flowers was abruptly halted in June, and a vigorous Antirightist Campaign was begun in which many of the critics who had stepped forward were attacked as antisocialist elements. One interpretation of this policy reversal has been that the Party set a trap for unsuspecting liberals in order to identify its enemies. A less sinister view is that Mao's enthusiasm for the project was not shared by many of the cadres who were to receive the criticism, and that when the full extent of dissatisfaction among bourgeois intellectuals became known, Mao was forced to accede to the wishes of his colleagues and halt the campaign.[24]

"On the Correct Handling of Contradictions Among the People" was published in *People's Daily* on June 19, 1957, after the conclusion of the Hundred Flowers Campaign which its oral presentation had done so much to encourage. Because Chinese have subsequently made so much of this work's contribution to an understanding of class conflict in socialist society, its discussion of class warrants a brief review. The passage quoted above (in contrast to the statement by Liu Shaoqi) insists that classes and conflict among them persist in socialism, at least for "a fairly long period of time."[25] Future class struggle, following unprecedented changes in society, will take place largely in the sphere of ideology, and will no longer be large-scale and turbulent.

Mao's assessment that class struggle will be of a new kind is linked with claims of a new cohesion among "our six hundred million people, united as one."[26] Awareness of unity, however, should not blind one to the continued existence of contradictions among the people of Chinese society; in fact, "it is these very contradictions that are pushing our society forward."[27] Here Mao attempts to solve a fundamental problem: if class struggle is the engine of history, what is to be the motor for progress after the socialist revolution brings about the ultimate end of classes? Mao's answer is to retain a notion of struggle detached from its connection with class. Contradictions include class contradictions, of course, but insofar as the concept also embraces many nonclass oppositions, it is a class-transcending idea.

This becomes clearer as Mao goes on to compare contradictions in two kinds of society.

> Contradictions in a socialist society are fundamentally different from those in the old socities, such as capitalist society. In capitalist society contradictions find expression in acute antagonisms and conflicts, in sharp class struggle . . . the case is different with contradictions in socialist society, where they are not antagonistic and can be resolved one after another by the socialist system itself.[28]

In this and similar passages, Mao never denied that class struggle exists in socialist society, but he clearly places it in a secondary position. The important contradictions are "among the people," and while there is "class struggle among the ranks of the people,"[29] it is a nonantagonistic struggle, different in quality from the conflict between the people and the enemy which dominated China before liberation.

What is different about such contradictions is that peaceful means may be used in their resolution. This is true also of the contradiction which Mao observed "between the leadership and the led; and the contradiction arising from the bureaucratic style of work of certain government workers in the relations with the masses."[30] This is, of course, the contradiction upon which Mao's support of the Hundred Flowers had been based, and which makes his Contradictions speech such an exceptional document in the history of socialist politics.

Although Mao did not dismiss the continuing presence of antagonistic class conflicts, with the socialist transformation he hoped that coercion might play an increasingly limited part in Chinese political life. Referring to his own 1950 comments on the People's Democratic Dictatorship, Mao claimed that the democratic part of that formula was for contradictions among the people, while dictatorship was for the now severely restricted enemy classes.[31]

The direction of the speech, then, is not to set up a scheme for analyzing China's classes and class struggle, as was claimed years after its delivery, but rather quite the opposite. Class and class struggle, while still acknowledged, are markedly diminished in importance, while the vaguer and more inclusive notion of "contradictions among the people" is raised to a position of primacy as a tool for comprehending conflict within Chinese society.

That Mao should step back somewhat from the concept of class is hardly surprising, given the difficulties which it posed after socialist transformation. In fact, it seems probable that Mao's attitude toward class was even more clearly one of rejection than is evident from the published text of his speech. I base this assertion upon the public discussion of the speech which took place throughout the spring of 1957, before it was published and before "certain additions" were made by the author.[32] No copy of the original text is known to exist in the West, and it is impossible to know exactly how the two versions disagree. But since the revised text appeared at a time when efforts were being made to restrain the ferment caused by the first version, it is not unreasonable to presume that they differ in significant ways.

Although one cannot specify what the first text actually said about class and class struggle, one can engage in some informed speculation about its import. The speech was given to an audience of 1,800 persons attending a Supreme State Conference in Beijing.[33] Later, recordings of the still unpublished speech were played to meetings throughout the nation as a basis for discussion.[34] The numbers of persons who had access either to the tape recording or to notes taken from it must have been quite large; for example, 682 Party and non-Party personnel attended one study conference in Shanxi.[35]

As Mao's speech was the subject of nationwide discussion in the period between the delivery of the talk and its ultimate publication, the press contained a surfeit of articles on the subject of contradictions among the people during those intervening months. There is a striking similarity of such published discussions, especially with reference to several points which differ from the June 19 text. I have found not a single article appearing in *People's Daily* or *Study* prior to the end of the Hundred Flowers on June 8 which presents classes and class struggle in the same terms as those used by Mao in the revised version of his speech. Unless one is willing to argue that the entire Party press was systematically distorting the content of the speech throughout the spring of 1957, one must conclude that Mao himself, by June 19, had decided to change the basis of the discussion.[36] I suggest that if the original text of Mao's speech is ever made public, it will be found to deemphasize class conflict even more than did the published version.[37]

The spring discussion presumed that class struggle was virtually over, and that socialism had won out in China. Whereas in June Mao asserted that the victory of socialism over capitalism in China was not yet assured, a few months earlier a *Study* article had claimed that the class struggles of liberation, suppression of counterrevolutionaries, and land reform, along with the socialist transformation of agriculture and industry "ultimately settled the question of which will win out, socialism or capitalism." This was an analysis which followed Liu Shaoqi's assessment in the previous year, and which most probably was in accord with Mao's own judgment in early 1957.[38]

Similarly, Mao's later and more equivocal view that "the large scale and turbulent class struggles of the masses characteristic of the previous revolutionary periods have in the main come to an end" is not found in the spring discussion.[39] This formulation is missing because the spring discussion assumes a sharp distinction between class struggle and contradictions among the people. For instance, a *Study* article published at the end of April states:

> with regard to the motive force and content of the historical development of society, we can put it this way: the history of class society is the history of class struggle; the history of socialist society is the history of contradictions among the people. No matter what history, it is all the history of contradictions; however, one is class contradictions and the other is contradictions among the people.[40]

This relationship is bolder, simpler, and more easily understood than Mao's subsequent "class struggle within the ranks of the people."[41] In the spring discussion of contradictions among their people, their origin was explicitly divorced from the origins of class conflict: "the birth of these contradictions is not from a basic conflict of class interests, but is from a contradiction between correct opinions and attitudes and incorrect opinions and attitudes."[42] Precisely because class struggle had appeared to diminish with socialist transformation, contradictions among the people were held to have come to new prominence in Chinese society. And if properly managed, these contradictions would replace the antagonistic clashes among classes of the recent past.[43]

This is not to imply that the February version of Mao's speech was completely different from the text which was finally published. In fact, the continuities between the spring discussion and the June text are considerable. Both emphasized the significance of ideological remolding, and both contain the important innovation about nonclass contradictions between leaders and those without official position.[44] I do believe, however, that Mao did back away from a February view of contradictions among the people as a socialist alternative to class conflict. The first version of the speech represents Mao's effort to broaden the class concept with a more inclusive unit of social cleavage, a task which seemed particularly appropriate at a time when the victory of socialism appeared to be secure. The revised version of the speech represents Mao's second thoughts on the subject.

Mao's initially optimistic interpretation of social tensions in socialist China was modified under the dual stimuli of Party resistance to the cadre rectification associated with the Hundred Flowers,[45] and his own realization that much of the criticism sparked by the movement was more bitter than he had anticipated.[46] By March, Mao spoke of the need to revise parts of his Contradictions speech in order to avoid provoking turmoil.[47] By April, Mao admitted that "in the past our alertness to class struggle was too high; now we are a bit conservative."[48] As Mao's fellow leaders had earlier compromised with his desire to encourage popular criticism through the Hundred Flowers, so Mao, perhaps somewhat chagrined by his miscalculation of public support for the Party, agreed to publish a tougher version of the speech. This version retained its innovations about contradictions between leaders and led in socialist society, but it strengthened the place of class struggle and weakened its expressions of confidence in the victory of socialism. The published speech enumerated six criteria "for distinguishing fragrant flowers from poisonous weeds," none of which had appeared in the public discussion of the preceding spring.[49] These steps all facilitated the ensuing Antirightist Campaign in which the Party attacked the harshest of its critics.

Communist attitudes toward class immediately after socialist transformation were complex and often confused, as the Party attempted to make an intellectual adjustment to the social changes brought on by the revolution. I have traced this process in some detail, not to belabor its complexity but rather to establish three points.

First, great caution must be exercised in dealing with Chinese materials about class. The bitter disputes of the Cultural Revolution inspired a misrepresentation of theoretical positions taken during the preceding decade, documenting conflicts and treacheries where none in fact existed. If Liu Shaoqi indeed urged in April of 1957 that "the term 'class' deserves to be reconsidered," he was merely expressing a view strongly held at the same time by Mao, whose followers would later take Liu's words out of their historical context as proof of his revisionist tendencies.[50] If the role of class struggle was an issue which separated Maoist from other leaders in the 1950s, it is certainly well concealed in public statements.[51]

Second, the broad consensus about class in the mid-1950s took the following course: all China's leaders agreed upon the continued importance of class until socialist transformation, when all agreed that the concept had outlived much of its former usefulness. Although there were divergent opinions about the need for a rectification of cadres in the Hundred Flowers, there was general support for Mao's theory of contradictions as an alternative to the class analysis of Chinese society. And the events of the Hundred Flowers Campaign persuaded all leaders that they had prematurely discarded the notion of class conflict, which was then restored to serve as the basis for an extensive antirightist movement. I do not mean to imply that there were never important differences among Chinese leaders on the subject of class. However, these disagreements occurred within a general consensus on the relative salience of class struggle. Disputes about class revolved around its content, not its existence.

Third, the renewal of interest in class which followed the Hundred Flowers was still centered upon the old property distinctions and their lingering ideological impact. Class as such was a weakened concept, useful only for considering old cleavages which would eventually pass into oblivion. This was not yet a reanalysis directing attention to social tensions rooted in the structure of China's new socialist order. Mao's encouragement of popular criticism of cadres did deal with the new inequalities, but neither Mao nor any other Party leader was then prepared to link this realm of inequality to a new theory of class.

The Attrition of Class Designations

Uncertainty about what to do with the class theory was reflected in an ambiguous treatment of this theory's institutional manifestation, the system of class designations. As I pointed out in the last chapter, that hierarchy of property-based "class" relations was eventually turned into a static ordering of revolutionary honor and shame. But the stasis was certainly not the plan of the Communist Party, which had anticipated that as individuals changed their economic positions, their class designations would be altered.

This issue was addressed clearly in the Party's plans for future treatment of the landlord class whose abolition was a primary purpose of land reform. "Decisions Concerning Differentiation of Class Designations in the Countryside" offered the following formula in 1950:

> Changes in the class designation of landlords: Landlords, who, since the completion of agrarian reform, have always obeyed the government's laws and decrees, devoted themselves strenuously to labor and production or other occupation, and have not been found guilty of any reactionary conduct whatever for over five consecutive years, may have their landlord class designation changed to that of laborer or other according to the nature of the labor or occupation they have engaged in, by decision of the township people's representative conference and with the approval of the county people's government.

"Those who have failed to conform to the foregoing conditions," the document warned, "should not have their class designations changed."[52]

Except for the final cautionary words, the impression conveyed by this and other land reform documents is that members of the defunct landlord class would soon cease to be distinguished from other rural people. After a decent interval in which former exploiters might rid themselves of old habits and ideologies, their class designations had to be altered, as class categories could not float freely above society, unanchored to ongoing processes.

A post–land reform modification of class position was also envisioned for the majority of rural residents who had received good class designations. While the Party held that eventually "the various strata among the peasantry will disappear," it also recognized that in the short run "new class differentiation is unavoidable and it should be permitted."[53] In the countryside, class struggle had moved from a battle between feudalism and a capitalist-socialist alliance to one between socialism and the nascent forces of rural capitalism. The redistribution of land and other property was not permanent; many poor peasants and former hired agricultural workers had improved their economic positions, but they did so at different rates, while a smaller number did not improve very much, if at all.[54]

Sensitive to changes in rural social structure, the Party attempted to analyze the shifting relationships in the peasant strata. A confusing array of new class nomenclature entered Party discussions, as distinctions were made between old and new middle peasants (the latter having risen, however precariously, to that position since land reform). Middle peasants were also divided, on the basis of relative prosperity, into lower- and upper-middle peasants. It became the policy of the Party to rely upon the poor peasants and the lower-middle peasants, the latter group now including both new lower-middle peasants (the post–land reform group) and old lower-middle peasants (who were given middle peasant designations during land reform).[55] The complexity of class in rural China was further demonstrated by the introduction of such concepts as "poor rich peasant," that is, a person who was classified as a rich peasant during land reform, but whose economic level had fallen to that of a poor peasant.[56]

Because of the continuing changes in rural stratification, many peasants and cadres anticipated a redrawing of class lines. Kenneth R. Walker observes that in 1953 middle and rich peasants in Guangdong were hesitant to produce to their full capacity, for fear of raising their economic levels just prior to a "second land reform" which would place them in uncomfortably high class categories.[57]

But there was no second land reform, or any systematic reevaluation of class designations. In fact, there is only limited evidence that significant numbers of landlords and rich peasants were ever allowed to abandon their economically inaccurate classifications. We know that persons identified in land reform as "overseas Chinese landlords" and "overseas Chinese rich peasants" (categories concentrated in Guangdong and Fujian) were allowed to change designations.[58] Evidence of other modifications is rare. By the end of 1955, 8 percent of the landlords and rich peasants of

Shanxi were said to no longer bear their land reform class designations.[59] Another Shanxi report from the following year said that in the Changzhi Special District, 80.5 percent of landlords and rich peasants had changed designations and joined cooperatives, while another 15.87 percent had become probationary cooperative members, but without change of class designation.[60]

But despite the second Shanxi report's prediction that all landlords and rich peasants would change their designations within the next two years, it is certain that such a general modification never took place. Whatever reclassification of landlords and rich peasants may have occurred was probably concentrated in the old revolutionary base areas of the North, since Cantonese emigrants to Hong Kong with whom I discussed this issue without exception denied that any change of class designation had ever been permitted.[61]

Similarly, the economic restratification among the other peasant strata was not reflected in a reassignment of updated class designations. No formal provisions were ever issued for applying the increasingly complex terminology employed by the Party to individual peasants. Class designations remained frozen markers of land reform position, while the changing analysis of the peasantry remained an intellectual abstraction. This abstraction was especially important at the time of agricultural cooperativization, but Mao Zedong cautioned that the analysis of the restratification of the peasantry "does not mean once again delineating class designations in the rural areas, but is a matter of policy . . . which should be publicly explained to the peasant masses."[62]

One of the reasons for the Party's failure to resolve the growing discrepancy between class designations and current economic positions no doubt was a recognition of the social costs of a systematic and large-scale reclassification. In land reform, class analysis had been expensive in time and energy, and had generated bitter strife among the subjects of the analysis. This was perhaps unavoidable during land reform, but must have seemed considerably less attractive at a time when the Party was eager to develop a new social cohesion. Moreover, the rapid pace of China's social change would demand that such investigations be performed with considerable frequency if they were to remain accurate.

A second deterrent to reclassification was that individual Communists had been especially successful in improving their economic levels since land reform, and were thus not inclined to support a broad reassignment of class designations by which their good revolutionary classifications might be exchanged for more prosperous ones. As Party members were often drawn from the most active, aggressive, and capable residents of an area, it is not surprising that they tended to profit from the economic changes after land reform. Tao Zhu observed in 1955 that more Party members had risen from poor to middle peasant status than had peasants outside the Party. Tao pointed to some deleterious effects this development had had on Party leadership, but his recommendation for improving the situation was not to redraw class lines but was rather the simpler method of diluting the newly prosperous Party membership in the countryside with a healthy mixture of (economically) poor peasants.[63]

The phenomenon of newly prosperous Party members was apparently widespread in the countryside.[64] Such cadres were often prejudiced against peasants who were still poor, whom they accused of laziness.[65] Had a serious effort been made to redraw rural classes, the Party would have found itself acting against the interests of its own local leaders, the people who had most clearly profited from the new system of social relations. And that the Party was unwilling and unable to do, for it would have meant penalizing the members of rural society who had shown the most courage and ability in the long struggle to destroy feudalism in the countryside.[66] This may be the first visible sign of a development of great significance for class in China: the self-interest which many cadres have in perpetuating the system of class designations, rather than analyzing the new patterns of inequality which have emerged since liberation.

A related justification for maintaining the increasingly outdated class designations was an anxiety about the rich peasants and landlords who had been overthrown. There were repeated exhortations to maintain an awareness of the distinction between former landlords and rich peasants on the one hand and poor and middle peasants on the other. The early forms of agricultural cooperatives were to exclude the former exploiters who might seek to sabotage socialism from within. Insensitivity to these class distinctions was held to represent "a great confusion of class standpoint."[67]

Party attitudes toward class designations prior to socialist transformation were complex and vacillating, and probably contributed to popular suspicions that the concept of class was neither straightforward nor easy to apply. Whatever pressures the Party may have felt to update the class designations were suddenly alleviated, however, following the socialist reforms of 1956..

For as the Party downplayed the notion of class in late 1956 and early 1957, so too was attention directed away from class designations. Following the new and optimistic assessment that the introduction of socialist institutions had dealt the former exploiters a fatal blow, the Party moved to soften its previous fixation upon class designations. This was most clearly visible in Deng Xiaoping's speech to the Eighth Party Congress on the revision of the Party Constitution. The old constitution, adopted in 1945, had treated applicants to Party membership differentially, by class designation.[68] The 1956 Constitution simplified these distinctions and divided the Chinese population into the broad categories of laborers and exploiters, allowing only the former group to be eligible for Party membership.[69] Deng's explanation of the reasons for this change is an articulate expression of the inadequacies which many Chinese apparently saw in the system of class designations.

The distinction that was hitherto made in the procedure of admitting new members has been removed because the former classification of social status has lost or is losing its original meaning. Both before the Seventh Congress and for a considerable period afterwards it was essential to have different procedures of admission for applicants of different social status and this served a very good purpose. But in recent years the situation has basically changed. The difference between workers and office employees is now only a matter of division of labour within the same class. Casual labourers and farm labourers have disappeared. Poor and middle peasants have all become members of agricultural producers' co-operatives, and before long the distinction between them will become merely a thing of historical interest. With the introduction of obligatory military service, revolutionary soldiers no longer constitute an independent social stratum. The vast majority of our intellectuals have now come over politically to the side of the working class and a rapid change is taking place in their family background. The conditions in which the city poor and the professional people used to exist as independent social strata have been virtually eliminated. Every year, large numbers of peasants and students become workers, large numbers of workers, peasants and their sons and daughters join the ranks of the intellectuals and office-workers, large numbers of peasants, students, workers and office-workers join the army and become revolutionary soldiers, while large numbers of revolutionary soldiers return to civilian life as peasants, students, workers or office-workers. What is

the point, then, of classifying these social workers? What is the
point, then, of classifying these social strata into . . . different categories? And even if we were to try and devise a classification, how
could we make it neat and clear-cut? [70]

Although this passage gained considerable notoriety during the
Cultural Revolution, when it was called "an outline for counterrevolutionary revisionism," such attacks were no more fair than
similar efforts to portray Liu Shaoqi's Political Report as an anti-
Maoist document. [71] The entire Party leadership, confident in the
power of socialism, began to resolve the dilemma of outmoded
class designations by downplaying their significance. [72] Class criteria for entrance into agricultural cooperatives were loosened, as
Deng Zihui, director of the Central Committee's Rural Work Department, told the Eighth Congress that the ultimate extinction of
peasant stratification was a process already under way. [73] After all,
as Deng Xiaoping had suggested, what standards could be used in
making meaningful class designations in a socialist society?

Not surprisingly, many persons with exploiting class designations responded warmly to this trend during the ensuing Hundred
Flowers period. Students from bourgeois families at Beijing University publicly and bitterly criticized the remaining influence of
class designations in a society in which their material bases had
been destroyed. [74] A critic from Jilin province argued that China
had been "proletarianized" by socialization, so that conditions distinguishing capitalists from the working class no longer existed. [75]
Capitalists had been given shares, bearing a fixed interest, for their
newly socialist enterprises; some capitalists evidently sought to
disown their rights to this interest in order to discard their class
designations. [76] Such activities were based upon official discussions
that in industry, "class struggle is already basically completed,"
and that "capitalists have already become office personnel." By
discarding exploitation and participating in labor, capitalists were
held to have "transformed themselves into self-sufficient laborers." [77]

But with the end of the Hundred Flowers period there was a
reaffirmation by the Party of the continuing significance of class
designations in the Antirightist Campaign. Even though socialization had seriously undermined the Party's standards for class
membership, there were severe criticisms of the "completely mistaken" view that socialist reforms meant that "there is no partic-

ular class struggle." [78] While the Party in 1949 had asserted with such simplicity that "We all know: people's ideological consciousness is determined by a definite economic foundation in society," by 1957 it was argued that "ideological questions cannot be measured according to changes in class structure, foundation, or work." [79] Not only were former exploiters still to be identified as such, but Deng Xiaoping now cautioned that even the expansion of the working class had brought former peasants, students, and urban paupers, to say nothing of landlords, rich peasants, capitalists, Guomindang military and police officers, and idlers and all their dangerous ideologies into the heart of the proletariat. [80]

But this renewed insistence upon the role of class designations, given the enormity of the economic changes which had accompanied socialization, was only as successful as most efforts at resurrection. Everyone watched the corpse very closely, but it soon became clear that new life could not be breathed into it. Socialist reforms had introduced new factors for the consideration of class inequality, but they were extraneous to the moribund system of class designations.

As originally constituted, the system of class designations provided the Party simultaneously with two sorts of information. It offered a view of the stratification of property and exploitation, and it concurrently served as a guide for distinguishing potential enemies and friends. But the failure to update the designations meant that they could no longer indicate ongoing economic positions of individual Chinese, and the system's identification of enemies and friends was useful only as a historical point of reference.

The stratification of occupational rank which was a by-product of socialist transformation offered an alternative for the first function of class designations. The work-grade schemes, although lacking a Marxist pedigree (and thus not a "theoretical" issue in Party discussions) nonetheless provided what postsocialist class designations could not: a changing index to economic rank. I do not mean to imply that there was a conscious replacement of the class designations by work-grades, but the introduction of an alternative (and more accurate) economic stratification established the conditions by which the majority of urban Chinese with good or middling designations might become less conscious of these memories of revolution.

Work-grades are ethically neutral, however, and thus the Party could not turn to them for immediate guidance for distinguishing enemies and friends. Hence much greater attention was given after 1956 to another classificatory scheme which I have not yet mentioned.

The System of Political Labels

The Party had long possessed a system for identifying politically deviant behavior, in which figurative "hats" *(maozi)* are placed on the heads of those who engage in socially disapproved conduct in order to set them apart from ordinary society.[81] While any society labels its deviants in some manner, the Chinese system is particularly systematic and official, which perhaps enhances the impact of labels upon social relations. A label may carry some form of punishment, including incarceration or loss of employment, or it may result in no penalty beyond damage to one's reputation.[82]

How is the system of labels administered? Most serious labels are assigned in the course of political campaigns, and they are often the responsibility of ad hoc organizations created to lead a campaign. During the 1957 Antirightist Campaign a special Antirightist Office was established, staffed by cadres on loan from Party and state personnel offices. The Cultural Revolution Group and the network of work teams which preceded it offer other examples. Labeled persons often appeal their cases to provincial or central Party authorities, as in the clamor over the "reversal of verdicts" which became a major issue during and after the Cultural Revolution. The supervision of labeled persons is the duty of the Public Security bureaucracy, which may also be able to initiate procedures to apply some minor labels.[83]

The lack of easily identifiable objective standards for determining labels facilitates their use as weapons in hard-fought political struggles, a function which is not always evident in the rhetoric about policy which often accompanies their application. To be sure, when class designations were assigned there were no doubt also frequent cases of political opportunism in judging who was to be called landlord or poor peasant. But unlike labels, for class categories there at least existed a set of relatively fixed objective criteria.

Three concepts related to labels should be mentioned here. First is a series of informal labels, which are not recorded in a person's dossier *(dangan)*, and are often little more than faddish terms of political abuse. Examples include such Cultural Revolution phrases as "political pickpocket" (one who relies upon deceit and trickery to attain political ends) and "little reptile" (one who pretends to be a revolutionary in order to amass political capital for personal advancement).

Second is the notion of "historical problem" *(lishi wenti)*, which encompasses both minor transgressions in one's political past (such as preliberation membership in the Guomindang Youth League) and having friends or relatives who are in some way politically dubious (through bad class designations, residence in Taiwan, etc.). Historical problems are a matter of official record, but are not as serious as labels.

Third is the positive counterpart to the basically negative label system. "Five-good commune member" or "five-good soldier" are designations periodically awarded for meritorious conduct. They are often related to specific campaigns, are officially recorded, and are a dynamic factor in Chinese political life. One can visualize the relationship of these "glorious appellations" to labels by imagining a spectrum of political designations, ranging from the most exquisite political purity to the greatest possible depravity. The glorious appellations are ranged at the positive end of this moral continuum, and the labels fall along the section marked "evil." Unsurprisingly, the forbidden end of this hierarchy of virtue and evil has captured more public attention, and the impact of labels on personal relationships is much weightier.

There is only a fuzzy boundary between labels and class designations; some hint of their complex interrelationship may be conveyed by discussing briefly two important labels. "Bad element" *(huai fenzi)* and "counterrevolutionary element" *(fangeming fenzi)* are not campaign-specific, and may be applied at any time in response to a broad range of activities. "Counterrevolutionary element" is one of the most severe labels, and "bad element" is usually described as one of the more gentle ones, as it seems to be relatively easy to remove. While I do not wish here to describe all the offenses which might make a person eligible for either label, there are many deviations to which either may be applied, such as robbery, murder, and a whole range of offenses which Americans might simply identify as crimes but which the Chinese are likely to characterize as offenses against socialism. How is it determined which of these two labels apply to a miscreant? Class designation may be a determining factor. It seems often to be true that a bad designation will assure treatment as a counterrevolutionary instead of as a bad element. Thus a bit of petty pilfering by a rich peasant is far graver than a similar crime by a poor peasant or worker.

But if a person with a good class designation comes out well in this comparison, one should note that even membership in the most reliable class will not provide insurance against labels. Indeed, one of the primary functions of the label system is to sanction penalties against those who have "good" class designations.

Another immediately obvious distinction between class designation and label lies in the scope of the two systems. Whereas the class designation system is nearly universal in its membership, only a portion of the Chinese population has ever been labeled. And because label is a concept which focuses attention on either criminal or political behavior, the persons who are most likely to be labeled are not ordinary Chinese but either felons or those who are in some way politically active. Thus label is a category which is often applied to "leaders," ranging from the famous personages who serve in the Political Bureau to the poor peasant activist who serves as head of a production team. These are the persons who are in positions in which they can most easily make political mistakes.[84]

Although label and class designation are analytically distinguishable, there is a danger of drawing a sharper separation between the two concepts than is sustained by Chinese social practice. The two concepts have become commingled, especially since socialist transformation. One of the terminological fruits of the 1957 Antirightist Campaign was the notion of the "five bad elements": landlords, rich peasants, counterrevolutionaries, bad elements, and rightist elements. These two class designations and three labels, often put into one Chinese neologism as *difufanhuaiyou* (from the first syllables of each category), often have been treated since 1957 as a shorthand conceptualization of the class enemy.

The system of labels gained new prominence after socialist transformation precisely because of its interpenetration with class designations. In a period in which class designations had become static, labels offered the Party a dynamic device for dealing with political evaluations. Because labels can be assigned and removed on an ad hoc basis, and because they focus attention directly upon current behavior, they offered an important device for relieving the pressure to reform the system of class designations. Through labels, persons of both good and bad designations could be treated without reference to the economic factors which seemed increasingly confusing to many cadres.

Although the Party had been unable or unwilling to consciously revise the property stratification, the new prominence of work grades and labels after 1957 accomplished this revision in a de facto manner. To be sure, class designations remained, but their static nature was made obvious by the contrast with these more malleable alternative windows upon Chinese society. That the most vital functions of class designations had been assumed by other measures made these designations, and the class concept upon which they were based, a weak but not quite empty shell. As a ranking of one-time relationship to the means of production, the class designations retained considerable historical interest. Socialist transformation had borne in its wake new and more meaningful bases for reckoning inequality, but these were not to collide with the now frozen class designations until Mao endeavored to reformulate the concept of class for a society without large-scale private property.

CHAPTER FOUR

The Maoist Revival of Class

When the Communist Party encountered harsh criticism during the Hundred Flowers Campaign of 1957, its leaders concluded that they had erred in presuming that class conflict would be ended suddenly through the establishment of socialist institutions. Mao and his colleagues responded to anti-Party criticism by adjusting their expectations: socialism would eventually result in the termination of class struggle, but the Party's leaders had discounted prematurely the influence of the formerly propertied classes. With the passage of time, the baleful class heritage of China's presocialist past would surely be eradicated.

"Beginning from now," Mao said in July of 1957, "this struggle may possibly go on for another 10 years, 15 years or longer." [1] Although Mao qualified this prediction with the thought that the end of class struggle must await the final destruction of capitalism and imperialism, he seemed to think that class tensions within China would be under control long before that day, as there was no longer an economic basis for the re-creation of bourgeois ideology within China.

Although the Hundred Flowers episode had forcefully reminded the Party's leaders of the importance of class, their understanding of class conflict as a question of private property had not been altered. Thus it is not surprising that attention to class resumed its decline toward the end of the decade. A 1958 article in the Party journal *Study,* for example, bore the title, "Must We Still Use the Method of Class Analysis in Handling Contradictions Among the People"? The affirmative answer provided to this query was unremarkable, but from the vantage of Cultural Revolution experience, it is rather startling that the question was raised at all, and that readers were warned that class analysis might be applied in an excessively "mechanistic" fashion.[2]

Within a decade, however, this seemingly hesitant attitude had been supplanted by a militant reaffirmation of the omnipotence of class struggle. Despite the ambiguities inherent in stressing "class" after the socialization of the means of production, Mao Zedong advocated the continuing relevance of class analysis as a means of arresting conservative tendencies and quickening anew the pulse of the Chinese revolution. This entailed a conflict-filled passage to a concern for the new inequalities generated by the institutions of socialist society.

Political Conflicts and Class Tensions after the Great Leap Forward

Although the socialist transformation of 1955–1956 eroded the pattern of Chinese class relationships, the implications of this change were not addressed by China's leaders for several years. Indeed, it was not until the early 1960s that Mao Zedong directed his attention to the issue of structured social inequality in a socialist society, and it was not until the Cultural Revolution of 1966 that he elaborated a political program for coping with this problem. Rather than attempt a survey of the social and political changes between the Hundred Flowers Campaign and the beginning of the Cultural Revolution, here I will sketch three factors which must be understood before examining the evolution of Mao's thinking about class in the early 1960s: the Great Leap Forward, the 1959 Lushan Plenum of the Central Committee, and the ensuing debate over how best to continue the Chinese revolution. A period which began in relative political unity ended with open conflict; through these years Mao and his associates increasingly interpreted leadership conflict in terms of tensions among classes in Chinese society. It is the progression from political unity to conflict which Mao had both to confront as a politician and to explain as a theorist.

Although the Hundred Flowers reminded the Party that the bourgeoisie's resentment of socialism had persisted beyond the socialization of the means of production, the Antirightist Campaign which followed was thought by many to have changed decisively the balance of classes in China.[3] Mao too felt that a decisive vic-

tory over the opponents of socialism had been won; upon this
perceived new unity he advocated a major new initiative in economic growth. Under the slogan of a "Great Leap Forward,"
Mao and his allies in the Party leadership proposed to forsake the
Soviet-style industrialization which had characterized the early
years of the People's Republic. Concluding that a capital-intensive
and bureaucratically administered program for economic growth
was poorly suited to China's needs, Mao favored compensating
for China's capital deficiencies by a massive program of popular
mobilization. By substituting labor, which China had in abundance, Mao envisioned not only a dramatic leap by which Brit-
ain's economic level could be attained in fifteen years, but also the
renewal of many of the Party's revolutionary traditions which had
gone into eclipse since liberation.

The Great Leap Forward promised a solution to the loss of revolutionary spirit among many cadres, a problem which had
eluded resolution in the Hundred Flowers period. Mao had then
been anxious about the ease with which many cadres had detached
themselves from the masses, and his 1957 focus upon contradictions between leaders and masses had stimulated a Central Committee directive which instructed leading cadres at all levels to participate in physical labor, as "not a few comrades who were
influenced by the thinking of the exploiting classes of the old society have now forgotten this excellent tradition and they look
down upon physical labour. A concern for fame, advantage, and
position is growing among them."[4] Such directives were insufficient to restore revolutionary vitality and commitment to the officials: Mao complained in 1958 that posters "have blown away
the stale atmosphere. Yet we always walk sedately with measured
tread."[5]

Little about the Great Leap was sedate. Mass mobilization of
untapped labor resources demanded constant cadre activity, as
thousands of small-scale industrial projects were initiated throughout the country. Officials were also taxed by a rapid administrative reorganization in which the smaller agricultural cooperatives
of 1956 were amalgamated into the new People's Communes.

Although the program of the Great Leap seems quintessentially
Maoist in many respects, its low attention to class is an anomo-
lous feature. That this burst of radicalism was not more explicitly
class-linked, in the manner of the past civil war or of the Cultural
Revolution to follow, is a consequence of Chinese enthusiasm

about the relative proximity of communist (and thereby classless) society. The building of communism was to be accelerated by the Great Leap, and thus lingering manifestations of class conflict would be diminished rapidly. No dates were ever given for the completion of the transition from socialism to communism, but many documents, later criticized for excessive "leftism," gave the impression that this might be in the forseeable future.

In Mao's "Sixty Work Methods" of February 1958, the Chairman first explained that classes and class struggle still existed in China—much in the spirit of the Contradictions speech—but went on to say that "the nature of struggle and revolution is different from the past; it is not a class struggle, but a struggle between advanced and backward among the people, a struggle between advanced and backward science and technology."[6] Less than two months later Mao optimistically concluded that although class conflict was not yet over, "there probably won't be more than a few more rounds in the struggle between the two roads."[7]

This complacency was shattered by events at the Lushan meetings of leading cadres during the summer of 1959. There Minister of Defense Peng Dehuai led an attack on the policies of the Great Leap.[8] Among China's leaders, many had not been very enthusiastic about the Leap from the beginning. Those who favored orderly, predictable, bureaucratic techniques for social change were not eager to undermine China's new and still delicate institutional structures by turning to what seemed to them to be old-fashioned methods of mass mobilization of millions of peasants and workers. Such cadres were inspired to criticize the economic policies of the Leap when these policies began to encounter difficulties. Inadequate planning and poor statistical coordination weakened the Leap from the beginning. Strong pressures from above encouraged lower-level cadres to demonstrate dramatic increases in production; when this could not be done, false reports were often submitted to central authorities, further undermining the efficacy of Mao's favored policies.

Just as the rightist criticism of the Party in 1957 shocked Mao into altering his analysis, so did the unanticipated demands of his adversaries within the Party in 1959 stimulate the Chairman to rethink the place of class struggle in society. The celebration of unity was no longer appropriate. Rather the analytical task was to explain how fellow Communists could have become opponents of the revolutionary line, or, as Mao asked of his enemies, "why is it that only yesterday they were men of great merit, but today they become arch culprits?"[9] Mao did prevail at the Lushan Plenum, and Peng was dismissed as Minister of Defense. But the experience was profound in its impact upon Mao's perception of the character of Chinese society. Mao said of his analysis of Lushan, "I consider these words to be extremely important," so I will quote what seems to me to be the core passage from his speech, delivered privately to members of the Central Committee.

The struggle that has arisen at Lushan is a class struggle. It is the continuation of the life-or-death struggle between the two great antagonists of the bourgeoisie and the proletariat in the process of the socialist revolution during the past decade. In China and in our party, it appears that such a struggle will continue for at least another twenty years, and possibly even for half a century. In short, classes must be completely eliminated before the struggle will cease. With the cessation of old social struggle, new social struggle will arise. In short, in accordance with materialist dialectics, contradiction and struggle are perpetual; otherwise, there would be no world. Bourgeois politicians say that communist philosophy is the philosophy of struggle. This is true. But the form of struggle varies with the times. In the present case, although the social and economic systems have changed, the reactionary ideology left over from the old times remains in the minds of a large number of people. This is also the bourgeois ideology as well as the upper-layer petty bourgeois ideology, and cannot be changed all at once. It may take time to change, and a rather long period of time at that. This is the class struggle in society, and the intra-party struggle has merely reflected the class struggle in society. This is by no means surprising. Indeed, it would be inconceivable if there were not such struggle.

"In the past," concluded Mao, "I have not spoken about it, and so many comrades still cannot comprehend it."[10]

Three aspects of Mao's discussion are noteworthy. First, he took the concept of struggle in society—which was perhaps the most constant element of his evolving ideology—and directed it away from a vague and unspecific concern with "contradictions," relinking it firmly and primarily with social class. Second, Mao's emphasis upon the varying forms of struggle, when coupled with his observation about the basic change in China's economic and social system, suggests that his restressed social class may well be a somewhat modified concept. Finally, Mao deliberately pointed to the novelty of his formulation, anticipating that his analysis might be difficult for many Communists to grasp easily, as he hinted either that such ways of thinking were new to him or that his was the first public exposition of a new theme.

Mao's initial effort to turn to class analysis to explain unanticipated political tensions not only concerned the internal opposition of Peng and his associates, but was also influenced by deteriorating relations with the Soviet Union. Maoist suspicion of the Soviet Party leadership had been aroused by Khrushchev's anti-Stalin speech of 1956, which seemed to many Chinese leaders to smack of liberalism and revisionism. Soviet failure to support China in the 1958 Taiwan Straits crisis appeared as further evidence of a decline of resolve to support revolution and oppose imperialism. On the Soviet side, Chinese eagerness to discard Moscow's advice in economic planning seemed foolish, and when Khrushchev ridiculed the new People's Communes in conversation with Hubert Humphrey, the Chinese were stung. The final end of amicable relations came with the abrupt termination of Soviet technical assistance to China in 1960, when Soviet advisers suddenly returned home with their blueprints, and action which looked to the Chinese like sabotage of their industrialization drive. For Mao and his colleagues, the Soviet Communist Party had ceased to be a model of socialism, and instead raised the specter of revisionism.

The concern to understand class which occupied Mao intellectually during the early 1960s was sparked by the double shock of Lushan and Soviet criticism. But Mao felt compelled to pursue and refine the links between political opposition and class conflict as he faced continuing frustration of his efforts to sponsor radical social policies. For all his desires to revolutionize Chinese society in the years immediately preceding the Cultural Revolution, practical administrative power basically remained in the hands of conservative bureaucrats, who continued to implement policies at odds with the increasingly radical rhetoric of the national press.[11]

Although this protracted political struggle was never so sharply delineated as Maoists subsequently claimed during the Cultural Revolution, it is apparent that resistance to Maoist programs did affect class interests and offered the major stimulus to Mao's reanalysis of class. I cannot here chronicle the complex policy conflicts of the early 1960s, but some hint of the sense of emergency which Mao apparently felt in this period can be gained by looking at what happened to rural policies. The Great Leap Forward had redressed the urban bias of Soviet-influenced development strategy in favor of the countryside; but the thrust of the Great Leap rural policies was clearly abandoned in practice in the following years. While Mao favored the expansion of rural health care centers, for instance, they declined from 280,000 to 70,000 between 1960 and 1963, while the 43,000 urban health clinics nearly doubled in the same period.[12]

Again, while the Great Leap embodied Mao's goals of higher levels of collectivization in Chinese agriculture, during the agricultural depression of the early 1960s, food production was again organized by household in some areas, a regression which Maoists regarded as a step that might easily lead to the restoration of capitalism. Indeed, at an enlarged meeting of the Political Bureau of the Party Central Committee in February 1962, Chen Yun argued for the decollectivization of land and its distribution to individual peasant households. Although this argument was not successful, the fact that it apparently won the support of Deng Xiaoping and other central leaders surely did little to reassure Mao about the security of the Chinese revolution.[13]

Maoist political goals were perhaps most frustrated in the realm of culture and education. In the schools, many of the reforms introduced in the Great Leap were circumscribed. As part-time and rural schools were limited, special preparatory schools were expanded in the cities, where they catered to cadre children. The proportion of college students of worker or peasant background declined as well; such students comprised 67 percent of the student body of Beijing University in 1958, but had declined to 38 percent by 1962.[14] Many artists especially resisted Maoist efforts to radicalize the content of their works in the early 1960s.[15] The most scandalous (to Maoists) example of this was the drama, *Hai Rui's Dismissal from Office,* written by Wu Han, Deputy Mayor of Beijing. In this allegory, a virtuous Ming Dynasty official (representing Peng Dehuai) loses his post for bravely criticizing the emperor's mistreatment of the peasantry.

Socialist China: The View from Mao's Study

After the Great Leap, Mao enjoyed an opportunity to think systematically about the links between class and politics in socialist

China. While he retained his chairmanship of the Communist Party, in April 1959 he was succeeded as head of state by Liu Shaoqi. Although Mao was under fire at Lushan, this withdrawal from daily political leadership was not intended to pacify his enemies. Rather the intent was partially to build up the prestige of other leaders in anticipation of a day when Mao would no longer be living.[16] But when the Central Committee endorsed Mao's pending retirement in December 1958, it also held that Mao would be able to devote more time to questions of Party and state policy, as well as "to set aside more time for Marxist-Leninist theoretical work. . . ."[17]

The events at Lushan provided Mao with a critical focus for such theoretical work, and for the next two years he devoted much energy to rethinking what was happening to Chinese society a decade after liberation. Lushan had persuaded him that the tensions of socialist China could not be understood without recourse to class analysis, but what *kind* of classes could be said to exist was by no means clear. The image which Mao's writings from the early 1960s offers is that of a mind which was working toward but had not firmly formulated a systematic theory of class struggle under socialism.[18] Although some of the major elements for such a theory had long existed in Mao's thinking, he began to recombine past insights in new ways.

Mao began his project with a conviction that the practice of the Chinese revolution had left its theory behind. In 1958 he had discussed the "fear of Marx" at the Second Session of the Eighth Party Congress. One should dare to go beyond Marx, Mao argued: "do not be afraid, because Marx was also a human being, with two eyes, two hands, and one brain, not much different from us, except that he had a lot of Marxism in his mind."[19] After his withdrawal as head of state, the appeal for the creation of new theories became even bolder. New theories were required because "In our work of socialist construction, we are still to a very large extent acting blindly. For us the socialist economy is still in many respects a realm of necessity not yet understood."[20]

In search of an adequate theory, Mao turned to the systematic study of Soviet experience. In a series of commentaries upon Soviet analyses of the problem of socialism, Mao contrasted Chinese conditions and practices with those in the Soviet Union.[21] Unsurprisingly, Mao was sharply critical of the intellectual assumptions which undergirded Soviet experience. While he certainly did not condemn all aspects of Soviet socialism, he was clearly stimulated in his studies to discover ways of avoiding similar harmful effects in China.

Of the many features of Soviet socialism which disturbed Mao, three points were particularly important for subsequent Maoist theorizing about class.

Soviet unwillingness to deal with contradictions which persist after a socialist revolution was a primary shortcoming in Mao's eyes. In his notes taken while reading a Soviet work on political economy, Mao complained:

> In studying socialist economy the text does not proceed from contradictions. In truth, it does not acknowledge the universality of contradiction nor that social contradictions are the motive force of social development. The truth is that in their own society there is still class struggle, that is, struggle between socialism and capitalist remnants. But this they do not concede.[22]

Another concern was the Soviet misunderstanding of the relationship between base and superstructure: "Stalin's book from first to last says nothing about the superstructure. It is not concerned with people; it considers things not people."[23] For Mao, however, the superstructure appeared increasingly as the critical point in a socialist society which had already transformed its economic base:

> Stalin speaks only of the productive relations, not of the superstructure, nor of the relationship between superstructure and economic base. Chinese cadres participate in production; workers participate in management. Sending cadres down to lower levels to be tempered, discarding old rules and regulations—all these pertain to the superstructure, to ideology. Stalin mentions economics only, not politics. He may speak of selfless labor, but in reality even an extra hour's labor is begrudged. There is no selflessness at all. The role of people, the role of the laborer—these are not mentioned. If there were no communist movement it is hard to imagine making the transition to communism.[24]

A third criticism was related to the other two: an unthinking emphasis upon cadres and expertise, at the expense of popular participation in economic construction. In the Soviet Union, "they believe that technology decides everything, that cadres decide everything, speaking only of 'expert,' never of 'red,' only of the cadres, never of the masses."[25] But of course without a grasp of the contradictions in socialist society, how could the Soviet Communists understand the tensions in the superstructure, and how could they avoid a narrowly administrative style of leadership?

> At every opportunity the text discusses individual material interest as if it were an attractive means for luring people into pleasant prospects. This is a reflection of the spiritual state of a good number of economic workers and leading personnel and of the failure to emphasize political-ideological work. Under such circumstances there is no alternative to relying on material incentives. "From each according to his ability, to each according to his labor." The first half of the slogan means that the very greatest effort must be expended in production. Why separate the two halves of the slogan and always speak onesidedly of material incentive? This kind of propanganda for material interest will make capitalism unbeatable![26]

This hostility toward the Soviet model of socialism was matched by Soviet disdain for Chinese attitudes; many of these tensions were revealed as the Central Committees of the Soviet and Chinese Communist Parties exchanged public letters in a bitter polemic throughout the early 1960s.[27] The letters from the Chinese side were planned, and in some places written directly, by Mao. The exchange was important for reasons of great power rivalry, of competing Soviet and Chinese claims to the leadership of the international communist movement, but also because the Chinese critique of Soviet society was offered as a negative example of what socialism should not become.

For example, the Chinese were especially upset by Krushchev's abandonment of the Leninist formulation "dictatorship of the proletariat" as a description of the Soviet state. Instead, Khrushchev had introduced the concept of a "state of the whole people," to indicate that Soviet power rested upon the support of the entire Soviet populace. Mao's outrage was that this Soviet innovation abandoned the Marxist theory of the state, which had stressed the state's function as an institution for class domination. After socialist revolution it was the proletariat which dominated the defeated former ruling classes, but the state nonetheless rested upon class distinctions. In Mao's logic, if there was a state, there must be classes: "It is only the bourgeoisie and its parties which in their

attempt to hoodwink the masses try by every means to cover up
the class nature of state power and describe the state machinery
under their control as being 'of the whole people' and 'above
class'."[28] And political events made Mao fearful that Soviet shortcomings were being replicated in China.

As Mao surveyed the changing shape of Chinese society in the
early 1960s, he was especially troubled by what had happened to
the Communist Party. Mao observed that 80 percent of the
Party's seventeen million members had joined since liberation,
and that there only remained a few hundred survivors of the veteran revolutionary cohort which had entered the Party in the
1920s. Tendencies toward individualism, bureaucratism, and sub-
jectivism were especially problematic among the newer members.
"All is not pure within the Party," lamented Mao. "We must see
this point, otherwise we shall suffer."[29]

After more than a decade of rule, the Communist Party was no
longer a band of radical revolutionaries, determined to transform
China's social institutions. Prior to liberation, the need for self-
sacrifice and the risks of death and torture had assured that large
numbers of Party cadres would be persons primarily motivated
by the goal of revolution. After 1949, however, the costs of Party
membership ceased to be so high as the Party became an establishment. Far from being a source of danger, Party membership had
become the primary path to personal success.

The rapid absorption of new members into the Party was accompanied by changes in its social composition. Between 1949
and 1961, members of peasant origin declined from 80 percent to
66 percent, while industrial workers increased from almost none
to 15 percent, and intellectuals grew from 5 to 15 percent. Indeed,
by 1956, a third of China's intellectuals had joined the Party,
whereas less than 1.5 percent of the nation's peasants were members.[30]

The Communist Party became the most important bureaucratic
organization in China because of its central position in the formulation and implementation of policy. Trends in other Chinese
bureaucracies only exacerbated the drift within the Party away
from the social groups which had provided the firmest support
during the revolution. Socialist transformation had increased the
need for officials to manage a state-controlled economy, and the
number of state cadres increased eightfold between 1949 and 1958.
Rather than police this growing bureaucracy with an external elite

of Communist cadres, the Party elected to control the new state organizations from within, by staffing them with its own politicized members. Implicit in this strategy was a risk that the revolutionary commitment of the Party's members might be undermined by the daily routine of administration.[31]

Mao had never been fond of bureaucratic ways, and part of his response to the bureaucratic consolidation taking place in China was to intensify a long-standing concern for the quality of administrative behavior. This is perhaps most evident in an undated discussion of "Twenty Manifestations of Bureaucracy." Four samples from Mao's bitter catalog will indicate the direction of his thoughts:

> They are conceited, complacent, and they aimlessly discuss politics. They do not grasp their work; they are subjective and one-sided; they are careless; they do not listen to people; they are truculent and arbitrary; they force others, they do not care about reality; they maintain blind control. This is authoritarian bureaucracy.
> Their bureaucratic attitude is immense; they can not have any direction; they are egotistic; they beat their gongs to blaze the way; they cause people to become afraid just by looking at them; they repeatedly hurl all kinds of abuse at people; their work style is crude; they do not treat people equally. This is the bureaucracy of the overlords.
> Documents are numerous; there is red tape, instructions proliferate; there are numerous unread reports that are not criticized; many tables and schedules are drawn up and are not used; meetings are numerous and nothing is passed on; and there are many close associations but nothing is learned. This is the bureaucracy of red tape and formalism.
> They seek pleasure and fear hardships; they engage in back door deals; one person becomes an official and the entire family benefits; one person reaches nirvana and all his close associates rise up to heaven; there are parties and gifts and presents. . . . This is the bureaucracy for the exceptional.[32]

This concern with the work methods of cadres led to a more general concern with privilege within the bureaucracy and with the system of work-grades that provided its underpinning. At several points in his writings between 1959 and 1962 Mao expressed discontent with the cadre grading system and wage reform of 1956. Cadres did not contend for wages and position during the revolutionary struggle, but "after liberation, we instituted a wage system and arranged all personnel in order of rank. On the contrary, more troubles arose. Many people frequently quarreled in their fight for a higher rank. As a result, this necessitated a lot of persuading."[33] Elsewhere, Mao asked, "Why must we grasp a wages system?"[34] Mao was here continuing an anxious theme which he first expressed shortly after the introduction of the work-grade stratification system:

One kind of problem arises among our own ranks. For example, some cadres now scramble for fame and fortune and are interested only in personal gain. In the discussion of the grading of cadres, there were instances where a cadre would not be satisfied with a rise of one grade, even a rise of two grades still left him weeping in bed, and perhaps only a three-grade promotion could get him out of bed. The fuss they kicked up has settled the question. This business of grading cadres, have done with it! Let wages be roughly evened out, with slight differences here and there. In the old days, the government of the Northern warlords had a prime minister by the name of Tang Shao-yi. Years later he was a magistrate of Chungshan County, Kwangtung Province. If a prime minister in the old society could serve as a county magistrate, why on earth can't our government ministers do likewise? In this regard, those who fuss over their rank and can be graded up but not down compare poorly, in my opinion, with this old mandarin. They vie with each other not in plain living, doing more work and having fewer comforts, but for luxuries, rank and status. At present, this kind of thinking has grown considerably in the Party and the matter demands our attention.[35]

After Lushan, Mao became concerned that the social distinctions manifested in the work-grade system might be associated with deeper cleavages in socialist society, as the following extract from his critique of Soviet political economy reveals:

[The Soviet textbook, *Political Economy*] says that in a socialist society a person's position is determined only by labor and individual capacity. This is not necessarily so. Keen-minded people are always coming from among those in a lower position. They are looked down on by others, have suffered indignities, and they are young. Socialist society is no exception. In the old society it was always the case that the oppressors had higher culture but were a little on the slow side. There is some danger of this today. The higher salaried strata of a socialist society have a bit more cultural knowledge but tend to be a trifle slow when compared to the lower strata. Thus our cadres' sons and daughters do not quite compare with the children of non-cadres.[36]

Elaborating further on the theme of the intergenerational transmission of privilege, Mao complained of the airs and "sense of superiority" of the children of cadres, despite their lack of practical experience.[37]

Such harsh criticism of cadre performance and its long-term implications was a well-established theme for Mao, the chief bureaucrat who felt a special need to discipline and inspire the officials of the political apparatus of which he was the head. Prior to Lushan, Mao had observed that "our central problem today is the work method,"[38] as he sought ever more powerful measures for leading a bureaucracy grown somewhat flabby without the invigorating pressures of revolutionary war.

In the years after Lushan, however, antibureaucratic sentiments assumed a new significance, as Mao began cautiously to move from an organizational critique to a class analysis of China's cadres. But once the decision had been made to incorporate cadres into a *class* analysis, there remained important choices about how this should be done. Two fundamentally different approaches presented themselves, and Mao entertained both of them. The easiest course was to distinguish proper from unacceptable bureaucratic behavior, attributing the former to proletarian consciousness and the latter to persisting bourgeois influence. Good cadres, according to Mao, "are frustrated by those comrades who are highly placed with fat emoluments and live in style, who are conceited and complacent and are only too glad to stick to the beaten track, and who are addicted to bourgeois metaphysics."[39] Such a perspective on class and bureaucracy leads logically to the type of reforms which characterized the Cultural Revolution: maintain constant pressure upon cadres to serve the masses, for in the absence of strenuous political attention, bureaucrats will succumb to bourgeois ways of conduct, and indeed will extend them.

But in the period between the Lushan Plenum and the Cultural Revolution, Mao also toyed fleetingly with a very different approach to the link between class and bureaucracy: bureaucrats themselves form a class, with interests "sharply antagonistic" to those of workers and peasants.[40] In this perspective, the issue is not simply ideological reform, but structural reform of the institutions created since socialist transformation. Mao complained in

1965 to André Malraux that "even today, broad layers of our society are conditioned in such a way that their activity is necessarily oriented toward revisionism. They can only obtain what they want by taking it from the masses."[41]

Mao had concluded that, following the socialization of private property, the source of class tensions was located in the superstructure, and that "politics" must be "in command." But did this imply a primary focus within the superstructure on the politics of ideology (with class defined in terms of political behavior), or on the politics of institutions (with class defined in terms of relationship to state administration)? The first alternative suggested a class conflict directed against a kind of cultural lag from the presocialist era, while the second choice led ultimately to a far more difficult task of using class struggle to reconstitute the organizational structure established by 1956.

Although Mao was to turn in another decade to a conception of class linked to the state institutions of socialist China, his choice prior to the Cultural Revolution was clear. With few exceptions, he emphasized the behavioral dimension of class as he tried to make a new class analysis, consistently holding back from a full-fledged examination of the structural roots of inequality in socialist society. Several factors guided this course, including Mao's continuing suspicions of the formerly propertied classes and unwillingness to remove them from the center of attention, and perhaps a realization that a more structurally oriented analysis of class might locate *all* cadres within a single hostile category. Not only was Mao uneager to identify himself and his followers as the class enemy, but his tactical sense was too shrewd to permit the political suicide which that manner of class analysis could well entail. All these issues could be handled more smoothly if class were revived not as a structural relationship but as a behavioral one.

An additional factor of some importance was the accepted Marxist tradition of interpreting bureaucrats as the agents of dominant classes, rather than as members of an antonomous social group. For all Mao's verbal derring-do about the need to surpass Marx, he was extremely cautious as he began to locate the bureaucrats within China's new socialist class system. Engels had long ago warned that the victorious working class, "in order not to lose its newly won supremecy," must "protect itself against its own deputies and functionaries."[42] Despite this and similar hints in the works of Marx, Engels, and Lenin, the most critical anal-

yses of socialist officials had come from the pens of such hetero-
dox Marxists as Trotsky or Djilas. Mao was understandably reluctant to render his analysis vulnerable to Chinese or Soviet
criticism as "unorthodox," however accurate such an assessment
might be. It is possible that Mao's hesitation may have included
an element of guile, as he sought to soften the break he was making in the Marxist-Leninist tradition.[43]

But it is perhaps more likely that Mao's hesitation grew from
an honestly uncertain evaluation of a still-evolving social situation. The Maoist revival of class was not an abstract intellectual
enterprise but was bound up in political conflicts of great immediacy. Unable to resolve at once all theoretical dilemmas, Mao
still felt compelled to turn again to the class analysis which had
served so well to win victory in the civil war: "whether in socialist revolution or in socialist construction, it is necessary to solve
the question of whom to rely on, whom to win over and whom
to oppose."[44] The categories may have remained obscure within
the first decade since socialist transformation, but Mao was certain
that "once we grasp class struggle, miracles are possible."[45]
Mao's confidence in class despite analytical uncertainty is apparent
in this 1963 remark:

> For 10,000 years there has been the question of whom to rely on.
> In the future there will still be idealism and materialism, the ad-
> vanced and the backward, and contradictions between the left, the
> center, and the right. Who should we rely on today? *There must al-
> ways be a class.* [Emphasis added.][46]

It was not until 1962, after Lushan, that Mao placed the class
issue squarely on the agenda of the Party. Why did he wait? As
we have seen, Mao spent part of the intervening period systematically composing his thoughts on the subject. In addition, wors-
ening relations with the Soviet Union seem to have occupied the
attention of central leaders through most of 1960.[47] Finally, Mao
may have awaited the end of China's economic crisis before beginning a new ideological initiative.

When Mao did determine, in 1962, that time had come to speak
to his Party comrades on class struggle, he emphasized its dual
nature. First, there were the "remnants" of the old exploiting
classes, still harboring desires for a restoration, despite the destruction of their economic foundation. Second, socialist society

itself gave rise to "new elements of the bourgeoisie." Because of this unprecedented combination, class conflict in socialist society "is protracted, complex, and sometimes violent."[48]

Mao advanced the theme of class struggle throughout 1962, reaching a climax in the Communiqué of the Tenth Plenum of the Central Committee, which met in September. In his speech to that meeting, he complained that at the Beitaihe conference of the preceding month, "I presented three problems: classes, the current situation, and contradictions. I raised the problem of classes because it has not been resolved yet."[49] In September Mao posed a question: "Are there classes and class struggle in the socialist countries? It can now be affirmed that class struggle definitely exists there." He went on to cite Lenin, to warn of degeneration and the continued existence of the defeated classes, and to cite the negative example of Yugoslavia, after which he concluded with an instruction that they learn to understand class struggle by talking about it "every year, every month, every day, at conferences, at party congresses, at plenary sessions, and at each and every meeting."[50] Mao's revival of class was encapsulated in the most famous slogan to come from this Tenth Plenum: "never forget class struggle."

Initial Ambiguities in the Rediscovery of Class

Mao's appeal to class struggle was the tactic of a politician acting from weakness, not strength. Mao hoped that he might rebuild lost influence by using the slogan to mobilize potential supporters who were then politically passive; perhaps he also imagined that his major adversaries might retreat under the threat of being stigmatized as class enemies. Mao's choice of issues and slogans was shrewd; his personal prestige was sufficiently high, and the heritage of class conflict was sufficiently glorious, that resistance to the revival of class was muted. There was criticism of this intellectual reorientation among academic historians in 1962,[51] and some central leaders indicated their displeasure at Mao's new fascination with class.[52] But the Chinese mass media were soon filled with articles employing the language (if not always the spirit) of class struggle. As the nation collectively recalled a vocabulary of class analysis which had been neglected in recent years, young people were offered "Little Lessons on Class

Struggle,"[53] while a more erudite audience was treated to discussions of such questions as "To What Class Do Eunuchs Belong?"[54]

In contrast to this ready acceptance of the superficial language of class, many Chinese were uncertain how they should use the newly reintroduced concepts. Local officials sometimes candidly admitted their bewilderment,[55] while Mao acknowledged that many highly placed cadres also found his new emphasis on class struggle difficult to comprehend.[56] Even Chairman Mao initially seemed to restrict the scope of class: in his Tenth Plenum speech he cautioned that class struggle should not affect ordinary work, but that the two "should be undertaken side by side. . . . Though class struggle is imperative, we need special persons to do this work. The Ministry of Public Security specializes in dealing with the class struggle."[57]

Such uncertainties only mirrored Mao's own ambivalence about the central focus of the new class analysis. Were the class lines to replicate the social divisions generated by the former private property system, or were they to follow the newer distinctions of socialist-bureaucratic China? Did the final analysis concern the distribution of wealth or the distribution of power? Of course, there could be no simple "final analysis," as elements of both kinds of class contradiction coexisted in Chinese society at that time. Class-based political programs had to take cognizance of that fact, even at the cost of analytical sharpness.

The lingering influence of the old propertied classes was a troublesome, if frustratingly diffuse, problem in the realm of ideology. A more concrete manifestation of persisting bourgeois strength was the overrepresentation of its former members in such critical occupational sectors as education and commerce. And there were even discernible material differences rooted in the former system of property relationships. Former capitalists, for instance, still received dividends from the shares of stock given in the socialization of 1956.

In the countryside, the pattern of income distribution still bore the imprint of the old class system, albeit in diluted form. Anne Thurston has shown that rural Cantonese classified as middle and upper-middle peasants prior to agricultural collectivization still enjoyed certain economic advantages over their poor and lower-middle peasant neighbors in the early 1960s.[58] Middle and upper-middle peasants, for example, had been allowed to retain ownership to such "minor means of production" as shovels, hoes, and rakes—tools necessary for successful cultivation of private plots, and which these peasants possessed in superior numbers and quality. In addition, middle and upper-middle peasant families tended to be large (presumably as a consequence of their presocialist prosperity, relative to their poorer neighbors), which entitled them to larger private plots. Such factors enabled these families to profit from the extension of rural trade fairs and weakening of collective agriculture in the aftermath of the Great Leap Forward.

The Maoist revival of class drew attention to such remaining manifestations of old class lines as it summoned the loyalty of the poor and lower-middle peasants in whose name the revolution had been made. Mao sought to remind the rural majority of the benefits secured by the revolution to mobilize their support against the erosion of the collective economy. Poor and lower-middle peasant associations, restricted to those so classified during land reform, were established as a means of encouraging consciousness of shared class position. A movement for peasants to research their family histories for three generations intensified the mood of remembrance of revolutions past. A delegate to the 1965 Guangdong Poor and Lower-Middle Congress bitterly recalled for the press how before liberation, his status as a cowherd led people "to treat him as the mud beneath their feet."[59] At the same time, official pressure increased against such symbols of the lifestyle of the old bourgeoisie as elaborate haircuts and pointed shoes.[60] The major political campaign of the early 1960s, the Socialist Education Movement, was characterized by Mao as a "second land reform," and as a "kind of class struggle involving all, both within the Party and outside the Party," which "has not been waged for over ten years."[61]

Against this attention to the lingering presocialist class divisions was a still unfolding set of inequalities associated with bureaucratic domination and the work-grade stratification system. While the two types of inequality were of political concern to Mao, especially as both the former bourgeoisie and the "new bourgeois elements" stood to gain from the elitist drift of the much social policy in this period, the Chairman nonetheless gave greater weight to the new class relations of socialism. To focus primarily upon the older class divisions of the property system would ultimately undermine the continuation of the revolution: "I have told you that the revolution is also a feeling. If we decide to make of it what the Russians are now doing—a feeling of the past—everything will fall apart. Our revolution cannot be simply the stabilization of a victory." [62]

Mao's own "Twenty-three Articles," written in 1965 to give direction to the course of the Socialist Education Movement, make clear that this movement was not, as the Chairman had hinted earlier, a simple replaying of the struggles of land reform. "The key point of this movement is to rectify those people in positions of authority within the Party who take the capitalist road," wrote Mao, who was certainly aware that such people were generally of good class designation. [63] In the dialectical reasoning of Chinese Marxism, there had been a division of one into two, as the winners of the civil war had split into true revolutionaries, those who remained underprivileged, and revisionists, those increasingly satisfied by the status quo. The liberation-era model of social cleavage and its associated class designations were decreasing in significance before the impact of a still poorly understood socialist cleavage.

Mao's unwillingness to challenge directly the structural roots of bureaucratized inequalities meant that the class conflict waged against the new bourgeois elements tended to be indirect. Rather than seek to reform the work-grade stratification system, for instance, Mao was content to restrict some of its symbols, as in the dramatic "abolition of ranks" in the People's Liberation Army in 1965. [64] Titles and insignia of rank were indeed eliminated, although the power relationships which they represented remained unaltered. This is not to slight the impact of the intensified application of such established Maoist techniques as ideological campaigns and personnel transfers as measures for limiting bureaucratic aspirations to privilege. More important, perhaps, was the mass mobilization which accompanied the Maoist revival. For many cadres preferred bureaucratic methods of policy formulation and implementation, finding mass campaigns distasteful for their active involvement of social groups the cadres tended to regard as the proper *objects* of administration. "Now that you have founded a party, entered cities, and become bureaucrats," challenged Mao, "you are no longer adept at launching mass movements." [65] The Maoist revival was accompanied by efforts to remove whole areas of social policy (notably health and education policies) from bureaucratic control by initiating mass campaigns.

Mao's revival of class endeavored to address simultaneously both types of class contradictions. In the process, however,

Chinese were given an opportunity to respond differentially to the appeal, "never forget class struggle." For example, the emphasis upon remembering past bitterness was relatively unthreatening to members of advantaged groups in socialist society. Those rural cadres who had prospered in the wake of land reform had little to fear from reopening discussion of class exploitation which had existed before liberation.

In contrast, except for the poor and lower-middle peasantry, the groups to which Mao made his greatest appeals against bureaucratic elitism were not discernible in the property-linked stratification of class designations: the People's Liberation Army (for its maintenance of the Party's revolutionary traditions within the state apparatus), youth (who had not yet entered the work-grade stratification order, and had fewer vested interests in challenging it), junior officials (often frustrated by the lack of promotion opportunities within the civil service hierarchy), and disadvantaged workers (temporary and "contract" workers denied the fringe benefits awarded their permanent colleagues). Even the peasant majority was placed against the work-grade system and its bureaucratized class relationships by virtue of its participation in the collective rather than the state-owned sector of the economy.

The tension inherent in Mao's revival of class was manifest most sharply in the question of what to do with the hierarchy of class designations, that troublesome epiphenomenon of the presocialist class system. Class designations, as we saw earlier, had not been altered since the discussion which followed the socialist transformation of 1956, even though they had diminished in salience for most Chinese. With the Maoist revival, however, these previously moribund markers were reinvigorated, as the Party recalled the past sins of the exploiters and the virtues of the oppressed. The sometimes confusing new attention to class designations redressed a decade of relative neglect:

> After the land reform, the landed elements did not have any land for rent; nor could they depend upon exploiting the peasants for their livelihood. Instead they were required to earn their livelihood through their own labor. Some persons were easily confused by this phenomenon and erroneously thought that landlords and peasants had become the same.[66]

But the renewed visibility of class designations also called attention to the fact that they were out of date. The issue was joined in the course of the Socialist Education Movement, a complex campaign originally designed to rectify improper political and economic practices which had arisen in the aftermath of the Great Leap.

The movement was to take as its class basis the poor and lower-middle peasantry: if the Party did not rely on them, "who else is there to rely upon?" asked a Central Committee document of 1963.[67] But who were these lower-middle peasants? As has been suggested above, this category came into being after land reform in many parts of China—which meant after the assignment of class designations. The task thus was one of retroactively identifying the middle peasantry, always a problematic stratum. Three categories were to be considered: the upper-middle peasants (the new term applied to the group given the land reform designation of well-to-do middle peasant), ordinary middle peasants, and "old lower-middle peasants." These last were originally designated middle peasants but could be retroactively distinguished—for membership in the new poor and lower-middle peasant associations—because at liberation they "possessed comparatively fewer production facilities and . . . had to sell a small amount of labor or borrow small loans, and were consequently living at a comparatively low standard."[68]

In order to make the distinctions accurate, rural cadres were instructed to study the same documents which had been used during land reform to differentiate classes, as well as for several new decisions.[69] "Of course, this does not mean that a new division of classes is going to take place in rural villages." Rural class designations were still to be "assessed on the basis of classifications carried out during the land reform with the changes of designation prior to collectivization taken into account."[70]

The extent of necessary adjustment was rather large. In addition to the lower-middle peasant problem, there was the fact that persons were given an opportunity to request corrections of mistaken designation—which must have inspired some middle peasants, rich peasants, and landlords to demand new evaluations in hope of improving their class positions. The class designations of Party members were to be specially examined, and although no extraordinary investigation was called for, it was pointed out that some landlords and rich peasants had been able to avoid their deserved designations during land reform, and that such persons, if they had engaged in destructive activities, should be properly identified during the Socialist Education Movement.[71]

As the movement intensified, so did the Party's zeal for rectifying the names of the old class designations. A 1964 revision of the Central Committee directive which had demanded the reassessment of class designations went much further:

> Since there is widespread confusion about class designations in the countryside, it is necessary to carry out a clarification of class designations as a part of the work of the socialist education movement. The designation of each rural household should be examined and classified after full discussion by the masses, and a class dossier should be established. [72]

The revised directive omitted the reassurance that "of course, this does not mean that a new division of classes is going to take place in rural villages," because that was precisely the suggestion. [73] A tougher line was also shown toward the landlords and rich peasants who had escaped the land reform classification: if located, they need not be reclassified if their behavior had been satisfactory, "but their original designations should be announced to the masses." [74] And for good measure, the Revised Later Ten Points took a harsher line than its predecessor toward the children of landlords and rich peasants, barring them "without exception from taking the positions of local basic-level cadres." [75]

Stuart Schram has assessed these documents as responding to "the need for the cadres to keep things under control." [76] Mao apparently concurred in the need for more precise class identification as an aid for leading the movement. However, in his 1963 "Instruction on the Socialist Education Movement," Mao cautioned against mechanically seeking out a predetermined quota of class enemies.

He underscored his own uncertainty in what now appears an understatement: "class struggle is still unpolished." [77] But by May 1964 he urged that "class identifications should be drawn in all units, factories, streets, schools, and official organs." [78] In that month he also demanded that "the cities must also differentiate class designations." Significantly, however, he was unsure about how they should be determined: "As to how they should be drawn, certain criteria should be formulated when we come to do this work in the future." Of one thing Mao was certain: "we cannot rely upon the theory of considering class designation alone." [79]

Mao amplified this remark in an "Instruction on the Question of Class Differentiation" (of unspecified date, but the context suggests that it is also from 1964).[80] In this instruction Mao affirmed that "it is necessary to differentiate classes," but that "class designation and individual behavior must be distinguished, with the more important being individual behavior."[81] Here Mao seems to have resolved in his own mind the dilemma of what to do with class designations. While unwilling to discard them outright, he determined that they be considered secondary to behavior, since the purpose of determining classes was "to clean out the bad elements."

Once again, theoretical uncertainty and practical hesitation were linked, as the Party held back from implementing its projected de facto reclassification of the Chinese population. Adjustments of class designations were made in some key areas, but the process was quite limited.[82] The absence of adequate standards for reclassification was no doubt a problem; it probably raised Maoist anxieties about the backward-looking thrust of an excessive concern for unreconstructed class designations. In addition, the Socialist Education Movement became mired in a dispute between Maoists and more conservative officials over how local cadres should be treated.

In the final directive from the Central Committee on the Socialist Education Movement, Mao's "Twenty-three Articles" of January 1965, there was little mention of class designations at all, much less instructions on how to update the identification of each household in China. By this time, Mao had chosen to emphasize political behavior as the measure for class, in preference to either the old class designations or some still embryonic (and undoubtedly politically costly) new classification which would account for social changes since 1956. The extent of confusion at the Party center is revealed in a transcript of Mao's conversation with several other Party leaders on December 20, 1964, twenty-five days before the issuance of the Twenty-three Articles.[83] The talk was wide-ranging, with one anonymous participant suggesting that "we should hold discussion on how to draw a line of demarcation and how to unify our language [in discussing class]. How should we discuss the principal contradiction?"

Mao responded to this query by saying, "Let's talk about power holders." A moment later, when another anonymous leader complained about those who had escaped class demarcation in the past, Mao again observed, "We need not concern outselves with class or stratum but with power holders. . . ."

A Comrade "X X" suggested some ways of identifying the corrupt individuals emerging in the countryside, to which Mao cautioned, "Don't mention strata; it suffices to call them elements or cliques," which advice he repeated a few minutes later. As most designations are the names of strata, Mao clearly seemed to be retreating from his earlier enthusiasm for stressing class designation in the Socialist Education Movement. Comrade "X X" agreed:

> We must not talk about strata. Otherwise, if you emphasize the bourgeois engineering and technical personnel, or the petty thieves and pickpockets, or students who come from uninfluential capitalist families, the cadres would be very enthusiastic. The consequence is that the cadres might slip away easily, and it will be impossible to strike at them.

Mao responded warily to this statement of the class problem in terms of the socialist cleavage, stressing again that "The focal point is the Party."

The conversation then turned to other matters, returning to class designations at the end. In an interchange which gives some measure of the confusion about class in socialist China, Mao, Premier Zhou Enlai, Li Xuefeng, and X X engaged in a brief but fascinating argument:

> X X: As what designation should we count those children of landlords and rich peasants who participate in labor?
> CHAIRMAN: As they are commune members, of course it should be peasant! Under socialism, how can you permit other people to participate while one family monopolizes all?
> XUEFENG: Poor Peasants and middle peasants are also called commune members, therefore this desigation cannot resolve the question of class designation.
> PREMIER: Ordinary peasant! Just call them peasants.
> CHAIRMAN: You had better argue some more!

Although Mao here saw the issue as one of equity—of course the children of landlords and rich peasants should be dealt with on the same basis as children of others—at least three of the leading members of the Party's Central Committee could not agree on the proper designation for such a straightforward case. Mao and Zhou argued that status as a commune member entitled one to the simple designation of "peasant." But Li Xuefeng pointed out that other commune members bear more specific class designation, as should these.

By the eve of the Cultural Revolution, then, Mao had succeeded in restoring the idea of class to a position of primacy in the Party's social analysis. But this had been so ambiguously accomplished that "class" might be interpreted in radically different ways. Mao's initial effort to resolve the ambiguity of class emphasized political behavior, an approach which allowed him to maintain attention to both types of class relationship in China. A second response to the question of class was more conservative, avoiding interest in peculiarly socialist inequalities in favor of a caste-like treatment of the class categories established prior to socialist transformation. A third and more radical response attempted to root class conflict in the institutional structure of socialist society, a perspective developed most elaborately by the so-called "Gang of Four" in the early 1970s, with the apparent endorsement of its patron, Mao.

CHAPTER FIVE

Class as Political Behavior

Early in the Great Proletarian Cultural Revolution (1966–1976), Red Guard publications frequently alleged that Liu Shaoqi, in opposition to the Maoist revival of class, had advocated a "theory of the dying out of class struggle." The charge was unfair, but its wide circulation underscored Mao's own success in persuading Chinese "never to forget class struggle." The complex currents of the Cultural Revolution did include sharp conflict among the still amorphous classes of socialist China, but they also embraced other types of social tension, such as a generational conflict between elders who had created the People's Republic and youth who had come of age there, as well as an intrigue-filled pattern of conflict organized along lines drawn by political factions.

In a situation in which all social conflicts were discussed as if they were aspects of class struggle, and in which the meaning of that class struggle was ambiguous, it is not surprising that contradictory interpretations of class arose during the decade-long sequence of conflict known as the Cultural Revolution. The revised theory of class initially put forth by Mao and his associates was the most anthoritative view.

The Maoist theory ultimately treated class in socialist society as a matter of political behavior. Political behavior was a standard which could encompass both the old inequalities of the liberation cleavage and the new ones associated with socialist institutions. It permitted movement away from attention to the stagnant class designations from the 1950s, but at the same time it did not require identifying a bureaucratic class as the major impediment to policies favoring workers and peasants. (The political dangers of the latter course were perhaps too great even for Mao to risk, as will be seen in chapter 7.)

The emphasis upon political behavior coincided with a concern for the superstructural aspects of society long characteristic of Chinese Marxism. The Maoist attack upon "persons in authority within the Party taking the capitalist road" reflects the critical role assigned to political leadership. And the Cultural Revolution was accompanied by a strengthening of many long-standing Party programs to prevent the alienation of bureaucrats from ordinary citizens. Along with the purge of such conservative Party leaders as Liu Shaoqi and Deng Xiaoping, senior officials found themselves less able to resist such radical demands as worker participation in management, the deemphasis upon professional expertise, physical labor by cadres, and other measures then advocated by Maoists as defenses against "bourgeois" behavior by officials.

The Maoist Theory of Class in Socialist Society

Although Cultural Revolutionary doctrine on class was identified as "Chairman Mao's great theory of classes, class contradiction, and class struggle,"[1] there is no single text in which Mao systematically developed his revised approach to inequality under socialism. There is instead a series of documents, some from the pen of Mao and some from other sources, which collectively acquaint us with this view. While Mao's statements generally may be treated as most authoritative, there are some important aspects of the theory of class struggle under socialism about which the Chairman had relatively little to say. Thus the doctrine cannot be specifically identified as the work of one person, although its tenor may be described fairly as "Maoist," with all of the ambiguities inherent in such a description. The new theory consisted of five major components.

1. *The persistence of class struggle.* Cultural Revolutionary Maoism insisted that class struggle does not end with the establishment of socialism and the concomitant weakening of distinctions among the relationships of citizens to the means of production. In part, this is because the impact of private property is felt long after its formal abolition: "Although the seal of the landlords and the bourgeoisie has been snatched away from them, and the means of production are not in their hands, these persons still live, and their hearts are not dead."[2]

In addition to these remnants from the old society there are two new kinds of forces that make continued class struggle necessary: first, the spontaneous tendency toward capitalism characteristic of China's millions of small producers, and second, degenerate elements created by the force of habit left over from the old society. This already dangerous mixture is brought to the point of combustion by the external pressures of imperialism. A critical state of class struggle persists until the destruction of imperialism and the universal establishment of a communist social order.[3]

That the class enemy will stir up trouble is inevitable. The "overthrown exploiting classes and their agents in the Party" match strength with the proletariat "once every few years. Urged on by their own class nature, ghosts and monsters feel compelled to pop out. This is an objective law which does not change according to the will of man."[4]

Under these circumstances, even large-scale political movements such as the Cultural Revolution are incapable of bringing class struggle to an end. "The floor may be swept for 24 hours, and yet there is still dust. The peasants hoe weeds every year, and yet new weeds still grow."[5] The numbers of the stubborn class enemy are small; one is continually told that they constitute "a small handful" (which may include up to 5 percent of the populace). But the danger they present to socialism in China is not a matter of numbers. "Their power to resist," observed Defense Minister Lin Biao, "is much larger than their ratio in the population."[6]

One must thus wage continuous warfare against the class enemy in order to protect Chinese socialism. "If you do not attack the class enemies and the tendency toward capitalism, they will attack you; if you do not criticize and repudiate them, they will corrupt you."[7]

But the battle is made more difficult because the adversary is often a "hidden class enemy"; "There are instances where the class enemies come out personally to fight the battle. But more frequently, they perpetrate sabotage by making use of their influence in the ideological sphere."[8] The covert activities of the class enemy are likened to a duck in a river: to look at it, the duck seems quite tranquil; but beneath the surface of the water its feet are constantly in motion.[9] The protracted and all-pervasive conflict among social classes can be won for the revolution only if Chinese "constantly ring the imaginary bell of class struggle in our minds."[10]

2. *The mixing of class and label.* In the early years of the People's Republic, the concepts of class and label were usually distinguished with some care. Class, a category of universal membership, was determined by the classical test of one's relationship to the means of production. Relatively few people had labels, and those who did had earned them through the quite different means of socially disapproved conduct. It was important to treat landlords and rich peasants (two classes) separately from counterrevolutionaries (a label), said a 1956 *People's Daily* article, in order to encourage the disintegration of the bad classes and the shrinkage of the social base of the bad label. Confusing them might thwart these goals.[11]

However, increasingly through the first decade of Communist rule, a tendency developed to group together the names of the bad classes and the worst labels. The common status of such people as real or potential enemies of socialism was apparently more important than theoretical niceties about the origins of the two concepts. The 1955 "Decisions on Agricultural Cooperation," for instance, complained of "feudal landlords, rowdies, counterrevolutionaries, and other bad elements," thus mixing in one breath one class and several labels.[12] This phenomenon became more pronounced in the Antirightist Campaign of 1957, which raised to greater prominence the idea of the "five-category elements," or "five bad elements," as the phrase is more frequently and less accurately translated. Landlord, rich peasant, counterrvolutionary, bad element, and rightist element *(difufanhuaiyou)* were, by virtue of the common suspicion with which they were regarded by the Communist Party, thrown together in a listing which dominated both popular and official consciousness until Mao's death.

This commingling of class and label in the 1950s was an empirical mixing, one which came about in an almost casual fashion. It was only with the renewed emphasis upon class struggle of the next decade that the breakdown of distinctions between the two categories was given a systematic theoretical foundation. As with many innovations in an established ideology, the label-class mixture, along with the rest of the new theory of class struggle, was initially offered as if it were the hoariest of traditions. Thus an important formulation by Mao in the course of the polemic with the Soviet Union in the early 1960s repeatedly and respectfully cited the authority of Lenin:

After the October Revolution, Lenin pointed out a number of times that:

(a) The overthrown exploiters always try in a thousand and one ways to recover the 'paradise' they have been deprived of.

(b) New elements of capitalism are constantly and spontaneously generated in the petty-bourgeois atmosphere.

(c) Political degenerates and new bourgeois elements may emerge in the ranks of the working class and among government functionaries as a result of bourgeois influence and the pervasive, corrupting atmosphere of the petty bourgeoisie.

(d) The external conditions for the continuance of class struggle within a socialist country are encirclement by international capitalism, and imperialists' threat of armed intervention and their subversive activities to accomplish peaceful disintegration.

Mao added that "Life has confirmed these conclusions of Lenin's."

> For decades or even longer periods after socialist industrialization and agricultural collectivisation, it will be impossible to say that any socialist country will be free from those elements which Lenin repeatedly denounced, such as bourgeois hangers-on, parasites, speculators, swindlers, idlers, hooligans and embezzlers of state funds; or to say that a socialist country will no longer need to perform or be able to relinquish the task laid down by Lenin of conquering 'this contagion, this plague, this ulcer that socialism has inherited from capitalism.' [13]

The Soviet response to this document (which had not then been attributed to Mao Zedong) was uncompromising. The Soviets dealt sarcastically with the roster of hostile class elements enumerated by Mao:

> It must be conceded that this is quite an original notion on the part of the Chinese comrades about classes and class struggle. Since when have these parasitical elements been considered a class? and what class? A class of embezzlers of public property, or a class of parasites? In no society have criminals comprised a particular class. Every schoolboy knows this. Of course, in socialist society, too, these elements do not comprise a class. These are manifestations of the vestiges of capitalism. [14]

Although the Soviet Communist Party had no better claim than the Chinese to represent a true and orthodox Marxism, its reaction exhibited an appreciation for the novelty of the Chinese position. Mao was unable to present a modified view of class and successfully pass it off as an ancient Marxist practice.

One need only examine the phraseology of class struggle in China to see that something had changed by the 1960s. What is the relationship to the means of production of "ghosts and monsters," or "chameleons and little reptiles," to cite two of the more colorful labels applied to persons seen as representing the bourgeoisie? The former phrase included all of the "five-category elements," thus making even landlords the servants of capitalism in China. Contrast this with the careful distinctions drawn even among bad classes at the time of liberation, when the landlord class was characterized as feudal in nature, unwilling to "develop along the capitalist road." [15]

An obvious effect of the blending of class and label was to increase the number of "classes," particularly during the Cultural Revolution, when new labels were devised with considerable zeal and imagination. [16] But some of the old class terminology was dropped to give way to the new and more fanciful class nomenclature of the 1960s. Here I refer mainly to the complex substratification of the peasantry which had presented so many problems after liberation. The old concern with new and old middle peasants vanished, and such terms as "new upper-middle peasant" were rarely employed after the early 1960s. The former distinctions among various sorts of landlords (enlightened, tyrannical, bankrupt, etc.) also became irrelevant.

In fact, although official class designations remained unchanged for the great bulk of the population, the officially perceived class structure of China underwent a process of simplification. Urban society had already been characterized by a tripartite division into the bad capitalists, the ambiguous petty bourgeoisie, and the good proletariat. With the Maoist revival, rural classes too began to fall into three groupings analogous to those of the city Chinese. Through their constant linkage as members of the five-category elements, landlords and rich peasants seemed to be fused in popular consciousness into a single bad class category comparable to the city's bourgeoisie. The middle category consisted of the "well-to-do middle peasants," a group proportionately much smaller than its urban counterpart, and all that remained, in practice, of the once important middle peasantry. The most important group in the countryside, both in numbers and in political purity, was the poor and lower-middle peasantry, a category which embraced three designations—lower-middle peasants, poor peasants, and hired agricultural laborers.

The English phrase "poor and lower-middle peasants" seems to denote two groups. However, one can date to approximately 1965–1966 a period in which the Chinese press stopped referring to "poor peasants *and* lower-middle peasants" (*pinnong xiazhongnong*) and began using the expression "poor and lower-middle peasants" (*pinxiazhongnong*), a transition which symbolized the blending of the two groups into a new classification of "rural proletarians" (actually three groups were so united, as the hired agricultural laborers had long since been subsumed into the poor peasant designation).

This is not to say that the official class designations of individual Chinese changed at all. These differences still continued to exist, and in spite of their new close association, it was and is still better to be a poor peasant than a lower-middle peasant. According to Cultural Revolution emigrants, the poor peasant, when asked his or her class designation, would simply reply, "poor peasant." The lower-middle peasant, however, trying to cash in on the greater prestige of the poor peasant category, would somewhat ambiguously respond, "poor and lower-middle peasant."

This simplification of the popular treatment of class designations complemented the growing reliance upon labels as a device which political authorities could employ flexibly to handle tensions in a rapidly changing society.[17] The static irrelevance of the class designations had demanded such an alternative form of classification.

3. *The complexity of class struggle.* As early as 1955, Mao advised that "We should never be so bookish as to regard the complex class struggle as so very simple."[18] The sense of a "complicated" class struggle rests on an image of a social process which is almost organic in nature, a self-sufficient social tension which has a life of its own: "It moves forward in a wave-like manner, rising at one time and falling at the other. Only when we fully know the twists and turns of class struggle can we foresee the trend of class struggle and retain the initiative in struggle."[19]

During the Cultural Revolution, those who attempted to thwart the natural course of conflict among classes were charged with vainly attempting "to keep the lid on class struggle." But if the natural development of class struggle could not be held back, neither could it be forced, as Mao explained in criticizing the premature formation of alliances among rival radical factions during the Cultural Revolution: because the laws of class struggle could not be abrogated by political intervention, such alliances could not endure.[20]

How could one come to an understanding of the laws and patterns of class struggle, so that such errors might be avoided? In socialist society, as in the revolutionary period which preceded it, the method of class analysis still remained "our most basic method for knowing conditions."[21] Class analysis was difficult, however, in a period in which the class struggle was characterized by complexity. And class struggle, as China progressed toward communism, would not become any simpler: "The closer is the all-round victory, the more complex and violent the struggle between the two classes, the two roads, the two lines becomes."[22] Only through persistent efforts to apply class analysis to Chinese society would one be able to understand the shape of the struggle. But once mastered, class analysis became a "magic weapon" with which the enemy could be defeated.[23]

A much-repeated phrase of Mao's held out encouragement: "the class struggle is effective once grasped." But the weapon of class analysis is double-edged, and may be wielded by the class enemy as well as by revolutionaries:

> They have long experience in class struggle, and they know how to engage in all kinds of struggle—both legal and illegal struggle. We revolutionary Party members must understand this aspect, and must study their tactics, in order that we may be victorious over them.[24]

With an understanding of the laws which govern class struggle, one can seize the initiative and cease being a pliant object, buffeted about by the currents of the struggle. Although the class struggle cannot be forced, its patterns can be mastered.

> Chairman Mao has said: 'There are laws governing swimming. It is easier to learn to swim if one masters them.' There are also laws governing revolution. Only by mastering them is it possible to acquire the ability to keep hold of the reins through all the developments and changes in class struggle.[25]

Of course, changes in the class struggle are not necessarily left to the analytical powers of individual communists to discover.

Party leaders point them out, and urge others to make appropriate adjustments in their own thinking. Such suggestions should assist those who are confused by the tortuous course of class struggle: "we should give these comrades a violent slap on the back so as to wake them up and make them catch up with the new situation in the class struggle today." [26] Merely because the high tide of a particular movement passed, one must not presume that class struggle is a process which "sometimes exists and sometimes does not." [27] In truth, the class struggle continues even when the class enemy has gone "deep in hiding." [28] The changing forms of class struggle combine with its "wave-like" motion to give the process a dialectical shape which must be comprehended before the larger pattern can be grasped. "Observing only the appearance and not the substance, one would likely consider the class struggle which rises and falls in a wave-like manner as occasionally non-existent." [29] Only constant analysis can reveal the changing material interests upon which successful revolutionary politics must be based.

4. *Line struggle.* The Maoist redefinition of class in terms of political behavior resulted in a constant emphasis upon a "struggle between two lines." In the phrase, "the struggle between two classes, two roads and two lines," one can easily identify the classes as the proletariat and the bourgeoisie, and the roads are obviously those leading to socialism and to capitalism. But what are the two lines, and how are they related to class struggle?

The two lines are the two sets of policies which promote either capitalism or socialism in China. The concrete manifestation of line, we are told, is policy, a fact which indicates that the arena of line struggle is more limited than that of class struggle, which embraces all social relations as its sphere. [30] "Line struggle is the reflection within the Party of the class struggle in society. So long as classes, class contradictions and class struggle exist in society, there must be the struggle between two lines within the Party." [31] Line struggle is thus a refinement of class struggle; because of its central locus within the Party, it is of special importance. In Mao's 1971 words, "The line is the key link; once it is grasped, everything falls into place." [32]

Line struggle is located not in the economic base but in the superstructure, where the behavioral consequences of material conflicts are evident. Mao is credited with teaching that class struggle in the superstructure is "in the last analysis, a matter of what ideological and political line" should be followed.[33] Attention to issues of line, centered as they are among Party members—whose class designations are likely to be good ones—is thus another step in the weakening of presocialist distinctions.

And as there are people in society who do not understand the ongoing nature of class struggle, so there are those who fail to comprehend that line struggle is also a continuing process. There must be efforts to counteract such tendencies as the "theory of the extinction of line struggle," or the view that "line problems have already been resolved."[34] The greater rarification of line than class struggle sometimes makes line struggle difficult to relate to the concrete conditions of daily life, thus giving rise to the "theory that line struggle is difficult to know."[35] Because of this *People's Daily* urged its readers to apply to line struggle Mao's advice about conflict among classes: "We must talk about it every year, every month, and every day."[36]

The modification of class analysis put a premium on a venerable tradition in Chinese Marxism: the insistence that a person can transcend a specific economic environment to serve a different class. Peasants could be seen as serving the proletariat, and renegade workers could assist the bourgeoisie, becoming class enemies, or "class alien elements." Much of the new theory—most notably the attention to issues of political line and the intermingling of class and label—underscored this conviction. Especially in a socialist society, Maoists held, class standpoint, the behavioral manifestation of consciousness, had become more basic than economic position in identifying class.

In 1962, Mao characterized the relationship among the three elements and the two bad classes of the five-category elements: "Counterrevolutionaries, bad elements, and anticommunist rightists represent the landlord class and the reactionary bourgeoisie. These classes and bad persons account for about four or five percent of the population."[37] The key word here is "represent," which indicates that whatever their personal class designations, these bad people will, in their behavior, serve the interests of the enemy classes.

Although the procedure is not easy nor are the criteria obvious, one can change class standpoint without change in property relationships by vigorously pursuing a revolutionary line. But even when an individual has changed his or her position in the production process, there is no reason to presume that a modification of

class standpoint must follow naturally. Mao pointed out that joining a labor union is not equivalent to becoming a proletarian.[38]
There is a great likelihood that a person entering a new class will
bear with him the ideology of a former economic group.

Mao's assessment of the situation of the intellectuals in 1956
seems consonant with his revised vision of class: "The intellectuals
serve the class they were born into. The classes of their birth have
now been destroyed, so they hang in mid air, they do not stand
on firm ground."[39] In Mao's new theory, the firm ground of a
reliable class standpoint could only be conceded when people
proved themselves through behavior.

5. *Two kinds of contradictions.* The final major element in the
new approach to class was the distinction, which Mao stressed in
1957, between two kinds of contradictions—those among the people, and those between the people and the enemy. Indeed, many
Cultural Revolutionaries claimed Mao's speech "On the Correct
Handling of Contradictions Among the People" as the basis for
grasping both theory and practice of class struggle in China.[40]

I argued in chapter 3 that Mao's 1957 speech on resolving contradictions among the people was intended to offer a class-transcending conception with which one might discuss Chinese social
cleavages after the basic socialization of the means of production.
In this interpretation, I suggested that Mao's second thoughts on
the subject caused him to modify his position somewhat in the
belatedly published text of his speech, where he left open the possibility for a still important role for class struggle in China.

The view of class struggle which dates from the early 1960s,
however, is certainly far more affirmative and thoroughgoing
than Mao's 1957 words on the subject. There is a definite tension
between the willingness to consider all kinds of social contradictions which Mao expressed in 1957 and the exclusive focus upon
class as the dominant social category of the following decade. This
tension was partially mitigated by the broadening redefinition of
class which was at the core of the Maoist revival, but the fact
remains that this new emphasis on class struggle was from the
outset placed within an analytical framework which had been designed to deemphasize the role of class.[41]

Some consequences of this become evident when one attempts
to understand just how the two kinds of contradictions are related
to the class struggle in society, a problem which became especially
prominent during the course of the Cultural Revolution. Proletar-

ian revolutionaries were to "use the viewpoint of class struggle and the method of class analysis to differentiate strictly the two different types of contradictions."[42] But after the socialization of the means of production, "confronted by the new situation of complex class struggle, many people were confused." This was in part because class struggle "permeated both types" of contradictions, and also because "the two different types of contradictions are often interwoven." Ultimately, the confusion between the two types could be clarified by relying upon the "political microscope and telescope" of Mao Zedong's thought.[43]

But even the Chairman had some trouble distinguishing the two kinds of contradictions during the Cultural Revolution: "The problem is that our contradictions with those who have made ideological mistakes and the contradictions between the enemy and ourselves can be mixed up and cannot be clearly separated for the time being."[44] Such analytical difficulties were often approached not by empirical investigations, but by following closely a series of "instructions" issued by Chairman Mao.[45] No matter if Mao was himself confused at times; his preferred politics of class struggle demanded that he issue authoritative glosses to his abstract writings on class.

If the fit between contradictions and classes as views of Chinese society was not always a smooth one, the distinction between two kinds of contradictions played an important role in Chinese class theory. The theory of contradictions, whether or not it was fully integrated into the theory of class struggle under socialism, helped to smooth the practice of class struggle in China.

The Behavioral Theory of Class as a Marxist Project

As a theoretical enterprise, the new approach to class was replete with ambiguities. Given both the ambitious scope of Mao's project and the still inchoate aspects of the rapidly changing society which he sought to comprehend, the achievement of scientific precision in class analysis would have been astonishing. In his search for a new theory of class, Mao had reinforced an older tendency within the Chinese Communist Party to value class standpoint above actual economic position as he directed attention away from the former calculation of individual relationships to the means of production. As he did so, the specification of personal class membership became highly problematic, as I will indicate later. But the fact that class membership was no longer predominantly a question of relatively unambiguous economic relationships does not imply that class had become instead little more than a set of arbitrary moral categories. One frequently encountered view holds that the Maoist revival of class turned Chinese Marxism into an idealist rather than a materialist doctrine. Here I will argue that the Maoist emphasis upon political behavior did establish some limits to the risks of subjectivity which it courted, and that Mao's revised approach to class may be interpreted as a serious restoration of concerns central to the Marxist tradition, rather than as an aspect of its decomposition.

Benjamin Schwartz has argued most thoroughly the moral dimension of class in China. In an early study, he noted the isolation of the young Communist Party from its desired proletarian base, a separation which Party leaders attempted to overcome through the acquisition of proletarian ideology.[46] Writing on the Cultural Revolution, Schwartz came to feel that even this tenuous connection between China's relatively small working class and the definition of "proletarian" had been broken. In discussing the idea of the dictatorship of the proletariat, he comments:

> In effect what has happened in China since 1957 is that the Maoist group in particular has come to use this phrase with ever-increasing vehemence as a designation of the dominance of the forces of good— whatever these forces may be—over the forces of evil, however defined. "Proletarian nature" now refers to a cluster of virtues, such as selfless submission to the collectivity, simplicity, austerity, unflagging energy, and single-minded hatred of the enemy, which can be thought of in detachment not only from its presumed class basis, but even from the Communist Party itself. . . . In fact "bourgeoisie" and "proletariat" have been transmuted in the Maoist universe into something like two pervasive fluids, one noxious and the other beneficial, which can find their lodgments anywhere.[47]

Schwartz holds that "the ultimate battlefield is the human soul," that "in the end the main criterion for assigning persons to the 'people' or 'nonpeople' is to be sought in their spiritual attitudes rather than in the facts of their class origin."[48]

At times, Schwartz seems almost ready to argue that class has become so arbitrary as to have no meaning at all: "The proletarian dictatorship is exercised by whatever groups or individuals behave in what Mao conceives to be a proper proletarian way." Most often, however, he resists the temptation to assert that class is merely the whim of Mao.[49]

An interpretation of class as a moral category is a useful one, as it stresses the movement from a basically economic conception, and it points to the strong evaluative component of the Maoist meaning of class. But to reduce class membership to a question of the mind is a misleading overstatement of an otherwise important insight. If class were in fact simply a matter of "a flash of illumination," or "a state of mind," then *all* Chinese should be capable of counting themselves as proletarians. But it is not that easy: class cannot be modified at will, a fact which is made evident through recurrent, intensive political debates over the statuses of former landlords, capitalists, and their children. Were class simply a matter of thought, why have such persons simply not willed themselves into the proletariat?[50]

Rather than being Schwartz's "clusters of virtues," "pervasive fluids . . . which can find their lodgments anywhere," classes in the new Maoist perspective represent a concept which directs attention toward neither economic position nor moral attitudes, but rather toward *manifestations* of such attitudes in the form of political behavior.

One reason to suspect that class may usefully be considered in terms of political behavior is that the Maoists continuously have told us to do so. Thus "the class struggle under the dictatorship of the proletariat, when reduced to a single issue, is still centered on the question of political power," but also "in class society all class struggles are political struggles."[51] What is politics? All class struggle is political struggle, according to one formula; in another, "politics refers to the struggle between classes."[52]

The practical method of identifying class membership is far removed from asking the relationship to the means of production, but it is equally distant from plotting the vague contours of struggle within the human soul. What is the alternative? "The most important way of judging a representative of a particular class is to see the line and policies he pushes and the interests of the class he represents."[53] Again, "We must see which class and line a thing serves and benefits. . . . Without class analysis and the class utilitarian standard, we would be more muddle-headed the more comparison we make."

This same article goes on to promote the six criteria offered by Mao in his Contradictions speech as standards for judging the quality of political behavior, adding that "the two most important concern the socialist road and Party leadership."[54]

This formulation of course begs the question of class criteria, as it is not necessarily evident what constitutes support for the socialist road or Party leadership. Of interest at this juncture, however, is not the relative nature of these class criteria, but rather the facts that there are criteria at all (which may appear much less relative to Chinese than to outsiders), and that these criteria are political ones. Here must be stressed the important distinction between arbitrary evaluation—which is done with no standards at all—and evaluation with political criteria, where the standards, albeit easily mutable and subject to abuse, are related to the goals one seeks to attain. The Maoist fascination with actual behavior and the interests which it represents made the new use of class political rather than merely whimsical.

Maoist emphasis upon labels and concern for political line both flow from this focus upon the behavioral dimension of class. Labels permit the continual fashioning of new class categories applicable to behaviors which represent the interests of classes hostile to socialism. The political line similarly draws attention away from economic position to force an examination of the potential consequences of the set of political acts which constitute Party policy.

However, the link between class and political behavior may be most apparent in the uses of Mao's theory of contradictions among the people. The political nature of class conflict and class categories is highlighted by the fact that the definitions of "people" and "enemy" are not constant. Mao asserted in 1957 that the content of these categories would vary and had varied in each period of the revolution and of socialist construction, and this impermanence has been stressed since.[55] One way of understanding Mao's behavioral conception of class struggle is to liken it to the Party's tradition of guerrilla warfare, with its attention to gathering the largest possible number of forces to attack the enemy where it is numerically weak—to determine the outcome of the war by manipulating the conditions of each battle so that in the shifting balance of forces, the enemy is always at a disadvantage.

That the class enemy is defined as "a small handful" means not only that the majority is a large one (95 percent is the almost magic figure one repeatedly encounters in the Chinese press), but that the formula by which that majority is to be mobilized and consolidated must be broadly based. The task is "to isolate thoroughly the most reactionary Rightists, win over the middle and unite with the great majority so that by the end of the movement we shall achieve the unity of more than 95 per cent of the cadres and more than 95 per cent of the masses."[56]

What emerges here is an image of class struggle where the good and bad classes (people and enemy) are defined ultimately by a quota. Persons are ranged according to political stance (actions and words which support the socialist road and the leadership of the Communist Party) along the political spectrum from left to right, the 5 percent on the extreme right being designated as the enemy and the other 95 percent being united through struggle against the minority. The key factor in identifying this 5 percent is not some absolute judgment of its political behavior, but the implications of its conduct for the majority.

The theory of contradictions among the people does not define classes, or even show how they are related; rather it provides a structure to the conflict, and if the structure is mastered, the course of struggle among classes can be guided. The contradictions doctrine offers a theoretical underpinning for practical wisdom which the Party learned long ago about building social solidarity through overcoming a common enemy.

In distinguishing class enemies from the people, this strategy focuses attention upon the often subtle gradation of political errors to the right of the political spectrum. It seeks to weaken opposition by offering differential treatment to its members, as in separating "the chieftains of the revisionist line from good people who made mistakes in line."[57] This means that in judging cadres and other leaders, one must consider entire careers, not just single mistakes. In Mao's words, "We must see not only every deed of a cadre at any moment, but also the whole of his history and work. This is the chief method for distinguishing cadres." And as for ordinary people who have made mistakes, such as joining conservative organizations in the Cultural Revolution, "through the class viewpoint" it is evident that "the hoodwinked masses are our class brothers."[58]

The ability to find this line by which one can separate the real and potential ally from the necessary adversary is a test of political astuteness.

Those with a Rightist way of thinking make no distinction between ourselves and the enemy and take the enemy for our own people. They regard as friends the very persons whom the broad masses regard as enemies. Those with a "Left" way of thinking magnify contradictions between ourselves and the enemy to such an extent that they take certain contradictions among the people for contradictions with the enemy and regard as counterrevolutionaries persons who are actually not counterrevolutionaries.[59]

When the line of division has not been properly identified, "a considerable section of the masses and especially those in the middle cannot be mobilized. Some people with ordinary problems are full of misgivings, while the genuine class enemies are full of glee."[60] But if the line of division has been correctly located, matters should follow the course laid out by Mao for the Socialist Education Movement, in which the class struggle was supposed to give unity to the forces of the people as it caused the enemy's ranks to disintegrate:

Throughout the movement, contradictions must be utilized to win over the majority and oppose the minority, and to knock down the enemy one by one. As is always the case, there are very few people who obstinately cling to the capitalist road. Some people have made mistakes, but they still can be corrected. We must be good at sowing discord among the targets of the four clean-up campaigns, deal with them according to their distinctions, and isolate people of the worst type to the maximum extent.[61]

In the politics of class struggle in China the most critical point on the political spectrum is that occupied by the small range of persons who hover between majority and minority. This is as true for whole classes and strata as it is for individuals within a specific unit. It is these borderline groups and individuals which will feel the greatest pressure to disassociate themselves from the minority on the right and embrace the majority on the left. This shaded section, stranded between the security of friendship and the certitude of enmity, may be largest at the beginning of a campaign, when the issues which are to unite the 95 percent are still unsettled. As the contours of the campaign take shape, however, the size of this section diminishes rapidly, as the strategy of the Party is to encourage the largest possible number of these doubtful cases in their hopes of finding safe refuge in the arms of the majority:

"We must not treat class enemies on the same basis, we must differentiate them, dividing them and disintegrating them." [62]

It is, of course, this need to divide the enemy which has always compelled the Party to adopt a policy of seeking the most broadly based compromise which is consonant with victory. The short-term goal is always that of uniting the most against the fewest, employing a program of common interests.

> The majority should be united on the basis of long-range interests. The demons and monsters are the landlords, rich peasants, counter-revolutionaries, bad people and rightists—the minority. Some people who have committed serious mistakes should also be saved so they may start with a clean slate. Otherwise, how can we unite more than 95 per cent of the people? [63]

None of this, of course, is entirely new. The same development of a majority to overcome a minority characterized the Party's theory and practice of the United Front in the years before liberation. Although the "class" of that time was much more strictly an economic category, at times the demands of fulfilling the proper numerical formula even then seemed to outweigh the economic factors. For instance, it is clear from Ren Bishi's well-known land reform speech of January 1948 that, rather than rely solely on objective economic conditions, the Party set quotas for class designations in the countryside. [64] And a tendency to value the relationship to the means of production less highly than the building of a majority was clearly expressed in 1954 by Deng Zi-hui. To the question "Why rely on the poor peasants?" Deng replied, "primarily it is because poor peasants . . . constitute a majority of the rural population . . . , and striving to obtain a majority of the masses is a basic principle of Marxism-Leninism." [65]

If such tendencies existed even when class was still relatively firmly bound to the relationship to the means of production, it is easy to imagine the greater slipperiness in visualizing class relationships which emerged after that bond was broken. Schwartz and others are correct in pointing to a greatly increased fluidity in determining "enemy" and "people." But mutable as these categories have been, the subjectivity of class has been limited in theory by the standard of real-life political behavior. This is rather different from conceiving of classes as exotic forces, occupying and doing battle over a marvelous spiritual universe of their own.

None of this is to deny the importance of the moral dimension of the Maoist theory of class. But there is no need to label this theory simplistically as "idealism" merely because the relationship between class behavior and economic position is not always a direct and vulgar one. In fact, Maoist thinking about class attempts to make sense of the complexity of this relationship in real life. Donald Munro suggests the subtleties involved:

> There is a general tendency in Maoism for the link between man's social nature (thought) and the economic base (so essential in the Marxist definition of social relations) to be sometimes fuzzy, sometimes nonexistent, and never as necessarily linked as in classical Marxism. There is no denial that the social environment influences people's thoughts. On the contrary, the greatest attention is paid the influence of regional practices and needs and group life-styles on the thought of citizens.[66]

Indeed, for all its imprecision, the Maoist behavioral approach to class is much closer to the spirit of Marx's own class analysis than was the formal hierarchy of class designations which it sought to supplant. The class designations had assumed an implausible accuracy in the calculation of individual class position, whereas only the most vulgarized forms of Marxism anticipate an *automatic* relationship between material position and political behavior.

By raising once again the opposition between class and stratification, it becomes possible to understand the complex interaction between Mao's revised theory of class conflict in socialist society and the static system of class designations as a dialectical one. Among Marx's few remarks on the character of socialist society is the well-known comment that it is "still stamped with the birth marks of the old society from whose womb it emerges."[67] Mao's revision of the theory of class was an effort to move beyond the birthmark of class designations to address new inequalities distinctive to socialist society. This enterprise may be seen as an effort to liberate "class" from the narrow confines of a social stratification which at best offered a pale image derived from a class structure which no longer existed.

One of the recurrent problems of Mao's new class theory has been its lack of specificity, the difficulty of locating individuals firmly within it. But in the effort to recapture the spirit of Marx's class theory, this problem is in fact a virtue, as it denotes a concern for the interests and behavior of broad social groups. In terms of the polarity between Marx's class concept and the ranking notion of stratification, Mao's "revision" of Marx, in moving away from the means-of-production test, is simultaneously a restoration of Marx, as Mao attempted to revitalize the dynamic, historical, analytic dimensions of Marx's class idea in a new social context.

Mao's Theory and the Practice of Class Conflict

Though the revised theory did not reduce class to the level of personal whim, neither was it wholly adequate for comprehending and managing the new class tensions of socialist society. In fact, the impact of this theory upon the practice of class conflict which it sought to analyze was ambiguous. While it contributed to Maoist political successes, it also exacerbated some bitterly divisive tendencies within Chinese society.

At one level, the Cultural Revolution, which developed both from and alongside Mao's new approach to class, was a period in which radical social policies flourished. Although no one can overlook the elements of continuity in Chinese policymaking which weaken official Chinese claims for dramatic shifts through the struggle between two lines, it is apparent that the Cultural Revolution strengthened prior Maoist efforts to limit bureaucratic privileges, to favor rural development over urban growth, and to expand the provision of health care and basic education to China's peasant majority.[68] These goals were central to Mao's motivation in initially deciding to revive the concept of class, and thus it is inappropriate to quickly brand Mao's effort a failure, whether on the basis of lack of intellectual rigor or because of practical difficulties in implementation.

Among the practical problems was the ironic undermining of Mao's favored political tactics through previous years of successful social reform. By the time Mao attempted to revitalize the Party's tradition of class analysis in the mid-1960s, China had become a very different society from the time of liberation. The thrust of Mao's reconceptualization of class was to honor the impact of socialist transformation and the decrease in inequalities based upon private property. But with socialization had come a second change which was less easily accommodated by Mao's new theory of class conflict: although class distinctions still existed in socialist China, a decade of vigorous social reform had ameliorated them. There was no longer an easily delineated and isolated privileged minority of 5 percent, which made problematic the Maoist challenge to build class alliances upon the shared interests of the vast majority. It is not that Mao's categories of enemy and friend had been made irrelevant, but that the tactics for class politics long associated with these categories had become more difficult to employ in the absence of a relatively clear-cut polarization around which mass mobilization could be organized.

The fact that class was not merely an arbitrary conception in Maoist theory did not protect against arbitrary applications of a difficult and often obscure doctrine. Distinguishing proletarian from bourgeois behavior was difficult, even when sincerely attempted. When applied hastily in the course of political struggle, the behavioral emphasis was often a source of mischief, as good socialist action may be variously defined. The repeated emphasis upon class struggle often encouraged the rhetorical escalation of routine social conflicts into life-and-death struggles between proletarians and bourgeoisie.[69] But when the official language of class conflict was superimposed upon local disagreements, there was often considerable uncertainty about how to use its class categories, a phenomenon which strengthened existing factional tendencies among Mao's youthful rebels.[70]

More ominously, the new class analysis was too easily used to turn weakened political adversaries into scapegoats, badgering old enemies in the name of revolution. In the absence of unambiguous guidelines for class identification, many cadres succumbed to the temptation to assign labels on the basis of personal animosities or ambitions. "Don't label people at random," Mao had warned in 1966. "Some of our cadres are fond of using labels to apply pressure to other people. Every time they speak, they let labels fly around, thus making other people dare not speak out."[71] Although Mao was apparently aware of the potential misuse inherent in his advocacy of labels as a dynamic alternative to the static system of class designations, he had not anticipated the weight these labels would acquire when buttressed by the cult of his own personality in the Cultural Revolution.

The Maoist stress upon superstructural phenomena was perhaps a necessary ingredient in the formula linking the class behavior of former property owners with that of new socialist bureaucrats. But it also encouraged a confusing tendency to treat some social groups as proto-classes, even when a common material basis was nonexistent. The Cultural Revolution's appeal to youth, for instance, often seemed to treat a particular age cohort as a component of a class alliance against the bourgeoisie. More narrowly drawn groups also attempted to utilize the call for class struggle to pursue very specific interests, as "rebel" organizations were sometimes composed solely of cooks, or drivers and conductors, or 1965 university graduates. Maoist leaders responded bitterly to the additional divisiveness introduced through these instances of interest-group politics.[72]

Perhaps even more disconcerting to the radicals was a related tendency for the language of class to be used to mask conflict organized by personalistic political factions. The Maoist focus upon political behavior was easily subverted by the long-standing Chinese propensity for factional conflict groups.[73] As this problem intensified in 1967 and 1968, the Maoist response was first, to seek a class basis for factional politics, and second, to supplant their reliance upon quarrelsome Red Guard groups with a new attention to industrial workers.[74] The class standing of industrial workers was relatively unambiguous, a feature which must have made them very appealing in the tumult of the Cultural Revolution.[75]

The superstructural emphasis of the Maoist focus upon political behavior also draws upon the Chinese Communist Party's tradition for self-criticism and thought reform. The violence of the Stalinist purges in the Soviet Union has been unacceptable to the Chinese, who have long been reluctant to take the lives of errant and defeated political leaders. Because incorrect behavior can be altered, labeled cadres can be rehabilitated. The Maoist conception of leadership assumes considerable movement in and out of authoritative positions, as may be seen in Mao's own image of the body politic:

> A human being has arteries and veins and his heart makes the blood circulate; one breathes through the lungs, exhaling carbon dioxide and inhaling oxygen afresh, that is, getting rid of the waste and letting in the fresh. A proletarian party must also get rid of the waste and let in the fresh, for only in this way can it be full of vigor.

Without eliminating waste and getting fresh blood the Party has no vigor.[76]

As labels have been assigned each year since liberation, large numbers of cadres (perhaps a majority in many units) have been labeled for major or minor transactions.[77] As career success depends upon the demonstrated quality of one's political behavior, cadres are eager to minimize the stigma of labels. This can be accomplished by proving through proper behavior that the original deviation has been corrected, or (more ambitiously) a direct challenge can be made to the legitimacy of the verdict by which a label was assigned.

During the Cultural Revolution, countless individuals and organizations responded to the Maoist appeal for class struggle by demanding a "reversal of verdicts," arguing that the political behavior for which they had earlier been labeled had been misjudged. This phenomenon has been repeated in other mass political movements; when radicals hold power, persons formerly labeled for "leftist" errors come forth to claim the injustice of their treatment, and when conservatives are dominant, behavior once classified as "rightist" is presented as truly revolutionary.[78]

Demands for the reversal of verdicts passed upon an entire category of persons are frequently organized around a few well-known cases, in which successful reversal would establish a precedent for many more people in similar situations.[79] Such test cases might win attention because of their sensationalism or emotional appeal. For instance, Chen Liang was a Guangdong language teacher who was labeled a counterrevolutionary in the early stage of the Cultural Revolution, allegedly by conservative cadres attempting to deflect criticism of their own shortcomings. He killed himself and his two sons after being labeled, and subsequently became a martyr in a major compaign for his rehabilitation.[80]

Demands for reversal might also be pressed on the grounds that recently discredited officials had been involved in passing the original verdict. One notable example is the "case of the two Chens." Chen Po and Chen Kun were two Guangzhou Public Security officials who were arrested in 1951 as spies, along with one thousand other persons alleged to be implicated in their activities. The campaign for their rehabilitation stressed the active role played by the purged Minister of Public Security Luo Ruiqing in determining their case, as well as the less direct involvement of such other targets of the Cultural Revolution as Deng Xiaoping, Peng Zhen, Liu Shaoqi, and Yang Shangkun. Some indication of the complexity of rehabilitation politics in China is found in the fact that this case, argued in 1968, had roots in the 1940s, when Chen Po is said to have exposed Luo Ruiqing's Yan'an lover as a secret agent for the Guomindang.[81] Official files were often raided during the Cultural Revolution, and documentation favorable to a campaign for reversal was often disseminated widely through the Red Guard press.

The confusion brought about during the Cultural Revolution by the large number of demands for reversal of verdicts was considerable. At a time when the old administrative offices had been paralyzed, the new Revolutionary Committees were overwhelmed by demands for rehabilitation. Of 847 letters and 168 visitors received by the Qinghai Provincial Revolutionary Committee, 422 letters and 130 visitors sought the removal of labels, which had become "the rage of the time." The head of the work unit of this committee complained:

> Right now, because there is an extraordinarily large number of people demanding rehabilitation, the normal development of work in the Revolutionary Committee has been affected. For a time, the officer on duty of the Standing Committee was unable to work. Quite a number of visitors demanding rehabilitation had been issued letters of introduction or official replies by the reception centers of various departments of the State Council and the Central Committee. Bringing with them such letters of introduction to the Revolutionary Committee, they tended to lose their temper, saying: 'How can you be called the Revolutionary Committee since you are unable to rehabilitate those with letters of introduction from the Central Committee?' Among the visitors demanding rehabilitation, quite a number were from other provinces, *chou* [prefectures] or *hsien* [counties]. After they came, they demanded immediate rehabilitation and refused to leave without getting what they wanted. In some cases, the whole family came at the same time, and the Revolutionary Committee could only direct them to the units to which they were sent and ask such units to provide the board and lodging. A small number of them did not belong to any work unit, and the Revolutionary Committee had to take care of them.[82]

Just when officals were especially susceptible to criticism for high-handed treatment of their constituents, cadres confronted by such demands were uncertain how to respond. Such anxiety was exacerbated by organized opposition to the reversal of many verdicts by those who hoped to see political adversaries permanently disabled.[83]

The official response to this problem of too many and conflicting demands concerning rehabilitation was fourfold. As the safest course, such cadres sought judgments by higher-level officials on the revolutionary status of individuals and organizations. Zhou Enlai and Kang Sheng were especially busy hearing the claims of different groups, and sometimes even the prestige of Chairman Mao was employed to give added weight to a decision on rehabilitation.[84]

A second step was to restrict the kinds of rehabilitation demands which could legitimately be pressed. This was attempted in two ways. First, May 16, 1966 was selected as a starting point for the Cultural Revolution: verdicts passed before this date were not to be reconsidered "until the later stage of the movement." Verdicts passed after this date included large numbers of early Cultural Revolution enthusiasts who had been labeled as counterrevolutionaries by conservative cadres eager to limit attacks upon the bureaucracy, and were thus appropriate for discussion. A second limit was to identify ten categories of persons who were not allowed to seek reversal of their verdicts. These included the five-category elements, former Guomindang supporters, corrupt officials, thieves, and others.[85]

A third line of cadre self-defense was to order the burning of materials gathered for purposes of seeking or opposing rehabilitation (including wall posters), in hopes of limiting the ammunition available for pursuing these battles.[86]

Finally, several documents were circulated which offered guidelines for treating the delicate issues of rehabilitation.[87] Such texts contained detailed local and central documents, transcripts of interviews with officials responsible for public security and rehabilitation, quotations from leading central cadres, and answers to detailed questions on the interpretation of Cultural Revolution policy concerning rehabilitation. These collections are reminiscent of guides published during land reform to assist cadres in implementing the then unfamiliar system of class designations. In the effort to pin down the obscure meaning of "ghosts and monsters," Maoists turned increasingly to a highly bureaucratized method for administering a campaign originally directed against conservative bureaucrats.

No approach to class is likely both to illuminate fully and to resolve decisively class tensions within a poor and rapidly changing socialist society. But even if Mao's effort is not judged against such a perfect standard, it is apparent that considerable difficulties were encountered in implementing the new Maoist theory of class. Many of these difficulties arose from the elusiveness of its central concept, political behavior. As we have seen, one reason why political behavior was appealing to Mao as a measure of class was that it permitted attention to be directed simultaneously against China's defeated propertied classes and the "new bourgeois elements" found within the socialist bureaucracy. Another source of behavior's appeal, however, was that it glossed over the politically difficult issue of specifying higher-level officials as a distinct class.

Although Mao's revival of class was in part an effort to move beyond the concern for individual class membership which marred the old system of class designations, in practice a focus upon political behavior again too easily brought the conduct of individuals, rather than groups, to the center of political conflict. Political behavior demanded examination of the conduct of individual cadres within organizations, with the immediate political solution to conflict being the replacement of errant officials with virtuous ones. A more structurally oriented theory would examine instead the institutional roots by which such individuals acquire and employ political power in a socialist society. But before such an approach could be tentatively formulated, it was necessary to play out a very different interpretation of class—one which insisted upon the continued primacy of the old system of class designations.

CHAPTER SIX

Class as Caste

The Maoist revival of class, as we have seen, attempted to encompass within one concept two different types of social inequality. Although the distance separating socialist cadres from socialist citizens was the most troubling to Mao, he also took seriously the continuing threat posed by members of the formerly propertied classes, even though the legal foundation of their power had been undermined by socialist transformation. Since two structurally distinct kinds of social relationships were simultaneously identified as "class," many Chinese could respond onesidedly to Mao's call for class struggle, focusing upon the old system of class designations, which, never having been updated, could be only frozen markers of social status, categories demonstrating one's historical location in a property-based stratification system which no longer existed.

This trend for the transmutation of class designations into badges of status was intensified by popular treatment of young Chinese. Although youth raised since liberation had not participated in the relationships represented by the class designations, the growing interest in class, coupled with the lack of any easy alternative basis for classification, encouraged many to regard class designations as inheritable. The treatment of children of landlords and rich peasants as landlords and rich peasants themselves further diminished the contribution of class categories to an understanding of current socioeconomic relationships. This tendency for class to degenerate into caste was most evident during the Cultural Revolution, with political rights and patterns of social interaction frequently following inherited class designation, especially in the countryside.

The appearance of revolutionary and counterrevolutionary "castes" flowed in some measure from the initial Maoist effort to revitalize interest in class struggle. Maoist leaders urged all Chinese to think about past class relationships as they "remember past bitterness." Formerly exploited peasants were organized into poor and lower-middle peasant associations, whose members recalled old scars inflicted by landlords and rich peasants more readily than they grasped such abstractions as "capitalist-roaders" inside the Communist Party. The perpetuation of legal disabilities against the formerly propertied classes, rather than against the shadowier capitalist-roaders, only reinforced the tendency toward caste. And when state policy sometimes similarly restricted the children of the defeated classes, ordinary Chinese found little odd in extending class designations to the second generation.[1]

From a Maoist perspective, the turning of class into caste was unwelcome. Mao's interest in restoring class as a dynamic conception was at odds with an approach to class which emphasized static patterns of inherited social honor. As consciousness of lineage connections had earlier impeded awareness of the class relationships which cut across them, so did class-as-caste obscure the contours of new class ties in socialist China. Conservative officials, under attack by radical activists, recognized this fact and turned it to their advantage. By interpreting class struggle to be a conflict among old class designations, they deflected criticism from themselves and onto a politically vulnerable group of former landlords, rich peasants, and capitalists.

The tendency toward caste assumed somewhat different forms in city and countryside. In urban areas, the issue was posed in a debate among Red Guards over the role of "bloodline" in measuring revolutionary credentials, while in rural areas, theoretical niceties were less important than the emergence of clear patterns of social interaction based upon the old class categories.

The Question of the Inheritability of Class

Among Mao's motives for reviving the concept of class in socialist China was an anxiety that young Chinese, lacking personal experience in revolution, would prove incapable of preserving their political heritage. In 1964, Mao cited imperialist analyses of China which maintained that revolutionary commitment would wane in the third generation after liberation: "In the Soviet Union it was the third generation that produced the Soviet Khrushchev revisionism. . . . How can we guard against revisionism? How can we cultivate successors to the revolution?"[2]

The juxtaposition of youth and class exposed the Party's indecisiveness on the issue of class designations, which had been fixed prior to socialist transformation. How did the Party's inability to determine how to assign new designations affect young Chinese? Theoretically, as young people came of age and entered the work force, they should have been assigned designations on the basis of their positions in the production process. In practice, youth appear to have decided for themselves what their proper class designations might be. This did not mean that young Chinese were free to select whatever class designations might strike their fancy. Class designation was a datum that had to be reported from time to time in the filling out of various forms, and the likelihood that a cadre familiar with a person's situation might discover a total fabrication was perhaps sufficient to discourage widespread and flagrant abuse. But young people received relatively little guidance on the subject, and were apt to give as their class their occupation, or, particularly among educated urban young people, the category of student.

The only discussion of this problem which I have located in the official press confirms the impression given by former residents of China. A 1962 article in *Chinese Youth* raised the question of what designations to apply to young people from bad class families who returned from school to their villages. The question "should be decided according to the chief means of support the individual has selected. Thus an individual who participates in agricultural production is counted as a peasant, one who participates in industrial production is counted as a worker, one who works in an organ is counted as a cadre, etc."[3] Although source of income is no adequate substitute for one's relationship to the means of production, there is no hint in this article that ancient Marxist principles were here being cast to the winds.[4] In fact, I suspect that it is because this was recognized by the Party as merely an expedient solution to the problem that it was so infrequently encountered in the press. In any event, the advice to young people seems to have been: if you must supply a class designation, offer your occupation, but don't worry too much about its theoretical implications.

The elusive character of the class designations of young people was a significant question on the eve of the Cultural Revolution because of the Party's increasingly intense appeals for attention to class struggle as the key to mass mobilization. In such an environment it became impossible for anyone to remain casual about the class identification of youth.

The emerging Maoist solution to the problem of imprecise class designations was of course to urge the examination of political behavior. But this was a new and difficult task for most Chinese. After all, in dealing with older people, officials could with much less trouble rely upon the established system of class designations. What simpler solution, then, for the busy cadre or uninterested employer who had to evaluate young people than simply to judge them according to their father's designations? This use of the father's designation (the Chinese presume that class, like filial obligation, is inherited through the paternal line) produces a distinct concept called "family background" *(jiating chushen)*. Although family background was not the same as class designation, it offered a relatively solid tag which could answer a need to categorize people grown to maturity since socialist transformation.

Whereas class designation identifies an adult's position in the production process, family background is an indicator of the social milieu from which one has come. In theory, every person should be identifiable by these two indices. In the common case of children following in their father's footsteps, they might be the same.

The problem of family background is one of determining the significance of the relationship of young people to the presocialist class positions of their fathers. Is the child of a worker to be given preferential treatment at the expense of the child of a landlord, or are they to be dealt with on a basis of equality? It will be recalled that class designations are fundamentally static; after their determination in the early 1950s, instances of modification were infrequent. In the years immediately following liberation, family background was primarily an academic question, as adults were judged by their own designations and the persons who eventually might have to worry about family background were still young children.[5]

But as these children became older, the problem received greater attention, particularly with regard to children of members of bad classes, who may have fallen under the influence of their reactionary parents. As most older Chinese had good class designations, the question of family background was threatening only to a minority of young people. In practical terms, the question of family background was usually reduced simply to "what should be the Party's attitude toward children from bad classes?" Although the hundreds of articles discussing this theme have varied in emphasis, two messages have usually been conveyed to those whose parents are of the exploiting classes. First has been the open message: follow the Party, draw a firm ideological line between yourself and your family, be active, and you will have a bright future. The second message usually has been veiled, but no less clear: no matter how hard you try to become a revolutionary in your thought and deeds, you will never be trusted quite as much as a child of a worker or a poor peasant.

The consequence has been a sense of ambiguity on both sides. Young people from formerly exploiting families could not easily determine how to find a course acceptable both to their families and to the Party's demands. And the Party tended to vacillate between welcoming such young people to its side and holding them at arm's length.[6] The Socialist Education Movement's Later Ten Points, however, criticized informal local prohibitions against the marriage of landlord and rich peasant offspring to poor and lower-middle peasants or to Party or Youth League members.[7] On the eve of the Cultural Revolution, the Party's public policy toward young people of bad family background may be characterized as "soft." In line with Mao's new initiatives in class theory, family background was neither to be ignored nor to be the dominant consideration in a policy which "places emphasis on behavior."[8] To demonstrate that persons with bad family background had a chance, much attention was given to model children from exploiting families who had attained Party or League membership. Doubters needed to be persuaded that such young people in fact could be acceptable, and the children of the exploiting classes themselves required prodding. Many of the latter felt that aspirations to political participation were unrealistic, akin to being "a toad who wants to climb the cherry tree."[9]

This new emphasis on persons of bad family background was associated with warnings that *all* young people were in need of continual ideological study, that even good family background was not enough to guarantee revolutionary purity.[10] Accompanying these ideological innovations in youth work was a drive to expand enormously the size of the Youth League, clearly lowering the family background requirements for membership.[11]

Implementation of this more open policy seems to have been

uneven. Many found it difficult to reconcile continued attention to class struggle with an attitude of welcome to children of bad family background. Teachers, cadres, and work leaders found it easier to presume the worst of young people of bad family background than to risk being deceived by apparently revolutionary behavior which might be superficial and insincere. Such a stance was perhaps tacitly encouraged by the Party's warning to these young people of the need to draw sharp lines between themselves and their families.

Thus in approaching class issues there was a tension between the new Maoist effort to focus attention on behavior and widespread popular readiness to rely instead upon the easier index of family background. But the history of class analysis in China, whatever its vagaries, had stressed the examination of one's own economic position, not that of one's parents. The fact that family background was an inadequate (and unfair) substitute for class designation was quickly realized by those young people who came off badly in the exchange.

A Cultural Revolution Debate over Family Background

The question of family background gained new prominence early in the Cultural Revolution. Maoist politicians, seeking allies in their struggle against more conservative bureaucrats, turned to Chinese youth for support. With fewer commitments than adults to the established social order, and with a long tradition of political activism in the twentieth century, students were willing to take risks on behalf of their ideals. As Red Guard groups were being formed in China's high schools and universities in the autumn of 1966, family background became an issue in discussions of who should be eligible to join the new revolutionary organizations. Two poles of argument were soon evident.

One group demanded that the limits of Red Guard membership be drawn according to the class of one's parents. Red Guards who urged the adoption of the readily identifiable standard of family background maintained that no one could join except the children of workers, poor and lower-middle peasants, revolutionary cadres, revolutionary soldiers, and revolutionary martyrs—the "five red categories." [12] The presumption underlying this position was that the five red categories were endowed with a *natural* redness which persons of nonrevolutionary family background could never attain. This doctrine became known as the "bloodline theory," or the "pedigree theory."

The contrary view rejected the implication that the five red category youths were necessarily more revolutionary than young people from other backgrounds. Instead, it was argued, the Red Guards should accept a wider range of members. Eligibility for admission to the rebel ranks should be determined by behavior loyal to the revolution and to Mao's thought, without reference to other factors.

Initially, the five red categories had their way, benefiting from the support of some important central Party leaders. But this success was transitory; it soon became evident that Red Guard groups organized on the principle of the five red categories often turned out to be conservative bodies, more interested in preserving the status of their members (and of the members' parents) than in launching a radical attack on social institutions.[13]

Some of the initial militance of the five red categories may have been fueled by resentment toward what they regarded as the Party's excessively tolerant policies on family background. In the autumn of 1966 many urban young people felt that the policy of emphasizing behavior was in conflict with Mao's Tenth Plenum injunction never to forget class struggle.

Some measure of the virulence of the five red categories toward those of bad family background may be seen in these lines from a Beijing handbill. Red Guards of the five red categories visiting from Jilin protested the presence in the capital of their provincial rivals with bad family backgrounds. These rebels of "pure" blood branded their rivals as "a litter of puppies," rejecting their right to participate in the Cultural Revolution.

Like a swarm of wasps, you sons and daughters of landlords, rich peasants, counterrevolutionaries, bad elements and rightists have descended on the capital with great pomp and speed! Let us tell you, we allow only the children of the five Red categories to come to the capital to establish ties and prohibit you to tour the capital and enjoy the scenic sights here. We allow only the left-wingers to rebel and prohibit the right-wingers to turn the sky upside down!

Some of your grandfathers served in the police force of Manchukuo, whom the people have long suppressed. Some of your fathers were members of the Kuomintang's San-min-chu-i Youth Corps or were Kuomintang officials, who have now been deprived of the right to vote and are being reformed under supervision. Some of you have the family background of capitalists; your relatives (uncles) had spent a number of years in the people's prisons, and some of your uncles were historically counterrevolutionaries. Some of your fathers have been ferreted out as members of the black gang! . . .

You, a bunch of bad eggs, the Red Guards and the 5-Red category children of Peking do not welcome you. We want you to get out of here, and at once. We give you 24 hours to do so.[14]

The social environment which generated the bloodline theory may be illustrated through a slogan, an organization, and a spokesperson.

The most famous slogan of the natural redness school was a bit of verse, a couplet: "If the father is a hero, the son is a brave fellow; if the father is reactionary, the son is a bad egg."[15] As these lines sum up the ideology of the pedigree theory quite succinctly, they were much cited during the ensuing debate about family background.

Perhaps the most notorious of the natural redness Red Guard organizations was Beijing's "Capital Red Guard United Action Committee," usually abbreviated as United Action *(liandong)*.[16] Composed of the children of officials, this and similar groups were more easily formed because of the existence of elite schools where most of the pupils were sons and daughters of high-level cadres.[17] The members of United Action apparently regarded their famous families with considerable self-importance, as they were said to wear insignia which corresponded to the bureaucratic ranks of their parents.

These important parents, often beleagered in the opening period of the Cultural Revolution, used their children's organization as a line of defense against those Red Guards who were more conscientiously attacking "reactionary power-holders." If natural redness meant that the young people of United Action had inherited revolutionary reliability, such reasoning went, then the parents from whom the pedigree had come must be red beyond question.[18] In its efforts to protect conservative cadres, United Action sought to divide their radical critics by attacking leftist leaders Chen Boda and Guan Feng, and by spreading (possibly accurate) rumors that Chairman Mao had criticized Jiang Qing.

As with other leading Red Guard groups, United Action's influence spread beyond its native city. In Guangzhou it was said that United Action was admired by the conservative Doctrine Guards *(Zhuyi bing)* of the August First Middle School, another elite institution for cadre children.[19] More radical Cantonese youth paid the Beijing organization the dubious honor of recognizing its special status by fashioning a new label, "United Action element."

As United Action was the best-known organizational embodiment of natural redness, so the theory's most famous spokesperson was a Red Guard leader of Beijing's Industrial University, Tan Lifu.[20] He was the son of Tan Zhengwen, deputy head of the People's Procuracy until his death in 1961, and his social contacts and political associates included the children of Chairman Liu Shaoqi, military leader He Long, and head of the Party's Southwest regional bureau, Li Jingquan. Young Tan became known as the "master of the theory of blood relationships" on the basis of a speech which he made in defense of the principle of natural redness. His speech was given on August 20, 1966, and is said (its contents are known only by the comments of Tan's critics) to have defended the early Cultural Revolution work teams, and may have included a defense of Peng Dehuai, as well as an exposition of the theory of blood relationships. In spite of its seemingly militant conservatism (or perhaps because of it) the speech was widely circulated and discussed. Leading cadres are alleged to have supported Tan, and the reorganized Beijing Party Committee supposedly telephoned Tan to give him encouragement as his words drew heated response. The speech was reprinted with the encouragement of Party leaders who perhaps entertained desperate hopes of being able to control the Red Guard movement by keeping their children in command. In Fujian, the speech was reprinted by the official New China Bookstore; Chen Boda asked of a group of Fujian radical Red Guards, "Do you know how to criticize Tan Lifu's speech?" But little assistance was needed, as Tan's words inspired many Red Guard organizations systematically to attack his ideas.[21]

The explicit advocacy of natural redness was severely hampered when the 1967 *Red Flag* New Year's editorial denounced the bloodline couplet and the views it symbolized. The editorial explained that the doctrine of natural redness initially had been accepted by misguided, yet innocent young people. Later, it had been exploited by enemies of the proletariat to deceive children of cadres and other students.[22] The ascendancy of forces within the Party leadership who opposed the pedigree theory was symbolized by Beijing's "Exhibition of the Crimes of United Action," visited by Zhou Enlai, Chen Boda, and Kang Sheng in March of 1967.[23]

Red Guards of bad family background were no doubt pleased that one set of persecutors had been restrained, but they still faced a dual problem. First, supporters of the pedigree theory were not necessarily convinced by editorials and exhibitions. Although they were unable to press their point so aggressively as in the autumn of 1966, their ideas were still held by many. Second, other Chinese occupied an intermediate position, disapproving of the elitism of the five red categories but nonetheless still deeply suspicious of the minority of young people who were children of capitalists or five-category elements. Emboldened by the New Year's editorial of Red Flag, some Red Guards of bad family background attempted to improve their situation by publicly criticizing the use of the family background concept. The most celebrated statement of this protest was a widely read essay, "The Theory of Family Background."[24] Its author, Yu Luoke, was a twenty-five-year-old factory worker whose ambitions for higher education had been frustrated by political problems in the pasts of both of his parents.[25]

Writing under the rather grandiose pen name of the "Beijing Research Group on the Question of Family Background," Yu complained that Marx, Engels, Lenin, and Mao all had bad family backgrounds, but became revolutionaries in part through struggling against their natal environments. By focusing upon the influence of family background, advocates of natural redness ignored the influence of society; in socialist China, this influence outweighed the more limited impact of parents from bad classes. The article complained that family background was a lazy substitute for class:

It's very easy to check on origin. One flip of the file, the problem's solved and all's well. Alternatively you can meet a person on the street, ask him "What origin are you" and thereby know everything about him. It's really simple and convenient. Checking a person's [political] behaviour is rather bothersome, particularly for that impossible group of doubters who don't believe either your everyday behaviour or your behaviour in times of turmoil; who doubt both your past and present behaviour and even prepare to doubt your future behaviour; who doubt until you die and only then, when the coffin lid is closed, give a final verdict. Finally, even they feel that they've been too suspicious.[26]

He enumerated instances of victimization of young people from bad family backgrounds who were blocked from educational opportunities or job promotions. "If things continue to develop like this, how will they differ from the caste system of the blacks in the United States [and] the untouchables in India?"[27]

"The Theory of Family Background" concluded with a query. Why was it that bourgeois elements sought to oppress young people of bourgeois family background? The fact that they did so was proof that they were not members of the same class. They had discovered that the five red categories were easier to control than young persons who had been raised in a personal environment of class struggle. They were the ones who had taken the formula, father's class designation equals child's family background, and changed it to father's class designation equals child's class designation. In so doing, they sought to confuse the contours of class struggle in China, and they had succeeded especially well in the case of cadre children who had adopted the theory of blood relationships. Under these conditions, two new social strata had been formed: one a privileged stratum and the other a stratum subject to discrimination. This situation hurt the will of many revolutionary youth, and it caused the revolutionary ranks to grow smaller. Those whose oppression at the hands of the bourgeoisie had been greatest should be able to offer the staunchest resistance.[28]

Yu Luoke had initially drafted his essay early in the Cultural Revolution, in the summer of 1966, and it had been distributed as far as Tianjin, Wuhan, and Guangzhou by October.[29] But it was not until early 1967 that family background became the subject of an important national debate. Following the *Red Flag* New Year's editorial attacking the "reactionary couplet," Chen Boda encouraged a public discussion of the family background issue, indication that the radical leadership of the Cultural Revolution was prepared to weaken the "royalist" Red Guard organizations by allowing five-category youth to express their grievances.

In the course of this national debate, millions of youthful Red Guards learned that the Maoist leaders regarded the bloodline theory's obsession with family background as a harmfully misleading substitution for the revolutionary tradition of class analysis. Defenders of natural redness were thereby deprived of their slogans and were compelled to advance their views more discreetly.[30] Yu Luoke's essay was widely defended, although many who recognized the injustice of only considering family background also criticized his article for reducing the question of parental influence to insignificance.[31]

This debate on family background was not resolved in a clearly decisive manner. Public discussion came to an abrupt halt after April 1967, when Qi Benyu criticized Yu Luoke's essay on behalf of the Cultural Revolution Group.[32] Although Yu's advocacy of completely disregarding family background proved unacceptable to the Maoist leadership, the condemnation of natural redness continued, and by April, the Maoist view that behavior was the ultimate test for measuring revolutionaries was apparently gaining in acceptance.[33] Young people of bad family background had won a partial victory in this episode. Nonetheless, their professions of revolutionary commitment were never accepted completely by the Maoists, who continued to tolerate massive discrimination against youth from five-category families. Although Yu Luoke had provoked the debate which rendered natural redness illegitimate, he was arrested at work in January 1968, and executed two years later.[34]

The controversy about family background highlights some significant aspects of the problem of fashioning a theory of class for socialist society. This debate was distinguished by the fact that the competing groups understood different criteria to constitute "class." The militant members of the five red categories insisted that the inherited factor of family background was the proper index of class, while Red Guards born of former exploiters quickly adopted Mao's new standard of political behavior. That neither side argued the relevance of strictly economic determinants underscores the limitations of the traditional means-of-production conception.

The early popularity of natural redness may be explained in part by the inexperience of the youthful Red Guards. A vast number of young people had reached the age of political awareness in the decade since socialist transformation, and they were often uncertain how to apply class categories to themselves and to others. The *availability* of family background as an easy way of coping with this uncertainty perhaps assured its use, especially as the great majority of young people were from families bearing favorable designations.

However, some others advocated reliance upon family background less naïvely. Cadres under fire often deliberately manipulated Red Guard politics in order to protect their positions. Note the words of Jia Qiyun, First Party Secretary of Guizhou:

> You are all sons and daughters of the five Red categories; the regime relies on you for protection. . . . Many of those in the liason teams [from Peking and other provinces that came to Kweichow] have bad backgrounds. Before, we battled with their parents and established our regime. Today, obviously, their parents are not reconciled to this and are using their children to struggle against us. You must battle against them.[35]

Vice-Premier Tan Zhenlin, who was particularly active in protecting senior officials against radical attack, sought to exclude from the Red Guard movement even young people of middling family background: "Red Guards must guarantee five red categories. They must not take in middle peasants and petty bourgeoisie!"[36] Like-minded officials had responded initially to the Cultural Revolution by deflecting its unprecedented assault upon new capitalist-roaders within the Party into yet another campaign against old capitalists within society. Their interest in extending this defensive maneuver to the children of the former exploiting classes may be seen as an effort to divide their Red Guard critics and to interpret the Cultural Revolution in terms of the liberation social cleavage in which their class designations of "revolutionary cadre" increased their distance from the target groups of the movement.

Orientation toward family background was closely related to the two models of social cleavage introduced above. Cadres such as Jia and Tan, finding themselves at the bottom of the socialist cleavage, had a powerful interest in perpetuating the liberation cleavage as the dominant image of Chinese society, as powerholders were largely drawn from its superior category. Many who insisted on the continuing salience of the cleavage between winners and losers of the civil war were consciously masking other social differences. Similarly, the children of members of the former exploiting classes had an obvious stake in encouraging the shift from the liberation to the socialist model, as they were clearly disadvantaged by the former, but at least had a chance at joining the good half of the polarity in the latter.

The militance of some of the five red categories suggests depth of feeling which might easily be manipulated by cadres seeking protection against Maoist attacks. At a simple level, the children of high-ranking cadres often were enrolled in elite educational institutions; many were seemingly headed toward influential careers of their own. These young people probably needed little encouragement to raise the standard of family background, as the defense of their own privileges was intimately connected with the retention of power by their parents.

More complex is the issue of the feelings of the larger number of Red Guards whose parents were members of good classes but were without political influence. Young people of bad family background often enjoyed cultural advantages which were resented by these children of workers and peasants. The pre–Cultural Revolution Chinese school system seems to have favored children of educated parents, regardless of family background. Many teachers, of course, were from bad classes, and were perhaps sympathetic to students who shared their class culture.[37] The charges and countercharges of discrimination which were raised in the course of the debate on family background cannot easily be sorted out. But although it is clear that there was massive discrimination against young persons of bad family background in many areas of society, at the same time they possessed advantages in the educational field.

Rather sketchy data suggest the following pattern: a decline in university and upper-middle school representation among children of workers and peasants and an increase among children of the former exploiting classes took place between 1960 and 1963, when considerable emphasis was placed upon academic achievement. Greater attention to political criteria in the next two years, however, led to a rise in the numbers of cadre children, who were favored both by family background and by prior educational achievement. Such a situation increased the resentment of worker and peasant offspring toward both cadre children and those of bad family background.[38]

Such resentment may have more easily been voiced against young people of bad family background in part because of a Chinese tradition of harsh treatment of the descendants of overthrown power-holders. There is ample precedent in Chinese history for the offspring of defeated social groups to be subjected to severe social disadvantages by their conquerors. Several of the "mean people" in China's past are alleged to be the descendants of the supporters of discredited regimes.[39] The temporary popularity of family background resembled earlier negative sanctions against the children of fallen enemies (such as restricting access to the civil service examination system). Such echoes of a stern tradition resounded to benefit cadres who were seeking to defend their privileges against Maoist attack.

The tradition of filiality, with its associated commitment to avenge wrongs done to one's parents, may cause Chinese to anticipate a higher degree of particularistic loyalty toward parents accused of political offenses than is true in the West. A popular imprecation of the Cultural Revolution period, "filial son and worthy grandson of the landlord class," suggests such a concern for filiality, as does the frequently expressed theme of class vengeance.[40] The constant demand that children from bad family backgrounds draw clear ideological boundaries between themselves and their families suggests that few believed that they really could do so.

But natural redness was suppressed, at least as an explicitly stated political position. And for all its practical problems, the behavioral conception of class was widely propagated, in large measure because of the prestige of Chairman Mao, even though he did not address publicly the issue of family background at the time of the controversy. Frequently quoted, however, were two formulas advanced by Mao during the 1960s as means of distinguishing revolutionary youth. The first of these is his "five requirements for worthy successors to the revolutionary cause.":

1. They must be genuine Marxist-Leninists;
2. They must be revolutionaries who wholeheartedly serve the overwhelming majority of the people of China and the whole world;
3. They must be proletarian statesmen capable of uniting and working together with the overwhelming majority;
4. They must be models in applying the Party's democratic centralism, must master the method of leadership based on the principle of "from the masses, to the masses," and must cultivate a democratic style and be good at listening to the masses;
5. They must be modest and prudent and guard against arrogance and impetuosity; they must be imbued with the spirit of self-crit-

icism and have the courage to correct mistakes and shortcomings in their work.[41]

There is nothing here about family background, nor is there in another statement of Mao's which was popular among opponents of the natural redness doctrine:

> What standard should we employ to see if youth are or are not revolutionary? How should we identify them? There is but one standard, and that is to see if they are willing, and moreover if they practice unity with the broad masses of workers and peasants. If they are willing and if they practice unity with the workers and peasants, they are revolutionary. Otherwise, they are nonrevolutionary, or they are counterrevolutionary.[42]

Again, the thrust of this statement clearly supports a conception of class which stresses political behavior, and is sharply at odds with any theory based on blood relationships. This is certainly in accord with Mao's then unpublished "Instruction on the Question of Class Differentiation." There, after insisting that behavior was to be valued about class designation, Mao continued:

> Class background and individual behavior must also be distinguished, with the emphasis on behavior. . . . The question is, do you have the class standpoint of your original background, or do you have a changed class standpoint, that is, do you stand on the side of the workers and the poor and lower-middle peasants? You must both avoid sectarianism and unite with the majority: you must even unite with a section of the landlords and the rich peasantry; you must unite with the children of landlords and rich peasants. There are some counterrevolutionaries and saboteurs who seek transformation; if they are willing to transform themselves, then you must take them, one and all. If you only appraise family background, then neither Marx, Engels, Lenin nor Stalin would make it.[43]

Mao might have added that his own family background had been used many years earlier to disqualify him from participation in the revolution.[44] But in spite of his disapproval of excessive reliance upon family background, Mao was not willing to discard it completely as one element to be combined with behavior in assessing an individual's reliability.[45]

Mao's attitude toward family background was also doubtless

influenced by his political position. The "royalist" backlash in the autumn of 1966 raised the threat that Mao's enemies within the Party, in defending themselves, might further consolidate the outmoded liberation cleavage. If this is so, Maoist harshness toward the doctrine of natural redness was not inspired by kind feelings toward a group of young people being wronged, but rather by the demands of Mao's revised perception of China's primary social cleavage. If one sought to have the socialist cleavage supplant its predecessor in popular consciousness, it would not do to advocate the hounding of children of a long-defeated adversary. But if one felt under attack as the negative member of a new contradiction (as did many Party bureaucrats), then by all means it was imperative to discourage popular realization of this cleavage by persisting in fighting an old battle in which glorious victory had already been attained.

But for Mao, the struggle which led to the Cultural Revolution was not a recapitulation of the civil war. One of the obvious purposes of the liberation cleavage, when new, had been to point to needed areas of redistribution of wealth in society. Mao long ago had recognized that this task had basically been completed with socialization, and that there was not much more to be attained by taking from the defeated classes and giving to the victorious rebels. But Mao was unwilling to accept this as a sign of a job well done, not in view of the continued existence of large-scale inequities unresolved by the revolution.

The second model of social cleavage opened up new if limited options for redistribution at the expense of the unwelcome restratification which had followed liberation. Not only were the exchanges already effected inadequate, but there was a growing tendency for their fruits to be concentrated in the hands of an ideologically lax and predominantly urban-based bureaucratic elite. Thus a continued thrust toward greater equity demanded that new developments in standard of living, health care, educational opportunities, and general access to privilege come at the expense of one sector of the winners of 1949. If the old system of class designations was not particularly relevant to the task of building socialism in an equitable manner, family background was even less helpful.

Class Designations and Social Honor in the Countryside

Red Guards who were relieved by the suppression of the doctrine of natural redness in the cities were often dismayed to discover that the transmutation of class designations into caste categories was far more advanced in rural China. Some of the legions of urban middle-school graduates sent to the countryside as "educated youth" were greeted by local cadres who claimed that "most educated youths are landlords or sons of a bitch. The sons you bear will also be landlords, and your sons' sons will be no exception." [46] The language in this case was extreme, but such attitudes were by all accounts common among peasants during the Cultural Revolution. Although rural residents were not treated to such intellectualized complexities as the Red Guard debate on family background, similar issues arose in the course of day-to-day social interaction, as class designations were raised to a new and different significance in response to the political pressures of the Cultural Revolution.

It will be recalled that in the early 1960s there occurred a simplification of the categories used to describe classes in rural life. This simplification was a logical response to the Maoist revival of class for a world in which individual relationship to the means of production was no longer a primary basis for economic differentiation. Although this classical Marxist test for class membership retained significant validity in the aftermath of the Great Leap Forward,[47] by the time of the Cultural Revolution and its renewed emphasis upon collective rural economy, individual class designations were an inadequate index of economic position in China's villages. While the determinants of material well-being in the Chinese countryside are complex, the most important factor seems to have become the ratio of family labor power to family dependents, a formula which is not related to class designation with great clarity.[48]

But even if family income was sometimes partially associated with class designation, income stratification could not be equated with class antagonism. Poor and lower-middle peasant perception of such income inequalities, however, may have enhanced a very nonbehavioral interpretation of the Maoist revival of class. The memory of sharp class distinctions in the countryside meant that Mao could not stress a new class struggle without rekindling old animosities toward persons with bad class designations. Unlike the cities, where class designations had never been rigorously assigned, and where urban anonymity further dampened the significance of presocialist class distinctions, Chinese peasants inhabit small communities where the reputation of past class position has been passed down from year to year. While urban campaigns were often directed against an abstracted notion of a class enemy, rural class struggle typically struck at concrete individuals. The Party's long effort to diminish the importance of rural lineage relationships was especially important in reminding peasants who had been a landlord and who had not.[49]

Far from representing economic classes, the three sets of rural classes (poor and lower-middle peasants, upper-middle peasants, and landlords and rich peasants) came to represent status groups, which Max Weber defines in terms of community:

> In contrast to classes, *status groups* are normally communities. They are, however, often of an amorphous kind. In contrast to the purely economically determined "class situation," we wish to designate as "status situation" every typical component of the life fate of man that is determined by a specific positive or negative, social estimation of *honor*.[50]

The role of class designations in shaping the boundaries of rural prestige systems may be illustrated by following Weber's identification of patterns of marriage and social intercourse as the primary manifestations of status communities.[51]

A developing status system tends to limit the frequency of intermarriage between status units. "The restrictions may confine normal marriages to within the status circle and may lead to complete endogamous closure."[52] Because marriage is a clearer indicator than less formal varieties of social interaction, it can be employed to identify a pattern in the chronology of status development since liberation. The acceptability of marriages between poor and lower-middle peasants and five-category elements has varied according to the level of attention given to ideas of class struggle in the society. The general trend I have described in discussing the theory of class seems to have been reflected in rural marriage practices: class categories were of paramount importance immediately after liberation and again between 1961 and the death of Mao, with a relative diminution of interest in class in the period between collectivization and the Socialist Education Movement.

At the time of land reform, interclass marriage was discouraged by the Party because it was feared that landlords and rich peasants might utilize it as a weapon. "If the parties really love each other, they will wait till after the reform, in order to prevent young farmers taking a sympathetic attitude towards the landlord family of their spouses thus softening the class antagonism between peasants and landlords."[53] Contrary to policy, such marriages did take place, although the poor and lower-middle peasants who made them may have paid some penalities for doing so. One informant described a popular and skilled lower-middle peasant who had been head of his production team for seventeen years, but who had consistently been denied Party membership because he had married the daughter of a rich peasant at the time of land reform. This ban persisted even during the early 1960s, a period of relaxed attitudes toward interclass marriage.[54]

Following the Maoist revival of class, the Party made a distinction between members of good classes who married members of the exploiting classes, which was held to be quite wrong, and those who married children of bad class parents. The latter was permissible, but required extreme caution, and demanded special attention to the behavior of the potential spouse with bad family background.[55] Although the Party criticized local restrictions upon marriages made across lines drawn by family background, a decade later Parish and Whyte found "a clear tendency for former poor or lower-middle peasant males to marry women of the same status, and for sons of former landlords and rich peasants to marry women with similar labels."[56]

It is not difficult to find explanations for this development. First, the Party was hostile to marriages of poor and lower-middle peasants to five-category persons. For instance, one *Southern Daily* article of 1970 brought up anew those marriages of landlord children to poor peasants at the time of land reform as devices to cover up the crimes of the class enemy.[57]

Second is the issue of the inheritability of class. Family background is transmitted by the father, a fact which put sons of landlords and rich peasants at a tremendous disadvantage in the competition for the daughters of poor and lower-middle peasants. In the words of one female informant, "If I were a worker, I would not be willing to marry someone whose family background was landlord, for our children would then immediately be landlords."

Third, in many areas of rural China, marriages are often partially arranged—not in the old manner in which prospective spouses never met before their wedding ceremonies, but with third parties serving as go-betweens, negotiators. Although it is difficult to gauge the extent of this practice,[58] in some areas even relatively activist peasants are said to rely on the assistance of traditional matchmakers. As peasant families continue to insure that the social stations of prospective matches are compatible, the marital isolation of five-category elements and their children is thereby reinforced.

It is somewhat ironic that the connection between five-category parent and child perhaps has been strengthened by some of the emphases of the Chinese Revolution. Thus attacks upon the idea of lineage have raised awareness of the nuclear family as economic changes have enhanced its functions. Young persons who seek to escape bondage to their parents' earlier misdeeds have been exhorted *not* to leave their homes, but to remain with their exploiting class parents and reform them, while at the same time taking care to draw a clear class line.[59] Although the policy of emphasis on behavior attempts to separate children from the errors of their parents, the Party often showed the shallowness of its commitment to that policy by sending whole families to live in the countryside during the latter stages of the Cultural Revolution, families selected merely because the father was a five-category element.

Male transmission of family background appears sometimes to have made sons of rich peasants and landlords (but not necessarily of the other three elements) almost unmarriageable. Not only have daughters of poor and lower-middle peasants and upper-middle peasants had little to do with them; even daughters of other five-category elements seem to have had little desire to perpetuate their stigma for another generation through an unfortunate marriage. But five-category daughters, on the other hand, have had a great motivation to marry into another group, as they can effectively lose their bad status after marriage; they and their children typically are identified by their husband's class category.[60] One informant suggested that the child of a five-category mother and a poor or lower-middle peasant father would have few difficulties, but that if he or she did encounter political problems later in life, the class designation of the mother might then be taken into account.

Thus men of the five categories were often only to be able to marry within their status group, while women had every interest in marrying beyond it. Compare the new pattern with that of preliberation China. The landlords then enjoyed concubines, while many of the poorest peasants were unable to afford wives. Although the top and bottom ranks of society have switched places, it is still the lowest status category which includes the most bachelors.[61]

Marital boundaries were often matched by class separation in other forms of social intercourse. Landlord and rich peasant families often lived together, at one edge of a village. In the evening, when members of the high status groups relaxed together after a day of agricultural labor, these families remained apart. And many landlords and their children were characterized by informants as silent and uncommunicative during the work day. Wishing not to stir up trouble, many perhaps reasoned that the safest course was that of quiet obedience.

The following incident from Jiangsu illustrates the social gulf between poor and lower-middle peasants and the five-category elements:

> One day, at a mass criticism meeting, Wu Wan-ch'uan, son of a rich peasant, came forward on his own initiative to uncover and criticize his father's counter-revolutionary crimes. At the moment, some people said: "This son of a rich peasant is tricky. He is putting on a disguise. You must not be day-dreaming. This is no time for you to play a trick." Wu Wan-ch'uan's face turned red with anger and he went away quietly. As he passed by the door of a landlord element, a bad element took him by the hand and said to him: "Little Wu, an old saying goes that when a man goes out of doors he should first see the weather. You also must see what period you are now living in if you want to be an activist." Wu found this quite sensible. Thereafter, he did not take part in study and did not labor vigorously.[62]

Wu's withdrawal to his own status group after the rejection of his overtures is not surprising in a climate of often harsh treatment of the five-category elements. They have been denied political rights,[63] and have often been excluded from rural welfare and health care programs;[64] their agricultural labor has commonly been remunerated with fewer work points than those received by poor and lower-middle peasants;[65] their property has sometimes been confiscated,[66] and there is even one account of a massacre.[67]

It is obvious that there was considerable variation, even within a single locality, in the treatment given five-category elements. Thus one middle-aged informant of landlord family background described the indifference displayed when he was discovered teaching his seven-year-old son to swim in preparation for an illegal flight to Hong Kong. But this desire to leave China had been fueled when that same son had been paraded through the streets to the sounds of a gong by his fellow students.

The transformation of class designations into markers of prestige may also be seen institutionally, in the failure of poor and lower-middle peasant associations to confront new socialist inequalities. Local peasant associations had been important organs through which land reform had been implemented, but they had become dormant after the destruction of landlord power. In response to Mao's 1962 call for a renewal of class struggle, these institutions were reconstituted as poor and lower-middle peasant associations, with membership restricted to the two best class designations. Among their purposes were the development of political and class consciousness and the supervision of cadre performance.[68] Mao hoped that the associations, as class-based organizations, would limit conservative influences from former landowners and rich peasants. But he also envisioned that they would correct cadre malfeasance, which also had grown in the years since the Great Leap Forward.

The supervision of officials was eventually weakened; by 1967, cadres as high as the commune level were entitled to join the associations which were supposed to oversee their work,[69] and by 1971 the associations could meet only if called together by the Party officials they were originally designed to superintend.[70] This devitalization of the associations' political autonomy heightened their character as a status group based upon the good class designations shared by ordinary peasants and their cadres.

Although the poor and lower-middle peasant associations lacked power, their symbolic role was indicated by the exclusion of all others from their meetings, which must surely have reinforced consciousness of shared status. These meetings have had their symbolic analog in regular convocations of a production brigade's five-category population, where public security cadres might explain Party policies to the assembled class enemies.

Beyond meetings, there have been other marked distinctions in the activities of the two major status groups. The five-category

elements in many areas have performed regular periods of con-
scripted labor, for which no work-points were recorded. In one
brigade, this was reported as half a day per week; in another, four
days monthly. The five categories also continued to work even
when the poor and lower-middle peasantry attended political
meetings.[71] As "controlled elements," the five categories typically
were required to make frequent reports to a public security cadre
and to request permission to travel beyond the brigade, or to miss
work because of illness. Visitors from other areas to the homes of
the five-category elements, including their children, also had to be
reported to the brigade.

Rural status distinctions which rest upon the system of class
designations often assumed a visually symbolic aspect. Bennett
and Montaperto were told by Dai Hsiao-ai how members of the
five categories worked in the fields of one county with cardboard
signs on their backs.[72] While this particular manner of physical
demarcation was probably not common (Dai found it remarkable,
after all) milder forms did exist. More widespread was the mark-
ing of the houses of poor and lower-middle peasants with large
couplets along the doors. On red paper, the sides of the door carried messages such as "Walk with the Communist Party," and
"Listen to Chairman Mao's words," which joined a top line such
as "Revolution to the end." Five-category homes, however, had
the status of their inhabitants indicated by couplets on blue, bearing such legends as "Become a new person," "Obey supervision," and "Undergoing reform."

The rural resurgence of class designations was a kind of conceptual second coming, or the raising of a ghost from China's not-
so-distant past. Even if the common economic basis of poor-
peasant or landlord membership had been obscured by collectivization, the renewed reliance upon old categories gave them a
rather different but still real quality as a social division and bond.
That supernatural imagery may perhaps capture the essence of the
use of class categories by Chinese peasants is some indication of
the elusive quality of their reality. The class categories did describe the borders of social interaction, but their frustrating and
illusory character is perhaps the most evident in the issue of the
reality of the class enemy.

Just as the two halves of a class contradiction form a unity,
defining one another through the tension between them, so consciousness of status is heightened by contrast with an opposite

status group. It seems that the poor and lower-middle peasants became sensitized to their common status through the separate identity of the five-category elements.

Here it becomes impossible to separate cause and effect. Did the poor and lower-middle peasants dislike the five-category elements because they were different and hated socialism, or did the lower status group reject socialism because its members were treated as five-category elements (treatment hardly designed to elicit warm support for the present order)?[73] The point here is not that the enmity of the five-category elements was artificial, but rather that once recognized and analyzed as the hatred of the class enemy toward socialism, that enmity may well have been perpetuated.[74] And if that analysis was based upon a perception of Chinese society divided into winners and losers of the civil war, then the reality of winners and losers may well have been sustained long after the revolution's victory would otherwise have been secure.

Family Background as "Proletarian Chauvinism"

Perhaps it is unavoidable that a Marxist revolutionary movement will show some signs of what has been called a "cult of proletarian chauvinism."[75] Consider, for instance, the boastful attitude of one Guangdong cadre toward his family origin: "Whenever I met a difficulty, I raised my head and looked at great leader Chairman Mao's brilliant image and recalled how my family had for the past three generations toiled as labor hands for the landlords."[76] The eagerness of officials to claim as their heritage the suffering of their ancestors is an aspect of a process described more generally by Weber: "Strata in solid possession of social honor and power usually tend to fashion their status legend in such a way as to claim a special and intrinsic quality of their own, usually a quality of blood; their sense of dignity feeds on their actual or alleged being."[77]

The Maoist revival of class certainly encouraged such a concern for "a quality of blood," as a way of enhancing the collective self-confidence of China's peasants and workers and as a basis for the legitimacy of Communist Party leadership. It is clear, however, that the thrust of Maoist class policy was to limit the scope of class designations to the revolutionary generation alone; tendencies to elaborate these categories into caste-like bonds between parents and their children undermined consciousness of newer material inequalities, and accordingly were resisted steadily by radical politicians.

Although both rural and urban areas have provided evidence for this transmutation of class designations into castes, the process seems to have been more easily restricted in the cities than in the countryside. Why should this be so?

One reason is that the system of class designations was never as firmly implanted in the cities as it was in China's villages through the process of land reform. And urban areas are characterized by looser political controls and less intimate personal contact; city-dwellers may know the class designations of few of the people they encounter in daily life, which is quite unlike the intimate familiarity of the village. It is only in urban accounts that one learns of efforts by young people to conceal bad family background, an impossibility in rural society, where details on one's life are more widely known by neighbors and associates.

A second factor is the different distribution of liberation-era classes. The great majority of peasants had good class designations or family backgrounds, and (although there is enormous local diversity) former landlords and rich peasant families typically made up only 5 to 10 percent of the rural population.[78] In the cities, however, the representation of the middling classes of the petty bourgeoisie was far greater, and even the industrial proletariat contained large numbers of former peasants or petty bourgeoisie. Urbanites thus had less incentive to emphasize a social hierarchy by which fewer of them would enjoy high rank.

A third cause lies in the fact that the rural economy is less socialist, and its work life is less bureaucratized than is true of the cities. Most urban enterprises are state-owned and fully "socialist" organizations where cadres and workers are fully integrated into the elaborate hierarchy of the work-grade stratification order. Property in the rural economy is collectively owned by members of producing units, and peasant labor is not structured by the work-grade career ladders of most urban workers. Thus the symbolic impact of the old class designations is not countered, as it is in the cities, by a more precise index to current economic position.

But in neither city nor countryside was the issue of caste settled unequivocably. The bloodline theory may have been suppressed in the 1960s, but it reappeared in practice repeatedly. For instance, a visitor to a May 7th Cadre School reported that young cadres of worker and peasant backgrounds regarded themselves as possessing a natural redness which should excuse them from the May 7th program of ideological reeducation.[79] Similarly, a report from a Guangdong factory complained that some young workers became arrogant because of their imagined "natural redness," while "those with a bad family background shouldered it as an ideological burden, with diminished spirit in work as well as in study."[80]

Against this, the Party stressed the need to unite with "educable" young people from bad family backgrounds. "Family background cannot be chosen, but one's road can be."[81] Young factory workers of bad family background were defended in terms echoing themes from Yu Luoke's essay: the environment of socialist China is a more potent force in shaping youthful ideology than the influence of bad class parents.[82] Similarly, stern warnings were also made to those of good family background, that they not rely complacently and uncritically upon "plain class feeling."[83] Although many Chinese have found reasons of their own to resist central political pressure to abandon the notion of family background, there has been nonetheless a clear trend toward weakening its impact in social and political life. The most recent wave of criticism of family background has come not from radical politicians, however, but from the more conservative administration which has held power since the death of Mao Zedong in 1976. But consideration of this important effort to put to rest both class designations and family background must follow an examination of a final Maoist twist to the theory of class, a radical effort to link socialist classes more directly to the apparatus of political power.

CHAPTER SEVEN

Class and the State

Although the transmutation of class into caste was resisted with considerable vigor, first by Maoists and more recently by the more conservative administration of Hua Guofeng and Deng Xiaoping, the ease with which the revival of class was subverted reveals the analytical weakness of Mao's behavioral theory of class. The emphasis upon political behavior failed to link action convincingly to the social structure. Caste-like interpretations did address the relationship of class category to social structure, but only by ignoring the impact of socialist reforms in favor of an obsession with a property system no longer extant.

Alongside the simple behavioral theory of class propounded by Mao in the 1960s, however, grew an alternative orientation toward class which did trace the roots of social conflict more deeply into the institutions of socialist society. In this view, socialist classes were based ultimately upon power relationships in a highly bureaucratized society. The central institution in the shaping of new class relationships was the state, the political apparatus recreated and strengthened by the Communist Party as a weapon for transforming society. As the treatment of class as caste directed attention to the old stratification by private property-based class designations, so the more radical interest in state power focused upon the work-grade stratification system as the leading manifestation of class inequality.

The Maoist revival of class was quite consonant with an effort to understand social inequality in terms of state power, but the Chairman was personally ambivalent about the desirability of elaborating such a theory. In chapter 4 I discussed Mao's fleeting identification of bureaucrats as an autonomous class prior to the

Cultural Revolution. He came closest to overcoming this hesitation on the eve of his death, when he complained of the contrast between workers and peasants who sought further changes since liberation and those Party members "who do not want to go forward." These Party members "have become high officials and want to protect the interests of the high officials."[1]

Anxious for the fate of the revolution he had helped lead, Mao extended his patronage to the important radical dissection of power and inequality which constituted the campaign to study the dictatorship of the proletariat of 1975–1976. While this campaign was accompanied by a sophisticated Chinese version of a "new class" theory of socialism, the first linkage of class to political power had been made earlier, during two other great radical moments in socialist China, the Great Leap Forward and the Cultural Revolution. Although Mao eventually chose to endorse such class analysis, it has since been repudiated vigorously as a part of the critique of the Maoist leaders labeled as the "Gang of Four."

State-Engendered Inequalities Through the Cultural Revolution

Mao's focus upon the state as the critical institution for the generation of inequalities in socialist society emerged only in the last years of his life, but this concern was grounded in issues which had provoked discussion soon after socialist transformation. Closely interrelated were the adoption of Soviet-style work-grades for cadres and workers and the question of how egalitarian should be the distribution of incomes in socialist China.

The introduction of a systematic hierarchy of work-grades for cadres and workers was marked by controversy. There were squabbles, for instance, over the assignment of ranks, and Mao complained in 1957 that the new system inhibited the promotion of able cadres against its rules.[2] Liberal critics of the Party objected to the new stratification as well,[3] although most cadres seem to have regarded this new system as a proper implementation of a successful Soviet precedent. Lowell Dittmer has described Liu Shaoqi's vision of society, for instance, as "a vast corporate hierarchy."[4] In such a world-view, the work-grade stratification must have seemed both appropriate and necessary.

Mao was more apprehensive about China's often uncritical emulation of Soviet experience in social organization; "To import Soviet codes and conventions inflexibly is to lack the creative spirit," he complained in 1958.[5] Such feelings were widespread within the Party during the radicalism of the Great Leap Forward, when the recently acquired work-grade hierarchy was seriously questioned. In anticipation of the creation of a communist society, egalitarian feelings were directed against this newly institutionalized form of material differentiation. Many leaders felt a need to prepare for the eventual change from Marx's socialist principle of distribution according to labor to the communist principle of distribution according to need.

The phrase "bourgeois right" was used to refer to the necessary presence in a socialist society (which is transitional to communism) of institutional inequalities inherited from capitalism. Important manifestations of bourgeois right were the commodity system, the use of money as a medium of exchange, and the formal distribution according to work (and the concomitant work-grade stratification system). Bourgeois right involved relations of remuneration and exchange, and it was a "right" to equal pay for equal work in socialist society as in its original capitalist context. But this equality was individualistic in nature, and although it was necessary for China's socialist present, it masked factual inequalities with a formal equality. Because physical and mental abilities differ, and because family sizes and numbers of dependents vary, some very real inequalities were inherent in socialist society.

During the Great Leap Forward, many cadres recalled with fondness the more egalitarian distribution arrangements practiced within the Party prior to liberation. At Mao's behest, a young Shanghai cadre named Zhang Chunqiao published an article in *People's Daily* questioning the desirability of the new wage system. Zhang's article was accompanied by an editorial note by his patron, although Mao's sponsorship was not indicated at the time.[6] In the ensuing discussion, Deng Xiaoping and others argued that such wage inequalities were a bourgeois right appropriate for China's current level of development.[7]

In the end, the wage system remained unaltered; some of the most radical impulses of the Great Leap were castigated as a premature "communist wind." Since 1958, notions of "absolute egalitarianism" have been illegitimate, as even the most radical Chinese leaders have recognized the need for unequal rewards during a prolonged period of socialism.[8] Marx's communist egalitarianism, which in fact demands not equal rewards but unlimited distribution according to individual need, rests upon the assumption of a materially abundant communist society, absent in China. There was also a need to use material incentives in some measure to motivate workers in production. The precise range of inequalities has, of course, been subject to considerable debate from that period to the present.

Although Mao maintained a public silence during the Great Leap discussion of bourgeois right, his personal and intra-Party writings and speeches between 1958 and 1961 reveal considerable dissatisfaction with the work-grade stratification system. He protested that China should not copy the extensive wage disparities of the Soviet Union, and complained of the widespread wrangling over social status which accompanied the assignment of bureaucratic ranks in the 1956 civil service reform.[9] At the same time, Mao recalled fondly the less hierarchical method of remuneration practiced within the Party prior to liberation:

> Our party has waged war for over twenty years without letup. For a long time we made a nonmarket supply system work. Of course, at that time the entire society of the base areas was not practicing the system. But those who made the system work in the civil war period reached a high of several hundred thousand, and at the lowest still numbered in the tens of thousands. In the War of Resistance Against Japan the number shot up again from over a million to several millions. Right up to the first stage of Liberation our people lived an egalitarian life, working hard and fighting bravely, without the least dependence upon material incentives, only the inspiration of revolutionary spirit.[10]

Mao was especially sensitive to the class implications of the new work-grade system: "In my view the rural area work style and the guerrilla attitude are still good. . . . Why must we grasp a wages system? This is offering concessions to the bourgeoisie." Mao went on to castigate as a bourgeois practice the giving of higher wages to mental than to manual workers, and to hope that China of the future would "show some consideration toward the elderly and the weak, but we don't want different classes for others."[11]

Despite these extensive reservations, Mao still recognized the necessity of the wage reform, even though it introduced a form of inequality which demanded constant attention. Criticizing those comrades who thought that bourgeois rights could be destroyed overnight, Mao upheld the introduction of the wage system as "basically correct."

> But there was a problem: we also took a step backward in the matter of grades. As a result there was a furor over this matter. . . . The grade system is a father-son relation, a cat-and-mouse relation. It has to be attacked day after day. Sending down the cadres to lower levels, running the experimental fields—these are ways of changing the grade system; otherwise, no great leaps! [12]

However impatient Mao may have been with China's work-grade stratification, he made few public appeals for its restriction. Even after he issued his dramatic call for a renewal of class struggle in 1962, he raised these issues only indirectly, through the increasingly intense polemic against Soviet revisionism. [13] Between 1959 and 1963, Mao supported some limited reductions in the salaries earned by high-level cadres, but by 1964, he felt that this approach had reached a limit, as it proved "difficult to further reduce wages at the upper levels." Rather, he concluded, high salaries should be stabilized while lower wages were gradually raised. [14]

When the Cultural Revolution began in 1966, such gradualism seemed out of harmony with the militance of this great mass campaign. *Red Flag* carried articles on the Paris Commune, informing Chinese readers of the egalitarianism of the Commune's cadres, whose salaries were no higher than those of ordinary workers. [15] Many of the newly mobilized Red Guards were inspired by their lesson in revolutionary history. "Why can't high salaries be lowered?" demanded one Hunanese group, but Mao did not join in raising this question. [16] In fact, apart from the limitation of bonuses for workers, the Cultural Revolution seems to have had little impact on China's distribution of personal income. [17]

Given the radically egalitarian mood of the Cultural Revolution, one must ask why Mao and his associates failed to pursue their well-established discontent with the work-grade system. [18] The stability of the 1956 hierarchy is one of the great continuities enduring through the often turbulent social history of the People's Republic, and it may best be explained by the Maoists' fears of alienating potential allies among officials by attacking too fiercely the perquisites of their offices. Instead of responding to Red Guard demands for greater equalization of incomes, the Maoists emphasized less direct ways of employing state power to reduce obvious inequalities. Status differences reflecting the values of pre-socialist China, for instance, were subjected to a relentless barrage of propaganda to redress inequalities rooted in social symbolism. And sidestepping the sensitive issue of individual incomes, Maoists advocated instead the expansion of *collective* material benefits. The extension of primary and secondary education and health care in the countryside, for instance, could be accomplished without taking away existing individual salary rights of cadres or industrial workers. Moreover, such reforms were typically based upon the self-reliant efforts of local communities, a strategy which further enhanced the appeal of an egalitarianism which did not level from the top but rather sought to raise the bottom of society.

Mao and his radical associates were even less supportive of Red Guard efforts to move beyond the admitted inequalities of the work-grade stratification to seek out an underlying system of class relationships. The boldest such attempt was made by the Hunan group, *Shengwulian* (a shortened version of the "Provincial Proletarian Revolutionaries' Great Alliance Committee"). The few documents which survive this radical organization date from late 1967 and January 1968, when it was suppressed. Their tone is one of frustration at the limitations of the Cultural Revolution, which Shengwulian faulted for holding back from a structural solution to China's political problems. The Hunanese radicals complained that the Cultural Revolutionary emphasis upon exposing the crimes of individual officials left untouched the social foundation from which these purged cadres had arisen. "Political power is still in the hands of the bureaucrats, and the seizure of power is only a change in appearance." [19]

Shengwulian demanded "a new analysis of China's society . . . so as to revise the class standings, rally our friends, and topple our enemies." [20] Without a new class analysis, there was insufficient popular awareness of the class nature of the enemy bureaucrats, whose power was rooted in control over the means of production through the mechanism of the state:

We really believe that 90 percent of the senior cadres should stand aside; and that at best they can only be subjects for education and uniting. This is because they have already come to form a decaying class with its own particular "interests." Their relation with the people has changed from that, in the past, between leaders and led to that between exploiters and the exploited, between oppressors and the oppressed. . . . Is it possible, instead of overthrowing this class, that they can be persuaded to give up the vested interests derived from their bourgeois legal rights, such as high salaries, and follow the socialist instead of the capitalist road? Chairman Mao's extensive concessions to the bourgeoisie are the pure expression of these efforts. However, the bureaucrats have once again launched a counterattack . . . , pushing themselves closer and closer to the gullotine. All this proves that no decaying class has ever been willing voluntarily to exit from the stage of history.[21]

Shengwulian went far beyond the standard criticism of Liu Shaoqi and Deng Xiaoping, identifying Premier Zhou Enlai as the leading representative of the capitalist-bureaucrat class, although the group treated with respect radical leaders such as Jiang Qing, Yao Wenyuan, and of course Chairman Mao. But these radical leaders were not eager to be linked to an organization which advocated armed struggle as a way of resolving the Cultural Revolution, and the perhaps inevitable campaign against Shengwulian was uncompromising and decisive.[22]

The tortuous politics of the Chinese ultra-left are of less interest here than the relationship between the ideas of Shengwulian and the Maoist political leadership which condemned them.[23] Although Mao and his associates had long been concerned with the inequalities of the work-grade stratification and although they had attempted to link class analysis to the problems of a socialist bureaucracy, they had never so explicitly identified high-level bureaucrats as an antagonistic class. There were both tactical and theoretical reasons for holding back from such a step.

In contrast to the ultra-left's indentification of bureaucrats as a class, the Maoist leadership insisted upon differentiating among cadres to locate a 95 percent who were good or basically good. True to the Party's preliberation United Front style, this Maoist tactic sought to weaken conservative opposition by narrowing the scope of attack and offering most cadres an opportunity to join the Maoist coalition. A uniform condemnation of all cadres would have assured an early defeat for the Maoist leadership. Even before the case of Shengwulian, the Maoist press had bitterly criticized similar notions as "anarchist" or "Trokskyite."[24]

To the slogan, "Overthrow all those in authority!" *Red Flag* replied that most cadres were in fact taking the proletarian road, and that the purpose of such a slogan could only be deliberately to confuse the revolutionary masses and strengthen the position of the "handful of Party people in authority" taking the capitalist road.[25]

Not only were Maoists concerned with mobilizing maximum support for dislodging their conservative opponents from power, but they were also eager to wield their own power effectively.[26] The castigation of all high-level bureaucrats as an enemy class would embrace Maoists as well, a possibility which the Chairman found unacceptable:

> The slogan of "Doubt everything and overthrow everything" is reactionary. The Shanghai People's Committee demanded that the Premier of the State Council should do away with all heads. This is extreme anarchism, it is most reactionary. If instead of calling someone the "head" of something we call him "orderly" or "assistant," this would really be only a formal change. In reality there will always be "heads." It is the content which matters.[27]

The theory of class propagated by Maoists in the Cultural Revolution was quite consonant with these tactical considerations. The interpretation of class as individual political behavior rather than as a system of collective structural relationships coincided with Mao's political needs. The emphasis upon policy outcomes (political line) permitted Mao's antibureaucratic attack to be justified in terms of the "force of habit" left over from the old society, rather than demanding a politically costly effort to dismantle the entire political apparatus.[28]

Although Mao failed to act in the Cultural Revolution upon his discontent with the remnants of bourgeois right in the work-grade stratification system, he did expand his critique of the division of labor in which the work-grades were embedded. Mao never denied that real economic benefits from the division of labor should be seized, but he maintained a skeptical attitude toward the extent of these benefits, arguing forcefully on behalf of measures to limit the social fragmentation which often accompanies occupational specialization.[29] Emblematic of this concern was the consistent Maoist opposition to the division of work and politics, which ought properly to be joined by workers who were "both red and expert."

Efforts to avoid the rigidity of occupational specialization led

Mao and his supporters to advocate policies in which individuals could at least temporarily experience other working environments. Through this method it was hoped that political consciousness might be raised as Chinese broadened their understanding of alternative laboring situations.

This movement of individuals throughout the occupational structure occurred along two dimensions. One emphasized the temporary change of ranks, as in the long-standing policy of sending cadres to work at the basic levels of their organizations. The other dimension stressed movement from one sector to another, either by transferring personnel to new jobs in new sectors or by combining the tasks of several sectors within a single organization. This had, of course, been among Mao's ambitions for the People's Communes in the Great Leap Forward, and he emphasized this theme anew in his "May 7th Directive" (1966). There he urged Chinese working within each of seven fundamental sectors of society (military, industry, agriculture, education, commerce, service, and Party and government organizations) to concentrate on the primary tasks appropriate to their own sectors, but also to master work skills associated with the others. "While mainly engaging in industrial activity, workers should also study military affairs and politics and raise their educational level. . . . Where conditions permit, they should also engage in agriculture and side-occupations, just as people do in the Taching Oilfield."[30] Similarly, soldiers were to run small factories and plant crops, as peasants were to diversify their activities to include education, industry, and military affairs. The matter was put in pithy terms in a campaign directed at commercial workers: "Cloth-dealers should learn to weave cloth; vegetable-mongers should learn to grow vegetables."[31]

Here one must underscore the limitations of such efforts. For all of the shifting around of persons from one locus to another, incomes continued to be derived from the original work-grade classification. Consciousness may well have been raised, but material interest remained unaltered in the absence of structural reforms. This sometimes resulted in anomalous situations, as when urban officials sent down to May 7th Cadre Schools retained their high incomes as they steeped themselves in revolutionary spirit by working temporarily in the countryside.[32]

"To Expose Our Dark Aspect Openly": [33] Mao and the Gang of Four

Given the caution exercised by Maoists during the Cultural Revolution in publicly pursuing the "bourgeois right" theme which had previously so intrigued them, it is noteworthy that bourgeois right formed the subject for the last great radical campaign before Mao's death in 1976. In this campaign to study the dictatorship of the proletariat, the behavioral emphasis of Mao's revised theory of class was subtly downgraded in favor of a new concern for the structural roots of China's "new bourgeois elements." Although the progression of Mao's shifting analysis of class conflict does not allow tidy periodization, the contours of this intellectual movement follow the course suggested by Paul Sweezy: "the class enemy . . . started out being the old ruling classes, increasingly became elites . . . still dominated by the ideas, values, etc., of the old ruling classes, and ended up being a 'new bourgeoisie' produced (and increasingly reproduced) by the social formation which had emerged from the revolution itself." [34]

After resisting for so long the temptation to focus upon the power relationships arising from the Chinese state, why did Mao and his associates turn to them in their class analysis of 1975–1976? One reason was certainly that the passage of a decade and a half since the weakening of private property in socialist transformation had increased the obvious centrality of contradictions between cadres and those without political power in Chinese society. With the growing intangibility of landlord and capitalist remnants in society, it became harder to avoid linking class to political power.

Maoist strategies for rapid economic growth also sustained this major intellectual shift. Here Mao's original revival of class honored very traditional Marxist logic: ruling classes impede great leaps in economic production by resisting the introduction of new relations of production and by consuming resources which might be used for capital investment. Mao maintained that class struggle would energize production, but the mass mobilizing techniques favored by Mao were often not well received by many high-level cadres. Landlords and capitalists had formerly resisted mass mobilization as a threat to their property; many bureaucrats disliked it as an erosion of their administrative domains. When Maoist demands to "grasp production, promote revolution" were met with cadre hesitation at transferring policy implementation to ad hoc groups beyond their control, radicals were quick to see this as the suppression of popular participation.

In addition, the Maoists were frustrated by many of the outcomes of the Cultural Revolution. This great movement had indeed toppled many power-holders whose policies were onerous to the radicals, but the Cultural Revolution's focus upon personnel changes and line struggle had failed to take up structural reforms. Without such reforms, radicals placed in new positions of power too often behaved in ways similar to the conservative power-holders they replaced.[35]

Worse, some of these errant rebels were not immediately obvious but were, as we saw earlier, "hidden" class enemies, invisible to the behavioral analysis of class. During the Cultural Revolution Mao was quoted in illustration of the problems of class analysis:

> The bourgeois representatives who have wormed their way into the Party, the Government, the armed forces and all cultural circles are counter-revolutionary revisionists. As soon as the time is ripe, they will seize the State power and change the dictatorship of the proletariat into a bourgeois dictatorship. Some of these elements are already known to us as what they are, others are not yet revealed to us, and still others are being trusted by us and trained to be our successors. Persons like Khrushchev are sleeping beside us. Party committees at all levels must note this carefully.[36]

One Khrushchev asleep beside the Chairman eventually turned out to be his closest comrade-in-arms: the shock of the Lin Biao affair may have done little to promote confidence in the analytic powers of a behaviorally defined concept of class.

The death of Lin Biao in September 1971 is still poorly understood, but was seemingly an important catalyst in the shadowy context of Beijing politics within which alternative theories of class have been shaped and propounded. I cannot hope to trace adequately these events here, save to refer to the division which occurred among the victorious radicals of the Cultural Revolution.[37] Lin Biao's mysterious plane crash had been preceded by the disgrace of Mao's former secretary and Cultural Revolution leader, Chen Boda; Lin's death reduced the radical leadership to a core whose most prominent figures included Mao, Kang Sheng, and four associates later to be labeled the "Gang of Four": Wang Hongwen (who had risen to central leadership as a local rebel ac-

tivist in the Cultural Revolution), Zhang Chunqiao (a former propaganda cadre and leader of the coalition which ruled Shanghai in
the Cultural Revolution), Yao Wenyuan (essayist, editor, and
drama critic, whose critique of "Hai Rui Dismissed from Office"
helped spark the Cultural Revolution), and Jiang Qing (Mao's
wife and advocate of radical reform in Chinese cultural life).

Lin Biao allegedly held that "once you have political power,
you have everything."[38] His conspiratorial efforts to seize this
power certainly drew the surviving radicals' attention more
sharply to the link between state and class. But a far more press-
ing consideration than the past example of Lin Biao was the question of who would succeed such senior Party leaders as Zhou Enlai, Zhu De, and of course, Mao Zedong (all of whom would be
dead by the end of 1976).

The logic of the behavioral approach to class demanded that
cadres once purged should be rehabilitated after they had corrected the erroneous thinking which had led them to advocate
wrong political lines. Amid the growing wave of rehabilitated
cadres of the 1970s was Deng Xiaoping, second only to Liu
Shaoqi as a radical target in the Cultural Revolution. Deng's influence increased during Premier Zhou Enlai's illness with cancer,
much to the discomfort of the radicals who had once driven him
from office.

Anxiety about the resurgence of conservative bureaucratic
power, as represented by Deng Xiaoping, probably provided the
final impetus for the radicals to initiate a large-scale campaign in
which the whole nation was to examine the linkage of state to
class. Zhang Chunqiao, Yao Wenyuan, and Jiang Qing all had
backgrounds in propaganda and cultural work, and their political
base rested too strongly upon their access to their patron, Mao,
and their control of mass media, rather than being rooted in some
critical institution of the economy or in the armed forces.[39] One
way of shoring up their own political vulnerability was to employ
as weapons social theories, the traditional stock-in-trade of leftist
intellectuals. Their apparent hope was that propagation of radical
ideas could inculcate radical behavior, even by those who otherwise would be disinclined to follow their policy preferences.

The radicals made a major effort to expand their influence by
using their near monopoly of the official press to propagate a
campaign against Lin Biao and Confucius in 1974. This seemingly
odd pairing provided opportunities for obscure and allusory criti-

cism of still-living political figures amid some very general discussion of the need to preserve the antibureaucratic innovations of the Cultural Revolution. The essentially defensive quality of this movement also characterized the more important campaign to study the Marxist theory of the dictatorship of the proletariat which began in February 1975.

One of Chairman Mao's characteristically delphic instructions initiated the campaign: "Why did Lenin speak of exercising dictatorship over the bourgeoisie? It is essential to get this question clear. Lack of clarity on this question will lead to revisionism. This should be made known to the whole nation." [40]

A selection of thirty-three statements by Marx, Engels, and Lenin on socialist society was published, prefaced by four new instructions by Mao. [41] The campaign was presented to the nation largely through commentaries which applied these statements to China's present situation. Besides Mao, other leading figures in the Communist Party who played prominent roles were Zhang Chunqiao and Yao Wenyuan, each of whom contributed a detailed and widely disseminated analysis early in the campaign. [42] The intensity of the movement subsided toward the end of 1975, although it was reinvigorated following the second purge of Deng Xiaoping in April 1976. It then persisted with increasing harshness until the death of Mao Zedong in September and the arrest of the four most famous radicals one month later.

"Dictatorship of the proletariat" is the formula by which Marxists have identified the transitional form of the state through which the victorious working class must turn socialism into communism. One of the thrusts of this campaign was to link state power to the unequal distribution of material benefits in socialist China. The quotation of Marx's comments upon the nature of communist society suggests that the radicals regarded egalitarianism as *ultimately* irrelevant for China: with the attainment of communism, the full development of the productive forces of society will create such abundance (while simultaneously diminishing bourgeois acquisitiveness) that all desires can be met. Calculations of equality will lose significance in a society which can "inscribe on its banners: From each according to his ability, to each according to his needs!" [43]

Until this golden age is reached, however, Chinese society cannot ignore the issue of inequality. Deeply imbedded in the institutions of transitional socialist society is the concept which Marx called "bourgeois right." The inequalities represented by this concept must be protected by the state, which, because it is a revolutionary state, must simultaneously restrict them over the long term. This revolutionary state, even though it is a dictatorship of the proletariat, is itself a vestige of bourgeois society.

Some forms of bourgeois right, such as the right to private property, had already been curtailed in China. Others remained, however, most notably in the realm of personal income.

> If such a state of affairs should be allowed to develop without any restrictions, the gap between those with more and those with less would become wider and wider to the extent that a polarization would take place. A few people would then convert their money into capital with which to engage in usury, set up underground factories or go in for speculation, all for carrying out criminal activities to exploit others.[44]

The danger was that China might become a captialist country, as had the Soviet Union. According to Mao, "Our country at present practices a commodity system, the wage system is unequal, too, as in the eight-grade wage scale, and so forth. Under the dictatorship of the proletariat such things can only be restricted." Mao went on to warn that should people such as Lin Biao attain power, "it will be quite easy for them to rig up the capitalist system."[45]

Throughout the campaign, however, great care was taken to assure people that this did not represent demand for the immediate abolition of all aspects of bourgeois inequality. Such an approach would be an ultra-left one, similar to the "communist wind" which blew during the Great Leap. Zhang Chunqiao explained:

> We have always held that, instead of having too big a supply of commodities, our country does not yet have a great abundance of them. So long as the communes cannot yet offer much to be "communized" with production brigades and teams, and enterprises under ownership of the whole people cannot offer a great abundance of products for distribution according to need among our 800 million people, we will have to continue with commodity distribution, exchange through money and distribution according to work. We have taken and will continue to take proper measures to curb the harm caused by these things.[46]

Thus these forms of inequality had to remain a part of Chinese social relations for a considerable period, and their envisioned restriction was intended to be very gradual indeed. In its barest form, the campaign was a reassertion of an older Marxist tenet that inequalities must be curtailed after a socialist revolution so that they may eventually be rendered meaningless.

More profound, however, were the ramifications of this campaign for the delicate question of the legitimacy of a Marxist state.[47] If a socialist government is to remain in power in a world which still contains the forces of its adversaries, it must convince its populace that its rule is just and proper, that its political power is the natural order of things, and that the social arrangements which it has brought forth are in fact legitimate ones.

This necessary task is incompatible, however, with the view of the state which is inherent in Marx's analysis of social development. Whether the state will wither away, as Engels imagined, or whether it will disappear in some other manner is irrelevant. The irreducible point is that the state, as a device of class society, *must* eventually be destroyed at the end of the progress toward communism. To Marx, all states—including the socialist state—are instruments of repression, and are only of limited duration. In such a perspective the state is by definition illegitimate. A socialist revolution thus faces a dilemma: if it is to remain in power in order to develop toward communism, it must convince people of its legitimacy. But legitimacy implies stability, permanence, and works against the abolition of itself, and even of particular institutional arrangements. Institutionalization is essential to protecting the revolution, but it at the same time is corrupting insofar as it works against further *movement*.

At one level, class struggle conveys legitimacy by involving individuals in the revolutionary process, by making them a part of the social order which is being created. But at another level, by improving the world, socialism diminishes the incentive of people to change it. The Maoist theory of class struggle under socialism was founded on a belief that the revolution had not gone far enough, that for it to be frozen into institutionalized patterns would exclude large numbers of Chinese from the fruits of liberation, and would have a deadening effect on future social and economic change.

The linkage of class to the state in this campaign was thus subversive of the new socialist order in a way which went far beyond the intellectually more limited appeals of the Cultural Revolution. Thus cadres had certainly been criticized earlier for the enjoyment of bourgeois pleasures, and this familiar Cultural Revolution theme was continued. What was different is the social basis suggested for the emergence of the "new bourgeois elements." This may be seen in the new assessment of the origins of Lin Biao's revisionism. As late as 1972 and 1973, the Party maintained that Lin betrayed socialism because of his family background, which made him weak and susceptible to the blandishments of hostile forces: "He was brought up in a big landlord, capitalist family. After admission into the Party, his bourgeois world outlook was never remolded." [48] This conception of the fallen revolutionary, incapable of maintaining a firm proletarian standpoint, is ultimately a psychological argument: Lin and his followers were covetous because of a weakness of the will.

Yao Wenyuan's analysis, "On the Social Basis of the Lin Biao Anti-Party Clique," was a major theoretical escalation in that it added to these psychological factors an important structural one. Lin's clique aimed at "grabbing the means of production they have never possessed," because "the existence of bourgeois right provides the vital economic basis for their emergence." [49]

If the "discrepancies between the various grades" and other aspects of social inequality were not reduced, but instead were consolidated and extended, "the inevitable result will be polarization, i.e., a small number of people will in the course of distribution acquire increasing amounts of commodities and money through certain legal channels and numerous illegal ones." Yao went on to catalog the consequences of such a course, which include the growth of acquisitive desires, increased corruption, the reintroduction of exploitation, and the eventual undermining of socialism. Yao maintained that when the economic power of the new bourgeoisie reached a certain (unspecified) extent, "its agents will ask for political rule, try to overthrow the dictatorship of the proletariat and the socialist system, completely change the socialist ownership, and openly restore and develop the capitalist system."

Because the desire for greater inequalities was built into the system of cadre ranks, the peril of revisionism could affect *all* bureaucrats, not only those with a weak ideological standpoint:

> As we now can see, the emergence of new bourgeois elements from among the working class, Party members or personnel of state and

other organs is inseparable from the fact that the areas or units they belong to are trying to preserve or extend bourgeois right and these elements themselves value and crave for it.[50]

In Zhang Chunqiao's analysis, some Communists and even leading cadres

> have reached the point of looking at everything as a commodity, including themselves. They join the Communist Party and do some work for the proletariat merely for the sake of upgrading themselves as commodities and asking the proletariat for higher prices.[51]

Institutions thus provided the motivation for avarice as well as the framework for its practice. How much more important, then, that the Party's leaders be sensitive to the need to restrict rather than expand inequality. Errant leaders such as Liu Shaoqi, Lin Biao, and Deng Xiaoping had been powerfully positioned to "consolidate and extend bourgeois right, protect their own interests, namely, the interests of the 'high officials' who practice revisionism, embezzle and squander huge amounts of social wealth, energetically engage in capitalist activities, undermine and disrupt the socialist relations of production."[52]

For all the quotations from Lenin which graced the documents of this campaign, it is obvious that they were not fully applicable to the situation of China in the 1970s. Many of Lenin's strictures against the bourgeois state, for instance, refer to the fact that the Soviet Communist Party literally took over the old Tsarist bureaucracy, giving the phrase "dictatorship of the proletariat" a rather different connotation that when applied against the political apparatus which the Chinese Communists had created for themselves in their prolonged struggle for power. This difference reminds us of the novelty of the radical position in China, which sought to relate class inequalities to roles in the state-directed organization of society.[53]

The critique of work-grade stratification was intended to appeal to those who were poorly situated within this hierarchy, and the radicals were especially concerned to expose high-level officials who used their positions as a means of securing advantages for themselves and their families. The press devoted considerable attention, for instance, to the problem of cadre children who relied upon their parents' political influence to gain entrance to desirable institutions such as universities or the People's Liberation Army "through the back door."[54]

The radicals did not dismiss all cadres as class enemies, but rather emphasized divisions among bureaucrats as a device for resisting cadre class cohesion. One such division was between local and state cadres, the former earning work-points (along with other peasants) and the latter regular salaries. As early as the Socialist Education Movement, Maoists had tended to protect local cadres, directing class struggle instead against the higher salaried officials. This trend continued through and after the Cultural Revolution. Another division of importance was between junior and senior officials. Wang Hongwen in many ways exemplified the young cadre propelled to power through Cultural Revolution activism (promoted "by helicopter" in the eyes of his critics). Unsurprisingly, he played a special role in criticizing veteran officials and demanding more authority for younger leaders.[55] There is also some evidence that the radicals were sensitive to the distinction between cadres specialized in technical and economic work and those engaged in political affairs, the former being regarded with considerable suspicion.[56]

Among industrial workers, the so-called "temporary" and contract workers probably found the radical appeals more compelling than their permanent colleagues, who were more firmly entrenched (and at a favorable level) in the work-grade system. The radicals sought to unite all workers, however, behind criticism of cadre authoritarianism in the workplace, insisting upon worker participation in managerial decision-making. The Gang of Four was later attacked for treating labor unions as "battle command posts of the working class," a curious charge to be made by one group of Marxist politicians against another.[57] Radical activities among the workers may have contributed to the industrial unrest in such cities as Hangzhou in the summer of 1975, which surely did not endear the Gang of Four to many managers. Even more threatening, however, was the radical effort to organize a worker militia, through which the radicals might achieve an institutional basis for enforcing their own interpretation of the dictatorship of the proletariat.

The campaign sought to protect peasant interests by preventing a growing gap between the bureaucratized incomes of urban Chinese and the collective incomes of rural workers. It was alleged that the continuation of bourgeois right would "be followed by a recurrence of the bygone situation when industry exploited agriculture, cities plundered the countryside, and mental workers ruled over manual workers."[58] In practice, the critique of bourgeois right was primarily an urban-based affair, and seems to have had limited impact in the countryside.[59] The radicals did encourage collective production, however, challenging the legitimacy of existing family-centered productive arrangements which might increase the range of material differences within villages. The radicals' model agricultural unit, the Dazhai Production Brigade, was distinguished not only for its exaltation of disciplined collective labor, but also by having abolished the so-called "private" plots. In general, the radicals seem to have deemed material homogeneity to be a protection for the political unity and autonomy of village communities.

It should be noted that this quest for unity extended to the old system of class designations, which the radicals, having witnessed its use to subvert class conflict, were not eager to retain. Thus one of the campaign's analyses of rural society pointed to the danger presented by "well-to-do peasants," a vaguer term than the landlord or rich peasant class designations targeted in past campaigns.[60] Chinese publications for foreign audiences emphasized that class designations did not represent current economic status, but rather were historical markers from land reform.[61] And the earlier anti-Confucian campaign had denounced the Confucian doctrine of "rectification of names." This theory held that a society is well ordered only when individuals rigorously adhere to the statuses appropriate to their positions, and its criticism was apparently directed by analogy against the caste-like use of class designations to resist radical change.[62] In addition, in some villages there were systematic public evaluations of former landlords and rich peasants, in which sanctions against them were lifted in a process of several stages.[63] There is no evidence that radical politicians initiated this process, but it is quite consonant with their interest in moving beyond the hierarchy of class designations to focus on actual material differences.[64]

The campaign to study the dictatorship of the proletariat did rest upon a conception of contradictory material interests, which the radicals sought to identify and mobilize as of old. The problem in this approach arises from the past successes of the revolution. Preliberation techniques of mass mobilization, in which potential supporters were aroused by the Party into large coalitions against privileged classes, are not easily replicable in a society in which the most offensive extremes of wealth and poverty have been limited through socialist reforms. Among the casualties of the revolution may have been the ease with which Maoist formulae for winning power may be applied.

To counter these changes in Chinese social structure, the radicals often seemed simply to state their case more frequently and more sternly, so as to bring a resistant society into harmony with their theories. Such a classically voluntarist position has been described by Berger and Luckmann, who argue that

> the relationship between 'ideas' and their sustaining social processes is always a dialectical one. It is correct to say that theories are concocted in order to legitimate already existing social institutions. But it also happens that social institutions are changed in order to bring them into conformity with already existing theories, that is, to make them more 'legitimate.'[65]

But the critique of bourgeois right was complex, and not easily established as a new element in the shared understanding of Chinese Marxism. "Some comrades, on the excuse that their level is low, regard grasping the superstructure and the line as the exclusive business of the leading cadres."[66] Against the difficulties of propagating a theory whose political significance was often wrapped in abstraction, the radicals supported the formation of worker and peasant "theoretical groups." Far easier is the situation of the "managers of a powerful Party-State bureaucratic apparatus which has a strong interest in its own self-preservation, and thus a vested interest in the political apathy of the masses."[67]

Mao Zedong died on September 9, 1976. Within a month, his most prominent radical colleagues were arrested and branded as a counterrevolutionary "Gang of Four." The precise relationship between Mao and these four will perhaps never be known. It is easy to reject the most extreme representations of this bond, however. Mao's intellectual intimacy with Zhang and Yao, and his personal intimacy with Jiang Qing, render preposterous assertions that the Gang of Four were his traitorous enemies. Similarly, Mao's political distance from the Gang's brand of radicalism (his caution about bourgeois right in 1958, and even in 1975, when he merely offered supportive statements rather than full-blown analyses of the dictatorship of the proletariat) makes one skeptical of the Gang's claims to be his true voice.

Between these extremes lie more plausible alternatives. Whisperings from Beijing hint that Mao, by the time of the Gang's rise to prominence, was weakened by senility, incapable of recognizing the harm done by a band of ambitious flatterers. Visitors' accounts and press photographs from Mao's last years certainly convey an image of increasing physical infirmity, but intellectual rigor is much more difficult to assess. Less contemptuous of Mao is a rather different interpretation: the aging Chairman, unsatisfied by the results of the Cultural Revolution and anxious about the ascendancy of conservative politics after his death, recognized the Gang's militance against the bureaucratic class and utilized it to strengthen one of his own intellectual bequests to China. In this view, Mao perhaps knowingly egged on the Gang into taking positions which would eventually bring about their political destructions, reckoning this to be a small and necessary sacrifice for the sake of raising the question of class and the state. No matter that the question was not resolved, as it is unresolvable without worldwide communist abundance; more important to Mao was to place the issue as firmly as possible within the emerging tradition of Chinese Marxism.

Mao had been cognizant of the possibility that his theories might allow him posthumously to influence Chinese politics, as can be seen from his 1966 speculation about "when the rightists come to power" after his death: "At that time, the rightists may prevail for some time by using my words, but the leftists may also organize some of my other words to overthrow the rightists." [68]

This organization of Mao's words in the last year of his life indicates his closeness to the Gang of Four. In a tense political climate, both radical and conservative politicians were eager to legitimize their positions as "Maoist." Deng Xiaoping attempted to downplay the focus upon class struggle by diluting Mao's directive on studying the dictatorship of the proletariat with two earlier instructions from the Chairman on promoting stability and unity and developing the economy. These three inseparable directives, said Deng, were "the key link for all work." To this, Mao responded angrily: "What 'taking the three directives as the key link'! Stability and Unity does not mean writing off class struggle; class struggle is the key link and everything else hinges on it." [69]

By contrast, when the Gang of Four was similarly accused of tampering with Mao's words for political advantage, the most damaging evidence was that the four had changed the phrase, "Act in line with the past principles," into "Act according to the principles laid down." This "sinister plot" was represented as a major distortion of Mao's thought, but the absence of more extensive "forgery" only strengthens the impression that Mao's views coincided with those of the Gang.[70]

CHAPTER EIGHT

China After Mao: More Inequality and Less Class Analysis

The extensive deradicalization of Chinese social policy which has taken place since Mao's death in 1976 may be taken by some as clear evidence that Mao was ultimately a visionary, who for all his revolutionary huffing and puffing proved incapable of "solving" the problem of the bureaucratic class. But Mao did not perceive the question of the relationship of state officials to the rest of society as a technical problem which one might someday resolve after hitting upon the correct formula. For him, this relationship was a constant feature of socialist society, demanding ceaseless intellectual and political engagement, not to eliminate the contradiction between leaders and citizens but to control the meanest manifestations of this contradiction. In the last year of his life, Mao asked rhetorically whether there would still be a need for revolution a hundred or a thousand years in the future. His response showed little hint of a vision of harmonious communist utopia: "There are always sections of the people who feel themselves oppressed; junior officials, students, workers, peasants and soldiers don't like bigshots oppressing them. That's why they want revolution. Will contradictions no longer be seen ten thousand years from now? Why not? They will still be seen." [1]

The years since Mao's death have been a period of restoration for the "bigshots" whom the Chairman had treated so harshly during the Cultural Revolution. With the arrest of the "Gang of Four" and the ensuing purge of leftists throughout the leadership of the Communist Party, these more conservative officials have felt free to act upon some very un-Maoist political principles. Under the aggressive leadership of Deng Xiaoping, the senior cadres of the post-Mao Chinese state have advocated social reforms often described as "moderate" in the West, but which are certainly extreme within the narrower tradition of the Chinese Communist Party.

Practice: A Campaign Against Equality

The changes in social policy which have taken place since Mao Zedong's death have been complex, but generally favored those social groups most restricted throughout the long arc of Maoist radicalism between 1962 and 1976. While the interests of state and Party cadres, technicians, and nonscientific intellectuals by no means always coincide, the thrust of recent Chinese policies has certainly been away from the Maoist emphasis upon less-skilled workers and poorer peasants. Although Mao's death was followed immediately by fervent declarations of loyalty to his preferred policies by the new Party Chairman, Hua Guofeng, many of these policies have been gradually supplanted by more elitist programs, especially as the power of Deng Xiaoping and his associates has increased. This pattern lends support to the notion that the last radical campaign to study the dictatorship of the proletariat was essentially defensive in nature, intended to deter the growth of new inequalities rather than to impose a spartan egalitarianism upon Chinese society.

In the language of the radicals, "bourgeois rights" have been extended through pay raises for 64 percent of China's cadres and workers.[2] In addition, bonuses are now used much more extensively in a national reward system that relies far more upon individual material incentives than in the radical years. Former discussions of the need to restrict bourgeois rights were replaced by a public campaign for remuneration "to each according to his work." This campaign was also extended to the countryside, where new work-point schemes were introduced which permit a wider range of peasant incomes. Of peasant families which appear unusually acquisitive, it is now said that "it is an illusion to build socialism through the method of preventing a part of the people from becoming well-to-do first."[3]

Other forms of material distinction have been awarded to

groups disfavored during the years of Cultural Revolution. The improvements in quality of life for intellectuals are especially obvious. New housing has been opened for teachers at all levels.[4] Recreational facilities (including swimming pools, movie theatres, and restaurants) formerly restricted to senior cadres have now been opened to "high-level" intellectuals.[5] And various systems of prizes have been established for academic research.[6]

Private property has been extended in unprecedented ways. Former regulations against the construction of new privately owned housing in urban areas have been revoked, and a new private corporation is constructing apartment buildings for private sale to overseas Chinese "or their relatives in Shanghai, as well as to the city's former capitalists who have housing problems."[7] How are these former capitalists to afford new apartments? The Party decided to restore to them assets confiscated early in the Cultural Revolution, as well as to give them back pay from the "high salaries" which were slashed at that time (many former capitalists were then employed as managers in the enterprises they had controlled prior to socialist transformation).[8] With this decision, an entire class which had recently seemed to be near extinction has been rejuvenated.

Initiatives favoring private property and individual achievement have been accompanied by a weakening of the collective economy. By April 1979, 46 percent of the Han production brigades on Hainan Island had dismantled their cooperative medical systems.[9] In Hunan there was extensive disbanding of pig farms run collectively by production teams.[10] And reports from Guangdong, Hunan, and Guizhou revealed that in many localities the production teams themselves had been disbanded, with collective property divided among "small groups" which often turned out to be families.[11] Such instances of decollectivization have not been without controversy, but they have apparently been encouraged by a powerful new emphasis upon family-based "sideline" production and an expansion of rural trade fairs where entrepreneurial peasants may sell their produce and wares.[12] All these changes have taken place in an environment in which the central authorities have tried to rehabilitate individual wealth, rather than the collective ascent to prosperity, as a legitimate ambition for China's peasantry.[13]

Another set of policy changes which has altered the thrust of past radicalism is a major emphasis upon respect for authority and its symbols. Cultural Revolutionary critiques of "capitalist-roaders" have given way to calls for deference to these same leaders as "veteran revolutionaries." Along with the rehabilitation of Confucius has come a more general restoration of Confucian attention to generational differences as a legitimate basis of human inequality.[14] Former encouragement of student criticism of teachers has been castigated as "anarchism," as such symbols of authority as formal titles of academic rank have been restored, "in order to teach more effectively."[15] Political activism by workers has similarly been discouraged amid new attention to the importance of management. The worker militia favored by the radicals has also been downplayed, as the People's Liberation Army asserts that "it is necessary for the army to stress discipline."[16] There have been many reports of an impending decision to reintroduce military insignia and rank (abolished on the eve of the Cultural Revolution) as a visible manifestation of that discipline.[17] Status-distinguishing occupational titles have already been restored in several other fields, including commerce and engineering.[18] Enthusiasm for the reestablishment of symbols of hierarchical distinction has even included a political post for Bujie, younger brother of Buyi, the last Manchu Emperor (who could be the pretender to the Qing throne if he were not a loyal member of the National People's Congress).[19]

Some of the institutions which most directly affect upward social mobility have been reformed since Mao's death in ways that are most likely to further restrict the already limited access of children from worker and peasant backgrounds to positions of relative power and affluence. The controversial down-to-the-villages program has been drastically curtailed, so that urban young people now find it much easier to remain in the cities after high school graduation. And although these urban youth face frequently enormous difficulties in finding jobs, new policies favor them with advantages not enjoyed by rural young people: an industrial worker, for instance, can retire early, with one child assured of replacing him or her on the payroll of the family factory.

More fundamental have been the reforms in the education system.[20] While there is considerable local variation in education programs, the broad pattern is clear: Maoist innovations have generally been supplanted by their opposites as pre–Cultural Revolution educational practices have been restored. Entrance examinations for university admission were reintroduced in 1977, ending the

radical method of selecting students according to a combination
of talent, social background, and political attitude. The achieve-
ment-oriented examinations are thought to work against applicants from underprivileged backgrounds, such as peasants, workers, and ethnic minorities, favoring children from already
educated families. The former system of "keypoint" schools has
been restored at all levels of the education hierarchy, placing superior material resources in a small number of institutions. There
has been a contraction of locally operated schools in the countryside, as control of educational institutions has been assumed by
state officials, in place of communes and production brigades.
Within the schools, tracking of bright and "slow" students has
become common, and the former emphasis upon integrating book
education with productive labor seems to be given little more than
lip service in many institutions.

The broad thrust of these reforms, with new advantages for the
upper strata within each of the sectors of Chinese society, shows
that class conflict is still very much alive as an issue in post-Maoist
China. Unsurprisingly, there is evidence of resistance to many of
these changes. The People's Liberation Army found it necessary
to issue a report to assuage the fears of "some individuals" who
"even believed that the Party's current policies were deviating to
the 'Right'."[21] When the Anhui Party School reopened in 1979,
it had to confront criticism that the Party was "backpedaling" in
social policy.[22] Letters to the editor of the *Jilin Daily* complained
of dividing students into classes of "quick" and "slow" learners.[23]
The *Workers' Daily* received letters unhappy about the restoration
of dividend payments to capitalists, complaining that "upon
drawing their dividends, some young workers from capitalist
families indulged in extravagant eating and drinking; some even
stayed away from work without leave and violated labor disci-
plines."[24] A report from Shanghai revealed popular complaints
about unprecedented displays of extravagance visible in the city's
restaurants.[25]

Such reservations from the Party's lower ranks have been expressed even in the face of a massive purge of radical leaders from
the Communist Party. Just as Maoists recruited young people and
workers into the Party during the Cultural Revolution, so has the
new administration sought to alter the character of the Party by
absorbing veteran intellectuals, even persons with bourgeois family connections. But half of the Party's members joined during the

radical years of Cultural Revolution, thus making it difficult to rapidly effect sharp changes in its social composition. This fact may help account for the great attention given to theoretical explanations for the policy departures since Mao's death, as the Party's new leadership must persuade a corps of members many of whom were enlisted precisely to oppose the kinds of policies now being introduced.

Theory: The Second Displacement of Class

Policy changes of such magnitude must surely rest upon a complex variety of motivations. These presumably range from a sincere conviction that the former radical program was economically and socially harmful to China, through a deep personal resentment at political setbacks and persecution at the hand of the former radical leadership, to simple desire to grab whatever advantages are available in a time of extensive political and social change. It seems apparent that the dominant social coalition in contemporary China has shifted markedly, from an alliance of radicalized central bureaucrats and their clients among the less-skilled workers and peasants (the last often represented through the army) to a new and still unsettled grouping of order-minded officials, skilled workers, intellectuals, and prosperous peasants.

Within the context of politics as practiced in China since 1949, these policy initiatives have been extreme, and they have required extensive justification to a population accustomed to the radical rhetoric which flourished between 1964 and 1976. The most fundamental such justification has been the national pursuit of the "four modernizations." These new inequalities are necessary, it is said, in order to transform China's agriculture, industry, national defense, and science and technology—in short, to attain "wealth and power," the cherished goal of Chinese reformers since the nineteenth century.

These measures also have been legitimized through a fierce campaign against the allegedly harmful influence of the Gang of Four. Just as the radicals themselves had earlier made Liu Shaoqi a symbol for all that they found wanting in Chinese society, so have present leaders attributed all current problems to the four fallen radicals (who have been bound by the press, for good measure, to their old rival, Lin Biao). Only in 1981 was Mao's ghost directly attacked; even now that his "errors" of class analysis and social policy have been acknowledged, the Gang of Four continues to receive criticism far harsher than that directed toward their patron. Some of the criticisms are certainly accurate (the Gang increased generational tensions among cadres), others are difficult to assess (the Gang was responsible for factional tendencies in Chinese political life), while others are clearly mendacious (the Gang sought to sabotage rapid economic growth and impoverish China).

As the terminology of social analysis in China has been so profoundly influenced by Mao Zedong, it is not surprising that much of the critique of radicalism has assumed the form of a discussion of class struggle. But because Mao's application of class analysis had become so threatening to high-level bureaucrats, it is even less surprising to see that the concept of class has again undergone alteration, as bureaucrats have deflected its critical thrust.

I do not wish to argue that the Gang of Four fell merely because its favored social theory was inhospitable to the interests of high officials. There is ample evidence that these four politicians were vain and sometimes nastily capricious, and that they unavoidably incurred not only their own political liabilities, but also acquired by extension the enemies of their patron, Mao. But their theory did not help, as no political stance may be trickier to maintain than that of the antibureaucratic official. Mao's prestige with the masses and his web of official links were sufficient to permit him to play that role. The Gang lacked both the mass base and the political clout, and thus did not survive the death of its sponsor. Charles Bettelheim's argument that the radicals were purged because they had too little class analysis is wrong—in the eyes of many officials, the radicals were discomforting because they had too much class analysis.[26]

There have been two distinct phases in the movement away from Maoist conceptions of class struggle. Initially there was no hesitation in turning radical class analysis against its primary proponents, as Jiang Qing, Zhang Chunqiao, Yao Wenyuan, and Wang Hongwen were identified as hidden "capitalist-roaders within the Party," as "new bourgeois elements" representing the interests of "landlords, rich peasants, counterrevolutionaries, the new and old capitalist classes, and imperialism, revisionism, and counterrevolution."[27] Further tarnishing the legitimacy of the Gang's exercises in social theory, the Gang's antibureaucratic politics were likened to the struggle of the Trotskyists after the death of Lenin in the Soviet Union.[28] Beyond their service as scapegoats for any shortcomings in Chinese society, the disgraced radical politicians were also charged with specific violations of Maoist class theory, including advocating the "theory of the extinction of class struggle" and promotion of "Liu Shaoqi's rightist opportunist line."[29] Although such charges were only obscurely documented (and at odds with attacks upon the Gang's alleged "anarchism" and "Trotskyism"), their extensive propagation was evidently intended to convey to the people of China the notion that these radicals had betrayed Mao's still-respected class precepts.[30]

The second phase of the abandonment of Maoist class theory began after the official conclusion of the campaign to criticize the Gang of Four (in December 1977), and intensified after the Third Plenum of the Eleventh Central Committee at the end of 1978. In this phase the problem was not that the radicals had been disloyal to Mao's theories, but that the theories themselves were dangerous, and at times counterrevolutionary. In a reversal of emphases, Mao was disassociated from his radical interpretations of class, responsibility for which was placed upon the Gang until 1981.

There was an important shift of political power which provided the context for this ideological change, as the purge of radical politicians and the rehabilitation of conservative ones had altered the distribution of power within the highest circles of Party leadership. In addition to the famous four radicals, other leftist leaders lost influence in the years after Mao's death, including Mao's nephew, Mao Yuanxin, who was arrested in 1976, and Chen Yonggui (the peasant Vice-Premier who had used the Dazhai Production Brigade as his political base). A protracted struggle against the surviving central leaders who had been on the winning side in the Cultural Revolution resulted in the purge of the so-called "little gang of four" of Wang Dongxing (once head of Mao's bodyguard), Wu De (Mayor of Beijing), Chen Xilian (head of the Beijing military forces), and Ji Denggui (overseer of Chinese agriculture) in 1979.

This "little gang of four" had been instrumental in conspiring to arrest its more famous namesake; at the same time, its members were quite eager to preserve some respectability for Cultural Revolutionary Maoism, as this radical ideology had given legitimacy to their past political successes. Castigated as the "whatever" faction for their fealty to "whatever" Mao had instructed, they resisted Deng Xiaoping's campaign to introduce social changes in the name of "emancipating the mind" (a phrase of Mao's, employed, as he once had predicted, to oppose his favored policies). As these leaders declined in influence, the power of Deng Xiaoping and his allies among the rehabilitated cadres reached the point where radicalism on class could be attacked directly, rather than merely twisted for use against the late Chairman's entourage.[31]

The pens of Party theoreticians were particularly busy concocting arguments that the scope of class conflict in socialist society is far more constricted than the radicals had allowed.[32] Among the tricks said to be employed by the Gang in pursuing its bourgeois goals was that it "muddled the people's thinking by spreading the notion that class struggle covers everything."[33] By "isolating the phrase of 'class struggle' from the complete system of Marxist theory" the radicals "used their so-called class struggle to undermine stability and unity."[34] In contrast, neither Lenin nor Mao ever "regarded the struggle between classes as the sole and whole content of politics, especially after the proletariat had seized power."[35] While it is certainly true that Mao did not reduce all politics to class struggle, such statements are clearly intended to counter the Chairman's intellectual preoccupations of the last two decades of his life.

The campaign to purge China's collective consciousness of Mao's concern for class in socialist society rather perversely utilized the publication of a new volume of Mao's *Selected Works* early in 1977. The first four volumes were drawn from the Chairman's speeches and writings prior to liberation. Volume 5 contains only works composed between 1949 and 1958. These years, of course, predated Mao's radical obsession with the emergence of new inequalities. By quoting extensively from these earlier writings by Mao, it is very easy to extract a 1950s theory of class.[36] Consider the communiqué issued by the Third Plenum, for instance, which sounds a nostalgic note as it recreates Mao's Hundred Flowers period approach to class, heedless of the fact that Mao himself had long since left it behind:

> Socialist modernization is therefore a profound and extensive revolution. There is still in our country today a small handful of counter-revolutionary elements and criminals who hate our socialist modernization and try to undermine it. We must not relax our class struggle

against them, nor can we weaken the dictatorship of the proletariat. But as Comrade Mao Tsetung pointed out, the large-scale turbulent class struggles of a mass character have in the main come to an end.[37]

We have already seen that "class conflict" can assume a variety of meanings, consonant with the needs of very different kinds of political actors in China. Thus it is not surprising that the post-Mao press has continued to contain frequent references to class. Defusing the final antibureaucratic twist to the Maoist theory of class does not require abandoning class altogether, but merely being more judicious in its use. To accomplish this, class analysis must again be rendered static, a taxonomy of China's past rather than a source of insight into its present and future. This need informs the bitter attacks upon the "vicious mastermind of the 'gang of four',", Zhang Chunqiao, who "instructed his hatchet men in Shanghai to investigate 'changes in class relations in the present stage.' " Zhang's apparently professed desire to write an "Analysis of Classes in China's Socialist Period" has been presented as a shameless rejection of Mao's preliberation analyses, as if Chinese social structure had remained unchanged.[38]

This movement away from Mao's understanding of socialism as a system which generates its own (sometimes fiercely antagonistic) class contradictions has given rise to a variety of other theoretical innovations. The radical critique of bourgeois right was subjected to especially bitter attack, as a sharp intellectual readjustment was dictated by the expansion of material inequalities.[39] In this campaign the radicals were further discredited by the suggestion that they had sought to keep China poor, for motives which remained rather vague.

There was also a clear reaction against the superstructural emphases of Maoist radicalism. The slogan, "Grasp Revolution, Promote Production," was criticized harshly as "un-Marxist" amid a more general attack upon the "idealism" of radical analyses of society.[40] This trend accompanied a new effort to exclude any political or ideological content from the "scientific" concept of class, which was held to be strictly economic.[41] When convenient, however, matters of voluntarism were still regarded as appropriate by many officials, as in the elaboration of some very unMaoist (yet equally noneconomic) standards for judging revolutionary behavior among young people. Far from urging a constant critique of old and new bourgeois influences in society, the head of the revitalized Communist Youth League insisted that "one important criterion for judging whether a youth today is really red is to see if he or she delves into his or her own field of work and diligently studies to master science and culture for the revolution."[42]

The allegedly "scientific" economic interpretation of class has facilitated a redefinition of intellectuals as members of the working class.[43] The allegedly "Maoist" basis for this step is apparently straightforward: after liberation, most intellectuals were associated with the bourgeoisie, but by 1979 the majority of intellectuals had been educated in a socialist environment, while most of the surviving members of the older generation had successfully reformed their bourgeois ideology. The new position does attempt to deal with the difficult problem of assessing the ideological influence of former classes. But Mao and the Gang of Four were never willing to follow this logic to the point of claiming that scientists, teachers, and cadres shared a common location in China's class structure with industrial workers. If all these people belong to the same "class," how could there be conflict of material interests among them?

The appeal to cadres of such conceptual expansion of the ranks of the working class to include mental workers is obvious. "No differences exist between the cadres and the workers in the ownership of the means of production," insisted one commentary, thus dismissing by definition the entire radical effort to grasp the contradiction between officials and masses in socialist society.[44] The flavor of nostalgia for the class doctrine of 1956, before Mao began to make matters difficult for bureaucrats, is nowhere more redolent than in Deng Xiaoping's remarks to the 1978 National Science Conference. Virtually quoting his controversial speech on the revision of the 1956 Party Constitution (discussed in chapter 3 above), Deng maintained that intellectuals (who include most cadres) "have become a part of the working class itself. The difference between them and the physical workers is only a difference of division of labour in society."[45]

Revisions of class theory have been accompanied by two important changes in the institutional apparatus associated with class politics in China. One of these is a limitation of the scope of labels. As a corollary to Mao's behavioral theory of class, labels have been the most important technique for both identifying and disciplining cadres. Hua Guofeng, Deng Xiaoping, and other current central leaders seem to be appealing to the mass of cadres now rehabilitated from Cultural Revolution labels when they accuse the Gang of Four of operating a "hat factory" in which labels were indiscriminately applied to veteran officials. There has been a new attention to legal procedures in dealing with cadre malfeasance, and as a symbol of the new administration's distaste for labels, the designation "rightist" was removed from the last group of persons so labeled during the aftermath of the Hundred Flowers Campaign.[46]

An equally wide-ranging reform was the severe restriction placed upon the old system of class designations. On January 29, 1979 it was announced that the Central Committee had decided to remove the class designations of former exploiters "who have, over the years, abided by state laws and decrees, worked honestly and who have done no evil, and to grant them the same rights as enjoyed by rural people's commune members."[47] In addition, the decision specified that these persons' class designations should become "commune members," and that their children should take "commune member" as their family origin, rather than "landlord" or "rich peasant." Nothing was said, however, to suggest that the positive designations of poor and lower-middle peasant should be altered in any way.[48] Minister of Public Security Zhao Cangbi made it clear that some landlords and rich peasants had evidently been judged not to have worked honestly, so the system of class designations remains in effect, albeit for a very small minority of the population.[49] But this reform was a major one, even if it only implemented procedures promised during land reform a generation earlier.[50]

The system of class designations had earlier been given new vigor, albeit as a set of status markers, in large measure by the efforts of newly privileged groups in China to legitimize their social positions and to deflect political criticism onto the shoulders of the defeated classes of the civil war. While at first view it may seem incongruous for a new and far less radical Communist Party leadership to circumscribe a status hierarchy which has tended to serve the interests of professional bureaucrats, it is in fact a logical step for a more conservative post-Maoist leadership to take. For the cadres are best served by a social theory which has no serious place for class conflict at all; their utilization of the old class designations in the Cultural Revolution was a skillful adaptation of Mao's call for class struggle. Following the purge of the Gang of

Four and less famous radicals from the Party leadership, the former constant pressure of leftist social criticism from the top has abated. And with internal criticism limited, there is less need for using the old class enemies to draw attention away from new ones.

In addition, the new administration actively courts the support of former capitalists, overseas Chinese, and others who might well be disadvantaged by attention to class designations. Nonetheless, there is considerable irony in the outrageously inaccurate charge that the Gang of Four was responsible for the caste-like developments associated with the bloodline theory.[51] There is ample evidence that it was the radicals, not their political adversaries, who sought most diligently to replace the outmoded class designations with new approaches to the problem of inequality in socialist China.

For all of the intellectual and practical problems associated with the radical efforts to come to grips with class—first as political behavior, and later as relationship to the organization of state power—more recent Chinese approaches to inequality are striking for their weakness. The problem of bureaucratic abuse of position has not gone away, for instance; it has intensified. But no longer is a serious effort made to cope with the social-structural roots of the problem, which has been reduced to "the desire for feudal prerogatives and the practices of royalty."[52] Similarly, Chinese discussions of Soviet society no longer seriously treat class relationships (which were used by the radicals as an implicit mirror for China), but have been reduced to diatribes against a rival power.[53] Like the Soviets they no longer choose to analyze, the Chinese seem likely further to remove class conflict from their examinations of social inequality.[54]

Conclusion

I will close this book with some last observations on the three themes raised in the introductory chapter: the character of class conflict in socialism, the sinification of Marxism, and the role of Mao Zedong as social critic since liberation.

1. *Class conflict in a socialist society.* The elusiveness of "class" in socialist China may be explained by both historical and theoretical factors.[55] The former include above all the freshness of the revo-

lution in the memories of the citizens of the first generation of the
People's Republic, along with the diverse social origins of political
leaders at all levels. Structural patterns which are still obscure will
perhaps assume greater clarity with the passage of another generation. Theoretically, it is apparent that a group such as the
Chinese bureaucrats is not a class in the same way as is capitalism's bourgeoisie. It has different tools at its disposal, and different linkages to the rest of society. This does not in itself disqualify
class concepts from application to contemporary China, but does
certainly demand that more sophisticated theories of class be fashioned. Charles Bettelheim reminds us that changes in legal forms
of ownership do not suffice to cause

> the conditions for the existence of classes and for class struggle to
> disappear. These conditions are rooted, as Marx and Lenin often em-
> phasized, not in legal forms of ownership but in *production relations,*
> that is, in the form of the social process of appropriation, in the place
> that the form of this process assigns to the agents of production—in
> fact, in the relations that are established between them in social pro-
> duction.[56]

This sounds like a call for understanding socialism as state capitalism, a task not apt to be accomplished any more easily in the
case of China than it has been for the Soviet Union. But as both
socialism and class conflict seem to be permanent features of the
modern world, we may hope that continuing observation of their
juxtaposition will inspire more penetrating analyses than yet exist.

The dual nature of the Chinese state which is so central to production relations has perhaps interfered with our perception of it.
The political apparatus used to destroy old inequalities has itself
given rise to a new set of social distinctions. In the dialectic of
inequality and the state, liberation and repression both stem from
the same institution; the concentration of power necessary to redress revolutionary grievances has facilitated the accumulation of
new sources for discontent. Political power has been employed to
transform Chinese society, but the process has undermined the
analysis which made that transformation possible. Class analysis
enabled the Party to socialize the means of production, but socialization turned its old class concept into an anachronism.

From this perspective, the problem becomes one of a Party
changing society faster than it has been able to modify its com-

prehension of a dynamic social structure. But, in Wallerstein's words,

> Classes do not have some permanent reality. Rather, they are formed, they consolidate themselves, they disintegrate or disaggregate, and are reformed. It is a process of constant movement, and the greatest barrier to understanding their action is reification. To be sure, there are patterns we can describe and which aid us to identify concrete realities and explain historical events. But the patterns themselves evolve over time.[57]

Class analysis thus must destroy itself: each time the fluid reality of class relationships is captured in a moment of frozen understanding, it gives rise to action by which that comprehension is subverted. But the process of analysis leaves behind a residue, shards of the mind, which impede the reanalysis of society by their attachment to material and symbolic interests. This process perhaps occurs in all societies (witness the confusing legacy of a once-useful economic distinction between white and blue collar labor in the United States). But the aftermath of revolution may compress this process in stark, sometimes painful ways.

As class analysis disintegrates, different social groups pick up these shards to use in their own ways. "Class" comes to assume multiple connotations as central bureaucrats see it as a weapon to restrict the former ruling elites, as peasants turn to the ennobling status legend implicit in the history of the revolution, as old class enemies find their designations to be stigmata blocking their children from social advance, as young people see a set of advantages or disadvantages in career mobility, and as discontented officials seek to turn the concept against their well-placed adversaries. Each of these disparate fragments of the old class analysis becomes a new social fact in its own right, further obscuring the class analysis of Chinese socialism.

2. *The sinification of Marxism.* This process is an ongoing one, and there is certainly little evidence from the shifting pattern of reinterpretations of class conflict suggesting that any fixed codification of Chinese Marxism will soon appear. Two trends, however, stand out with some clarity.

First is the movement within Chinese Marxism's attention to superstructural phenomena from a focus upon ideas and values to a concern for political institutions. This trend may be traced to both radical and conservative impulses in Chinese politics. Conservative leaders have consciously eschewed Mao's "heaven-storming" style of mass mobilization through ideological appeals, as this approach to political life tends to disturb the orderly life of bureaucratic organizations and therefore endangers the stability of the state. Radicals, on the other hand, have been compelled to turn, however reluctantly, to the question of the state as they have sought to identify the new material interests by which the revolution might be redefined and continued.

A second trend is the broad adaptability of Marxist theory to the needs of an incipient class of socialist bureaucrats. What could be more seductive to such a social group than a theory which, because it was initially fashioned for a radically different time and place, obscures the autonomous power associated with state office in this century? Socialism subverts the political theory of classical Marxism:

> Extended state interventionism becomes a source of "politicization of the economy," and begins to alter the relations between the economic base and the political superstructure. If ownership in an economic sense is understood as actual and relatively permanent disposition over means of production, the direction of dependence begins to be modified here, since in some areas power no longer stems from ownership, but rather ownership stems from power.[58]

Even the propagation of a new theory of class struggle has been inadequate to prevent many cadres from profiting by their new posts, created in the name of revolution. Radical perceptions of social structure in medieval Europe, revolutionary France, and Stalinist Russia were all co-opted for use by newly privileged classes.[59] In People's China, the mere suppression of anti-class views has not been enough; "radical" symbols have easily been subverted to conservative uses by cadres less eager than Mao to devise ways to continue the revolution. Of "positively privileged status groups," Weber observed that "they live for the present and by exploiting their great past."[60] When Mao sought mass mobilization by reminding ordinary citizens of the revolutionary struggles of the Jiangxi Soviet, the Long March, and Yan'an, bureaucrats less dissatisfied with the course of social change expropriated the same symbols to justify their positions in the new order. Conservative officials may prefer not to be bothered by an antibureaucratic theory of class conflict, but even such a theory can be imbued with a static interpretation which will support power-holders as easily as can a vision of society which does not raise the question of class at all.

Even much of the Maoist application of Marxism to processes of social change in China is quite compatible with the pursuit of bureaucratic interests. Consider Mao's fundamental pair of questions. "Who are our enemies? Who are our friends?" The social content of the "our" is ambiguous, and may refer either to the loosely conceived revolutionary proletariat of Mao's vision or to the workers' self-declared political agents in Beijing today.

3. *Mao Zedong as critic of socialist inequality.* Already, in the few years since his death, much of the heroic cult built around Mao's person has been dismantled. Chinese may now acknowledge his flaws, and his words are no longer printed in boldface type to set them apart from the surrounding texts of greater mortality. I have not written this book as an effort to resurrect a fallen deity, much less as an apology for any of the extensive political abuses made in the name of continuing the revolution. But I have emphasized a side of Mao which is not held in high honor by the present Chinese administration. I must here repeat that Mao simultaneously defended and attacked the new order in China which he helped bring forth; to counterrevolutionaries he said that it was good, and should be protected, yet he prodded old revolutionaries, saying that it was not good enough.

This latter aspect of Mao is less popular in Beijing today, where Mao the bureaucrat, leader of industrialization and builder of national power, is esteemed. Thus it is appropriate to heed Stuart Schram's caution against

> the most natural, but at the same time the most inexcusable error into which one can possibly fall in interpreting Mao's thinking: taking at face value the one-sided actions or statements into which he is constantly led by his passionate and impulsive temperament, and forgetting that somewhere in the background there is surely lurking an antithesis which will bring the picture into focus again.[61]

The chief cadre and the leading rebel were bound together especially clearly in the seriousness with which Mao took the Marxist goal of a classless society. During the Cultural Revolution, Mao inquired of his comrades, "I should like to ask: have you ever carefully thought about how socialism is going to graduate into communism?"[62] Perhaps unlike some of his fellow leaders, Mao did think carefully about this question, which he sought to answer in a way at once both radical and conservative. By turning to class analysis, Mao sought to preserve and build upon a central tradition of the revolution. Although the nature of property relationships had changed, the purpose of class analysis remained the same, the construction of alliances and the discrimination of adversaries. At one point in the course of the revolution, the relationship of individuals to the means of production was the most efficient way to discover enemies and friends, but after 1956 the spirit of the Chinese revolution was poorly served by retaining outmoded class categories. Mao's search for a new conception of class was in one important sense conservative, in that it sought to recapture his own role as the grand tactician of revolutionary struggle, an image which may describe his Marxism better than that of the theorist of economic relationships in the European tradition. For Mao, the value of the concept of class was never its immediate (and inherently transitory) economic content, but its potential utility as a building block for understanding and then energizing material conflicts in a changing society.

Some readers may find it tempting to read the story of power and ideas told here as a tale of tragic failure by a romantic Mao, his visionary eglitarianism inevitably crushed against an intractable reality of natural hierarchy. Especially given the conservative drift of official Chinese Marxism since Mao's death, it may seem to many that Mao's case is closed, that the issues which dominated his political consciousness are now being supplanted in importance by a new set of primarily economic concerns.

Such a view would be unduly short-sighted. However unpopular Mao's revival of class theory may now be among the current Communist Party leadership, it is difficult to imagine that Maoist views of class will leave no heritage in Chinese political life. Industrialization in a poor, still predominantly agrarian society is unlikely to proceed without controversy over the control of China's limited productive assets and the distribution of their fruits. Of course, campaigns against radical interpretations of the social structure may well force the class issue to be raised again in different terms. But more specific evocations of elements from Mao's class analysis might be heard if China again faces the situation which sustained the Maoist revival of class in the 1960s:

widespread discontent outside the top and middle ranks of the bureaucracy, and a central leader frustrated by bureaucratic resistance to policies of collectivism and redistribution. But even if no future Party Chairman ever finds the need to turn to Mao's class analysis to discipline a recalcitrant officialdom, the fact that Mao himself once did so is likely to form a less conscious undercurrent to new directions in Chinese ideology, exercising by its past example a continuing pressure for bureaucratic rectitude in action, if not in thought.

APPENDIX

The Two Stratification Systems

I. The Hierarchy of Class Designations

Below are listed some of the more important of the more than sixty class designations which were assigned to individual Chinese in the early years of the People's Republic.

A. Noneconomic Class Designations
    Revolutionary cadre *(geming ganbu)*
    Revolutionary soldier *(geming junren)*
    Dependent of revolutionary martyr *(geming lieshi jiashu)*
    Military officer for an illegitimate authority *(weijunguan)*
B. Urban Class Designations
    Worker *(gongren)*
        Enterprise worker *(chiye gongren)*
        Transport worker *(banyun gongren)*
        Handicraft worker *(shougongye gongren)*
        Sailor *(haiyuan gongren)*
        Pedicab worker *(sanlunche gongren)*
    Idler *(youmin)*
    Petty bourgeois *(xiao zichan jieji)*
        Urban pauper *(chengshi pinmin)*
        Peddler *(xiaofan)*
        Small shop-owner *(xiao shangye dianzhu)*
        Small factory-owner *(xiao gongchangzhu)*
        Office employee *(zhiyuan)*
        Liberal professional *(ziyou zhihyezhe)*
    Capitalist *(zichan jieji)*
        Commercial capitalist *(shangye zibenjia)*

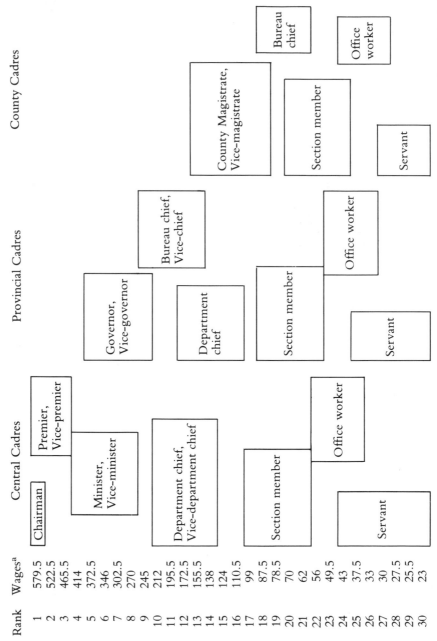

Central Cadres — Provincial Cadres — County Cadres

Rank	Wages[a]
1	579.5
2	522.5
3	465.5
4	414
5	372.5
6	346
7	302.5
8	270
9	245
10	212
11	195.5
12	172.5
13	155.5
14	138
15	124
16	110.5
17	99
18	87.5
19	78.5
20	70
21	62
22	56
23	49.5
24	43
25	37.5
26	33
27	30
28	27.5
29	25.5
30	23

Central Cadres: Chairman; Premier, Vice-premier; Minister, Vice-minister; Department chief, Vice-department chief; Section member; Office worker; Servant

Provincial Cadres: Governor, Vice-governor; Bureau chief, Vice-chief; Department chief; Section member; Office worker; Servant

County Cadres: County Magistrate, Vice-magistrate; Bureau chief; Section member; Office worker; Servant

[a] Monthly wages in renmin bi (1956: 1 renmin bi = US$0.42)

Industrial capitalist *(gongye zibenjia)*
Compradore capitalist *(maiban zibenjia)*
C. Rural Class Designations
Hired agricultural laborer *(gunong)*
Poor Peasant *(pinnong)*
Middle peasant *(zhongnong)*
   Old middle peasant *(jiuzhongnong)*
   New middle peasant *(xinzhongnong)*
   Well-to-do middle peasant *(fuyu zhongnong)*
Rich peasant *(funong)*
Small land lessor *(xiao tudi chuzuzhe)*
Landlord *(dizhu)*
   Enlightened landlord *(kaiming dizhu)*
   Overseas Chinese landlord *(huaqiao dizhu)*
   Landlord who is concurrently an industrialist or merchant
      (dizhu jian gongshangyezhe)
   Sub-landlord *(erdizhu)*
   Hidden landlord *(erlu dizhu)*
   Bankrupt landlord *(pochan dizhu)*
   Despotic landlord *(eba dizhu)*

II. The Hierarchy of Work-Grades

The ordered neatness of China's work-grade stratification is suggested in the chart opposite, which shows the range of bureaucratic ranks and wages appropriate for government employees from the head of state to the most menial service worker in a state organ. Selected offices are shown for central, provincial, and county-level workers. The wages shown are those given in Beijing, Tianjin, Shenyang, and Kunming. Ten other wage scales exist, to compensate for differences in the cost of living in various parts of China. These wages were fixed in 1956, and have varied only in minor ways since then, although the grades 26 through 30 have been dropped from use. Source: *1956 nian zhongyang caizheng fagui huibian (Compendium of 1956 Central Government Financial Regulations)* (Beijing: Finance Press, 1957), pp. 223–47.

Notes

Titles of Chinese articles have been provided only in English translation, dispensing with awkward and lengthy romanizations. Chinese publications and their authors are identified in *pinyin* romanization, although I have retained Wade-Giles romanization in citing English-language publications that used it.

The following standard abbreviations are used:

ECMM	*Extracts from China Mainland Magazines*
FBIS	*Foreign Broadcast Information Service*
JPRS	*Joint Publiations Research Service*
SCMM	*Survey of China Mainland Magazines*
SCMP	*Survey of the China Mainland Press*

One: The Problem of Class in Socialist China

1. André Malraux, *Anti-Memoirs* (New York: Holt, Rinehart and Winston, 1968), p. 373.

2. Franz Schurmann's comment is typical: "The Communists now speak of the need to continue the 'class war' during the Cultural Revolution, yet the open struggle between real segments of the population, in my opinion, ended sometime in the 1950's." "The Attack of the Cultural Revolution on Ideology and Organization," in Ping-ti Ho and Tang Tsou, eds., *China in Crisis* (Chicago: University of Chicago Press, 1968), vol. 1, book 2, p. 541.

3. See Ezra F. Vogel, "From Revolutionary to Semi-Bureaucrat: The 'Regularization' of Cadres," *China Quarterly* (January–March 1967), 29:36–60.

4. John Philip Emerson, *Nonagricultural Employment in Mainland China: 1949–1958,* U.S. Department of Commerce, Bureau of the Census, International Population Statistics Reports, ser. P-90, no. 21(1965), p. 205.

5. *Ten Great Years* (Beijing: Foreign Languages Press, 1960), p. 183.

6. Ying-mao Kau, "Patterns of Recruitment and Mobility of Urban Cadres," in John W. Lewis, ed., *The City in Communist China* (Stanford: Stanford University Press, 1971), pp. 98–99, 106.

7. Christopher Howe, *Employment and Economic Growth in Urban China, 1949–1957* (London: Cambridge University Press, 1971), pp. 42–44.

8. Michael Oksenberg, "Political Changes and their Causes in China, 1949–1972," *The Political Quarterly* (January–March 1974), 45(1):111.

9. Zhang Chunqiao, "On Exercising All-Round Dictatorship over the Bourgeoisie," *Peking Review* (April 4, 1975), 18(14):6.

10. The recently popular antisocialist polemic by Simon Leys, *Chinese Shadows* (New York: Viking, 1977) distorts the image of Chinese politics through its utter lack of sympathy for the ambiguous situation of state administrators in a revolutionary society.

11. There still exists no adequate theory of socialist class relationships. I have argued elsewhere the utility of focusing upon the bureaucrats' collective control of the means of production as a way of viewing Chinese political life. See "The Chinese State and its Bureaucrats," forthcoming in Victor Nee and David Mozingo, eds., *State and Society in Contemporary China*.

In recent years there has arisen a literature which treats patterns of inequality in socialism, but to date, these studies have focused upon the relatively industrialized Soviet Union and Eastern Europe. For example, see Frank Parkin, *Class Inequality and Political Order* (London: Palladin, 1971); David Lane, *The End of Inequality?* (Harmondsworth: Penguin, 1971); Mervyn Matthews, *Class and Society in Soviet Russia* (New York: Walker, 1972); Anthony Giddens, *The Class Structure of the Advanced Societies* (New York: Harper Torchbooks, 1973); Charles Bettelheim, *Class Struggles in the USSR: First Period, 1917–1923* (New York: Monthly Review Press, 1976); and Walter D. Connor, *Socialism, Politics, and Equality: Hierarchy and Change in Eastern Europe and the USSR* (New York: Columbia University Press, 1979). The Chinese experience is somewhat different, and while this book is not explicitly comparative, it bears some relevance to the general problem of the impact of socialism upon class conflict.

12. Benjamin I. Schwartz, *Chinese Communism and the Rise of Mao* (Cambridge: Harvard University Press, 1951), and *Communism and China: Ideology in Flux* (New York: Atheneum, 1970); Stuart R. Schram, *The Political Thought of Mao Tse-tung* (New York: Praeger, 1969), *Mao Tse-tung* (Harmondsworth: Penguin, 1967), and "Introduction: The Cultural Revolution in Historical Perspective," in *Authority, Participation and Cultural Change in China* (London: Cambridge University Press, 1973); and Maurice Meisner, *Li Ta-chao and the Origins of Chinese Marxism* (New York: Atheneum, 1970), and "Utopian Socialist Themes in Maoism," in John W. Lewis, ed., *Peasant Rebellion and Communist Revolution in Asia* (Stanford: Stanford University Press, 1974).

13. Aidan Foster-Carter, "Neo-Marxist Approaches to Development and Under-Development," in Emanuel de Kadt and Gavin Williams, eds., *Sociology and Development* (London: Tavistock, 1974), p. 92.

14. See especially Bertell Ollman, *Alienation: Marx's Conception of Man in Capitalist Society* (New York: Cambridge University Press, 1971); and Alan Swingewood, *Marx and Modern Social Theory* (New York: Wiley, 1971).

15. Andrew G. Walder, "Marxism, Maoism, and Social Change," *Modern China* (January 1977), 3(1):101–18; and Donald J. Munro, "The Malleability of Man in Chinese Marxism," *China Quarterly* (October–December 1971), 48:609–40.

16. On voluntarist and determinist strands in political Marxism, see Lewis A. Coser, "Marxist Thought in the First Quarter of the 20th Century," *American Journal of Sociology* (July 1972), 78(1):173–201.

17. Jerome Ch'en, "The Development and Logic of Mao Tse-tung's Thought, 1928–1949," in Chalmers Johnson, ed., *Ideology and Politics in Contemporary China* (Seattle: University of Washington Press, 1973), pp. 79–89, discusses the attitudinal dimension to class analysis prior to liberation.

18. The question of working class purity has persisted after liberation: "We know that within the working class there are many new workers who were still small producers not long ago; petty bourgeois ideology and the force of habit of small producers have followed them and been carried into the ranks of the working class." Lin Zhen, "Some Points of Understanding on the Question of Contradictions Among the People," *Xuexi (Study)* (1957), 7:11.

19. An important institutional manifestation of this trend has been analyzed in Martin King Whyte, *Small Groups and Political Rituals in China* (Berkeley: University of California Press, 1974).

20. The evaluation of Mao's thinking on class would be impossible without the hundreds of his speeches, reading notes, and records of conversation which appeared in unofficial and semiofficial form during the Cultural Revolution. The indispensible guide to these writings is John Bryan Starr and Nancy Anne Dyer, *Post-Liberation Works of Mao Zedong: A Bibliography and Index* (Berkeley: University of California Center for Chinese Studies, 1976). Considerably more problematic are the texts offered in volume 5 of the *Selected Works of Mao Tsetung* (Beijing: Foreign Languages Press, 1977). This important volume contains edited versions of Mao's speeches and writings between September 1949 and November 1958, supplementing the other 4 volumes, published by 1960 and limited to Mao's preliberation works. The fact that this volume was published after Mao's death raises questions about some of the changes which have been introduced. Even alterations which may have been endorsed by Mao may anachronistically spice 1950s texts with 1960s phrases and concerns. Because of this problem, I have generally relied upon the unedited and unofficial collections from the Cultural Revolution, save in a few cases where works not otherwise available were revealed and which contained points unlikely to have been added by editors after Mao's death. Mao's fulminations against bureaucratic abuse, for instance, are not likely to have been concocted in an effort to de-radicalize his works by a successor regime of more conservative officials.

21. Some samples are given by Martin King Whyte, who discusses

Chinese bureaucracy from the perspective of classical Western organization theory. See "Iron Law Versus Mass Democracy: Weber, Michels, and the Maoist Vision," in James C. Hsiung, ed., *The Logic of "Maoism"* (New York: Praeger, 1974), pp. 37–61; and "Bureaucracy and Modernization in China: The Maoist Critique," *American Sociological Review* (April 1973), 38(2):149–63.

22. Mao Tse-tung, *Selected Works* (Beijing: Foreign Languages Press, 1967), 1:291.

23. An overview of official Soviet thought on class is found in Mervyn Matthews, *Class and Society in Soviet Russia* (New York: Walker, 1972), pp. 32–51.

24. Extended discussions of Mao's theory of social change may be found in Schram, *Political Thought of Mao Tse-tung*, pp. 84–110; and John Bryan Starr, *Continuing the Revolution: The Political Thought of Mao* (Princeton: Princeton University Press, 1979).

25. The published version of this speech was revised to place a greater emphasis upon class. See my discussion in chapter 3 below.

26. For a detailed analysis of these events, see Maurice Meisner, *Mao's China: A History of the People's Republic* (New York: Free Press, 1977), pp. 167–254.

27. *Peking Review* (March 12, 1976), 19(1):4.

28. "Talk Opposing Right-Deviation and Conservatism," in *Miscellany of Mao Tse-tung Thought (1949–1968), JPRS,* 61269-1 and 61269-2 (February 20, 1974), p. 27.

29. James Peck has criticized "the most popular scholarly image of Mao—that of a deeply frustrated visionary, applying revolutionary values to a post-revolutionary society." "Revolution Versus Modernization and Revisionism: A Two-Front Struggle," in Victor Nee and James Peck, eds., *China's Uninterrupted Revolution* (New York: Pantheon, 1975), p. 75.

30. The Chinese situation fits the more general characterization by Stanislaw Ossowski: "In the social sciences theoretical conceptions sometimes anticipate life, and become a guide for men of action. In periods of violent change, however, the theorist cannot keep pace with life. Reality then changes more rapidly than does reflective thought, which is left breathless by the rate of change at a time a deep breath is most needed." Stanislaw Ossowski, *Class Structure in the Social Consciousness* (New York: Free Press, 1963), pp. 3–4.

Two: Two Models of Social Stratification

1. *Selected Works of Mao Tse-tung* (Beijing: Foreign Languages Press, 1967), 1:13.

2. On the application of class analysis before liberation, see Lyman P. Van Slyke, *Enemies and Friends: The United Front in Chinese Communist History* (Stanford: Stanford University Press, 1967); Jerome Ch'en, "The Development and Logic of Mao Tse-tung's Thought, 1928–49," in Chalmers Johnson, ed., *Ideology and Politics in Contemporary China* (Seattle: University of Press, 1973), pp. 78–114; Tso-liang Hsiao, *The Land Revo-*

lution in China, 1930–1934: A Study of Documents (Seattle: University of Washington Press, 1969), pp. 103–14, 254, 284; and Trygve Lotveit, *Chinese Communism 1931–1934: Experience in Civil Government* (Copenhagen: Scandanavian Institute of Asian Studies, 1973), pp. 145–84. On the development of class theory, see Arif Dirlik, "Mirror to Revolution: Early Marxist Images of Chinese History," *Journal of Asian Studies* (February 1974), 33:193–223; and James P. Harrison, *The Communists and Chinese Peasant Rebellions* (New York: Atheneum, 1971), chap. 2.

3. By "class designation" I am freely rendering the Chinese phrase *jieji chengfen*, which may be translated more precisely as "class element" or "class composition." It is perhaps most commonly turned into "class status," which unhappily suggests a commingling of economic and prestige dimensions which Western social scientists often take great pains to distinguish.

4. Lenin, "A Great Beginning," *Selected Works* (Moscow: Foreign Languages Publishing House, 1952), 2:224. The definition has been quoted often in China, including Jun Lin, "The Principles and Standards of Class Differentiation," *Xuexi (Study)* (October 1950), 3(1):23.

5. See the discussion in *Xuexi* (November 1949), 1(3):19–20.

6. Nicolai Bukharin, *Historical Materialism: A System of Sociology* (Ann Arbor: University of Michigan Press, 1969), p. 284. For a discussion of Soviet difficulties in identifying class membership, see M. Lewin, *Russian Peasants and Soviet Power: A Study of Collectization* (New York: Norton, 1975), chaps. 2 and 3.

7. Attention to the political component of class is by no means as unMarxist as is sometimes imagined, since Marx too shifted "his use of 'class' to sometimes include political as well as economic categories." Anthony Giddens, *The Class Structure of the Advanced Societies* (New York: Harper Torchbooks, 1975), p. 98. This point is often overlooked in Western writings on Chinese Marxism, where Mao is presented as the voluntarist theoretician of the superstructure, in contrast to a Marx whose analyses alledgedly are rooted only in the economic base of society. For a critique of this view see Andrew Walder, "Marxism, Maoism, and Social Change," *Modern China* (January–April 1977), 3(1–2):101–18, 125–60.

8. The classification of the Chinese populace into economic categories by political authorities is not a Communist innovation. For instance, see the discussion of the registration and grading of households in the eleventh, twelfth, and thirteenth centuries in Brian E. McKnight, *Village and Bureaucracy in Southern Sung China* (Chicago: University of Chicago Press, 1971), chap. 6.

9. For example, Meng Xianzhang, "The Development and Mutual Relations of the Classes and Strata of Modern Society," *Xin zhonghua banyuekan (New China Semi-Monthly)* (August 1951), 14(15):8–12; Jin Can, "Old China's Colonial, Semicolonial, Semifeudal Society," *Xuexi* (February 16, 1951), 3(10):9–11; and Hu Sheng, Yu Guangyuan, and Wang Huide, "China's Semifeudal, Semicolonial Society and New-Democractic Society," *Xuexi* (July 1, 1951), 4(6–7):61–63.

The answers to readers' questions published in *Xuexi* in this period often explain class distinctions in considerable detail. For example (October 16, 1950), 3(2):17–18 relates the work of a Chinese opera singer to the theory of surplus value.

10. Mao's article was reprinted in *Xuexi* (July 1, 1951) 4(6–7):3–6. Study aids include Li Chi, "Read 'Analysis of the Classes in Chinese Society' " *Xuexi* (March 1, 1951), 2:20–27; and Xiao Wu, "Study the Method of Class Analysis," *Xin jianshe (New Construction)* (February 1952), pp. 16–19.

11. Xiao Wu, "Study the Method of Class Analysis," p. 18.

12. A concise description of land reform procedures concerning the determination of class designations may be found in Chao Kuo-chun, *Agrarian Policy of the Chinese Communist Party, 1921–1959* (Bombay: Asia Publishing House, 1960), pp. 122–23. The classic account is William Hinton's *Fanshen* (New York: Vintage, 1968). See also John Wong, *Land Reform in the People's Republic of China* (New York: Praeger, 1973); and Jack Gray, "Political Aspects of the Land Reform Campaign in China, 1952," *Soviet Studies* (October 1964), vol. 16, no. 2.

13. "Decisions Concerning the Differentiation of Class Status in the Countryside," in Albert P. Blaustein, ed. *Fundamental Legal Documents of Communist China* (South Hackensack, N.J.: Fred R. Rothman, 1962) pp. 291–324. This document was in fact a revision of an earlier aid prepared by Mao in Jiangxi in 1933. See Hsiao, *Land Revolution in China,* pp. 103–14 and 255–82.

14. See Wong, *Land Reform,* pp. 41–44.

15. In a 1939 work, "The Chinese Revolution and the Chinese Communist Party," Mao had analyzed rural class structure as 5 percent landlord, 5 percent rich peasant, 20 percent middle peasant, and 70 percent poor peasant. He was offering an overview of the national distribution of classes, which, of course, could not describe the reality within each village. *Selected Works,* 2:323–26.

16. The Five Antis campaign of 1952 criticized the bourgeoisie for bribery, tax evasion, fraud, theft of government property, and theft of state economic secrets. It is sometimes viewed as an urban analog to land reform, in that it was the first major effort of the Party to mobilize lower-class residents against the former economic elite in the cities. Kenneth Lieberthal informed me that he interviewed two persons from Tianjin who were assigned class designations in a political study group in December 1951, at the outset of this campaign. Such designation may well have been widespread; nonetheless, precise and universal class identification was not an integral aspect of the movement. See John Gardner, "The Wu-fan Campaign in Shanghai: A Study in the Consolidation of Urban Control," in A. Doak Barnett, ed., *Chinese Communist Politics in Action* (Seattle: University of Washington Press, 1969), pp. 477–539.

17. See Yeh-lu and Ho-shih, "A Preliminary Analysis of the System of Feudal Serfdom in Tibet," *Min-tsu yen-chiu (Nationalities Studies)* (March 4, 1959), no. 3, trans. in *ECMM* (June 8, 1959), 171:1–18. This article was brought to my attention by John Dolfin.

18. The class designations of South China fishing people were gleaned from the following articles: "Fish Market and Fishing People," *Nanfang ribao (Southern Daily),* July 10, 1959; "Looking at the Problems of Guang-

dong's Fishing People from the Coastal Work Conference," *Huachiao ribao (Overseas Chinese Daily)*, August 9, 1951; "How Could the Fishing People of a 'Fish and Rice' Township Starve to Death?" *Nanfang ribao*, January 21, 1951; and "How Have the Boat People and Fishing People of *Shima* Harbor Carried Out Democratic Reform?" *Fujian ribao (Fukien Daily)*, March 10, 1953. These data were supplemented by interviews in Hong Kong in 1972.

19. As my present task is to explain the meaning of class in China rather than catalogue its seemingly infinite varieties, I have not searched extensively for other, even more exotic kinds of class designations. It is likely, however, that the herding people of Inner Mongolia and the salt workers of China's coastal regions have their own sets of class designations. For the former, see the discussion of the "two opposing classes of herd-worker and herd-master" in "Thoroughly Expose the Exhibition of the Achievements of the North China Four Clean-ups Movement," Beijing *Dongfang hong bao (East is Red Bulletin*, Beijing Geological Institute), April 28, 1967. The latter possibility is hinted at by Tao Zhu's separate treatment of "salt people" *(yanmin)* in his 1957 speech on contradictions among the people in Guangdong, *Nanfang ribao*, May 5, 1957.

20. See the examples in Dorothy J. Solinger, "Minority Nationalities in China's Yunnan Province: Assimilation, Power, and Policy in a Socialist State," *World Politics* (October 1977), 30(1):21. For evidence of villages where classification was incomplete or nonexistent, see "Decisions on Agricultural Co-operation" in Blaustein, *Fundamental Legal Documents*, pp. 355–56; and Richard Baum and Rederick C. Teiwes, *Ssu-Ch'ing: The Socialist Education Movement of 1962–1966* (Berkeley: University of California Center for Chinese Studies, 1968), p. 110.

21. Liu Shaoqi discussed difficult cases of class designation in his "Report on Land Reform," in *Tudi gaige xuexi ziliao (Land Reform Study Materials)* (Guangzhou, 1950), p. 15; see also Baum and Teiwes, *Ssu-Ch'ing*, pp. 92 and 116.

22. Ralf Dahrendorf, *Class and Class Conflict in Industrial Society* (Stanford: Stanford University Press, 1959), p. 8. And in fact, Marx was writing a chapter of *Capital* entitled "The Classes" at his death (ibid.).

23. Anthony Giddens, *Capitalism and Modern Social Theory* (London: Cambridge University Press, 1971), p. 36.

24. Stanislaw Ossowski, *Class Structure in the Social Consciousness* (New York: Free Press, 1963), p. 73.

25. The following discussion is based upon my reading of Marx, and upon these commentators: Shlomo Avineri, *The Social and Political Throught of Karl Marx* (London: Cambridge University Press, 1971); Dahrendorf, *Class and Class Conflict;* Giddens, *Capitalism and Modern Social Theory;* Giddens, *The Class Structure of the Advanced Societies;* Henri Lefebvre, *The Sociology of Marx* (New York: Vintage, 1969); George Lichtheim, *Marxism: An Historical and Critical Study* (New York: Praeger, 1961), pp. 380–92; Georg Lukács, *History and Class Consciousness* (Cambridge: MIT Press, 1971); Bertell Ollman, "Marx's Use of 'Class,' " *American Journal of Sociology* (March 1968), 73(5):73–80; Ossowski, *Class Structure;* Nicos Poulantzas, "On Social Classes," *New Left Review*

(March–April 1973), no. 78; Rodolfo Stavenhagen, *Social Classes in Agrarian Societies* (Garden City, N.Y.: Anchor, 1975); and Alan Swingewood, *Marx and Modern Social Theory* (New York: Wiley, 1975).

26. Dahrendorf, *Class and Class Conflict,* p. 19.

27. Ossowski, *Class Structure,* p. 141.

28. Marx, "The Eighteenth Brumaire of Louis Bonaparte," in Marx and Engels, *Selected Works* (New York: International Publishers, 1968), p. 172.

29. Ollman, "Marx's Use of 'Class,' " p. 578.

30. E. P. Thompson, *The Making of the English Working Class* (New York: Vintage, 1966), p. 9.

31. In 1934 the Soviet-oriented Returned Student Clique attacked Mao's class investigations as mechanical. The Returned Students may have scored a theoretical point, but they were unable to lead the Party to victory. See Hsiao, *Land Revolution,* p. 110.

32. A classic statement is Robert A. Nisbet, "The Decline and Fall of Social Class," *Pacific Sociological Review* (Spring 1959), vol. 2.

33. For example, see Harry Braverman, *Labor and Monopoly Capital: The Degradation of Work in the Twentieth Century* (New York: Monthly Review Press, 1974), pp. 27–30; and Reeve Vanneman, "The Occupational Composition of American Classes: Results from Cluster Analysis," *American Journal of Society* (January 1977), 82(4):783–807.

34. Stavenhagen, *Social Classes in Agrarian Societies,* pp. 33–34.

35. The impossibility of combining urban and rural wage scales is discussed in Tso Chun-t'ai and Fang Wei-t'ing, "Several Questions Concerning the Reform of the Wage System," *Cheng-chih hsueh-hsi (Political Study)* (June 13, 1956), no. 6, in *ECMM* (August 13, 1956), 47:8–11. The basic work on wages in China is Christopher Howe, *Wage Patterns and Wage Policy in Modern China, 1919–1972* (London: Cambridge University Press, 1973). On the issue of wages and motivation, see Carl Riskin, "Maoism and Motivation: Work Incentives in China," *Bulletin of Concerned Asian Scholars* (July 1973), 5(1):10–24.

36. Important nonwage income sources have included bonuses and piece-rates for industrial workers, and private plot and agricultural sideline income for peasants. The use of piece-rates declined during the Cultural Revolution, at which time bonuses were also severely attacked. Their reintroduction has been as an automatic and equal year-end payment, which of course heightens the role of work-grades in income differentiation. See Carl Riskin, "Worker's Incentives in Chinese Industry," in United States Congress, Joint Economic Committee, *China: A Reassessment of the Economy* (Washington, D.C.: Government Printing Office, 1975), pp. 199–224. No data about peasant supplementary income are available, but it is reasonable to hypothesize that those peasants with high work-point ratings for collective work are also likely to cultivate the most productive private plots, in which case the supplementary income would reinforce rather than undercut the work-grade stratification. Some other nonsalary income sources have been stock dividends for China's remaining capitalists, and royalty payments for writers. Although large amounts of money may have been involved here, the total number of persons eligible to receive it has been quite restricted.

37. The Chinese word I translate as "sector" is *jie,* which is commonly rendered as "walk of life," or "circle" (as in "people of all circles"). It might also be translated as "situs," its equivalent in the language of American sociology.

38. More specific sectors can be identified, such as the attention given during the Hundred Flowers period (1956–1957) to "personages of the industrial-commercial sector, the cultural, scientific, and artistic sector, the journalist and publishing sector." "Correctly Resolve Contradictions Among the People," *Renmin ribao (People's Daily),* April 13, 1957.

39. A. Doak Barnett, *Cadres, Bureaucracy, and Political Power in Communist China* (New York: Columbia University Press, 1967), pp. 6–9.

40. The following discussion of civil and military cadre work-grades is based upon Barnett, *Cadres, Bureaucracy, and Political Power;* Vogel, "The 'Regularization' of Cadres"; John Philip Emerson, *Administrative and Technical Manpower in the People's Republic of China,* United States Department of Commerce, International Population Reports, ser. P-95, no. 72 (1973); and the detailed regulations governing cadre and other work-grades in *1956 nian zhongyang caizheng fagui huibian (Compendium of 1956 Central Government Financial Regulations)* (Beijing: Finance Press, 1957), pp. 223–72.

41. Access to information (such as a limited edition of Anna Louise Strong's book on Stalin), medical care, and even desks and waste-baskets is apparently governed by a cadre's grade. See Peking Students' Union, *Look! What Kind of Talk is This?,* trans., and ed. by Dennis J. Doolin as *Communist China: The Politics of Student Opposition* (Stanford: Hoover Institution, 1964), pp. 26, 31–32.

42. A practical reason for having comparable scales is that army practice in placing demobilized personnel in civilian jobs usually includes promotion to one grade higher in the civilian scale than one's last grade in the armed forces. Thus a similarity in ranking systems is necessary to make them compatible. The two scales cannot be perfectly interchangeable, however, as Chinese military personnel, like American and others, receive housing and clothing benefits beyond those available to civil servants. Useful discussion of military ranks may be found in Harvey Nelson, *The Chinese Military System* (Boulder: Westview Press, 1977), chap. 5.

43. The stratification of industrial labor is discussed by Charles Hoffman, *The Chinese Worker* (Albany: State University of New York Press, 1974); Peter Schran, "Unity and Diversity of Russian and Chinese Industrial Wage Policies," *Journal of Asian Studies* (February 1964), 23(2):245–51; Peter Schran, "Institutional Continuity and Motivational Change: The Chinese Industrial Wages System, 1950–1975," *Asian Survey* (November 1974), 14(11):1014–32; *1967 feiching nianbao (1967 Bandit Affairs Yearbook)* (Taibei, 1967), 2:1361–66; Riskin, "Worker's Incentives in Chinese Industry"; and Lynn T. White III, "Workers' Politics in Shanghai," *Journal of Asian Studies* (November 1976), 36(1):99–116.

44. Information gathered in Hong Kong interviews, and from the *1967 Bandit Affairs Yearbook.*

45. *1967 Bandit Affairs Yearbook* (Taibei), 1:1363–65.

46. Prior to the Cultural Revolution, many artists were less bureau-

cratically organized. Writers received piece-rate *(gaofei)* payments, which were sometimes quite high. Examples, including a payment of over US $80,000 to the novelist Ba Jin, may be found in "Shocking High Manuscript Payments," Guangzhou *Wenge fenglei (Cultural Revolution Wind and Thunder),* March 1968. For labor reeducation camps, see Martin King Whyte, *Small Groups and Political Rituals in China* (Berkeley: University of California Press, 1974), p. 200.

47. This discussion draws upon Frederick W. Cook, "Chinese Communist Agricultural Incentive Systems and the Labor Productive Contracts to Households: 1956–1965," *Asian Survey* (May 1973), 13(5):470–81; Byung-joon Ahn, "The Political Economy of the People's Commune in China: Changes and Continuities," *Journal of Asian Studies* (May 1975) 34(3):631–58; Martin King Whyte, "The Tachai Brigade and Incentives for the Peasant," *Current Scene* (August 15, 1969), vol. 7, no. 16; Jack Chen, *A Year in Upper Felicity* (New York: Macmillan, 1973), pp. 156–65; and Whyte, *Small Groups and Political Rituals,* pp. 145–46 and 151–53.

Three: Socialist Transformation and the Displacement of Class

1. "Speedily Correct Mistaken Propaganda about Socialism in Some Villages," *Xuexi (Study)* (December 5, 1951), 5(3):29.

2. Mao, *Selected Readings from the Works of Mao Tse-tung* (Beijing: Foreign Languages Press, 1971), p. 389.

3. Kenneth R. Walker, "Collectivisation in Retrospect: The 'Socialist High Tide' of Autumn 1955–Spring 1956," *China Quarterly* (April–June 1966), 26:1.

4. Limited but economically significant holdings were retained for several years in private hands, especially in agriculture, where private plots were an issue throughout the next decade. Trees, tools, and livestock were also often under private ownership, with consequences for rural income patterns, On this subject see Kenneth R. Walker, *Planning in Chinese Agriculture Socialization and the Private Sector, 1956–1962* (Chicago: Aldine, 1965). In industry, former capitalists were given shares in the newly nationalized firms, the "public-private joint enterprises." These shares did return interest at a fixed rate and were held until 1967. See Mao's comments at a meeting of business representatives in 1956, in *Miscellany of Mao Tse-tung Thought (1949–1968)* (hereafter *Miscellany*), *JPRS,* 61269-1 and 61269-2 (February 20, 1974), pp. 41–45. See also Audrey Donnethorne, *China's Economic System* (New York: Praeger, 1967), pp. 145–47; and David S. Buck, "Directions in Chinese Urban Planning," *Urbanism Past & Present* (Winter 1975–1976), 1:29. But in spite of these remnants, private ownership of the means of production existed after 1956 only in severely truncated form.

5. Yu Lin and Liu Huan, "Ideological Problems of Rural Cadres," *Xuexi* (October 16, 1951), 4:14.

6. Li Zongyang, "Rely Upon Whom to Run Cooperatives? Rely Upon What to Run Cooperatives?" *Xuexi* (April 1956), p. 9.

7. "Comrade Deng Zihui's Report to the Youth League Central Rural

Work Conference," *Zhongguo Qingnian (Chinese Youth)* (September 1954), 17:9.

8. Hua Guofeng, "Fully Research the Development of Each Rural Stratum," *Xuexi* (November 1955), 11:30–31.

9. Liu Shao-ch'i, "The Political Report of the Central Committee of the Communist Party of China to the Eighth National Congress of the Party," in *Eighth National Congress of the Communist Party of China* (Beijing: Foreign Languages Press, 1956), 1:15.

10. "Resolution on the Political Report of the CCP Central Committee to the 8th National Congress of the Party," in *Documents of the Chinese Communist Party Central Committee Sept. 1956–Apr. 1969* (Hong Kong: Union Research Institute, 1971), 1:32.

11. A *People's Daily* editorial noted with pride in the following year that "in a very brief seven years, the ranks of the working class have been enlarged from over seven million to over twenty million persons." *Renmin ribao,* April 23, 1957.

12. For representative Chinese use of the Soviet example, see the questions-and-answers column in *Xuexi* (May 16, 1950), 2:13; and Liu Jichen, "Introducing the Second Chapter of 'How the Soviet Union Eliminated Exploiting Classes and Class Differences,' " *Xuexi* (August 1953), 8:36–37. See also Zou Shumin, "Is Class Struggle in the Transitional Period Increasingly Acute?" *Xuexi* (June 1956), pp. 22–23; and Zhang Jing, "Rural Class Struggle in the Transitional Period Is Not Increasingly Acute," *Xuexi* (July 1956), p. 42.

13. Adapted from "More on the Historical Experience of the Dictatorship of the Proletariat," *Renmin ribao* editorial, December 29, 1956, in *Communist China 1955–1959: Policy Documents with Analysis* (Cambridge: Harvard University Press 1962), p. 267.

14. See Mao's introductory notes and comments upon the three batches of materials on the Hu Feng "anti-Party clique," in *Renmin ribao,* May 13, May 14, and June 10, 1955; his speech "On the Question of Agricultural Co-operation" (July 31, 1955), in *Selected Readings,* pp. 389–420; and his editorial notes to *Zhongguo nongcun shehui zhuyi gaochao (The Socialist Upsurge in China's Countryside),* 3 vols. (Beijing: People's Publishing House, 1956). Mao's authorship of several anonymously published works (such as the Hu Feng materials) is established by John Bryan Starr, "Mao Tse-tung's Theory of Continuing the Revolution Under the Dictatorship of the Proletariat: Its Origins, Development, and Political Implications" (unpublished Ph.D. diss., Department of Political Science, University of California, Berkeley, 1971), and in Jerome Ch'en, *Mao Papers* (London: Oxford University Press, 1970).

15. See the text in Stuart R. Schram, ed., *Chairman Mao Talks to the People* (New York: Pantheon, 1974), pp. 61–83. This speech was in 1977 published in the Chinese press for the first time, and was the subject of intensive political study. But the version presented to the populace contains obvious revisions to bring it into accord with subsequent Maoist thinking about class. These changes are minor and may well have been made by Mao prior to his death. The amended text is in *Peking Review* (January 1, 1977), 20(1):10–25.

16. Mao, "Speech at a Report Meeting," in *Long Live Mao Tse-tung Thought* (n.d.) trans. in *Current Background* (October 8, 1969), 891:72. Mao's reference to Deng Xiaoping concerns the speech discussed in the second half of this chapter.

17. *Selected Readings,* pp. 463–64.

18. Peking *Hsin Pei-ta (New Peking University)* (February 25, 1967), in *SCMP Supplement* (May 1, 1967), no. 180.

19. For examples concerning Liu Shaoqi, see *Renmin ribao,* August 20, 1967; Beijing *Dongfanghong (East is Red),* January 4, 1967; Beijing *Jinggangshan (Jinggang Mountains),* January 1, 1967; *Beijing gongshe (Beijing Commune),* April 15, 1967; *Nanfang ribao (Southern Daily),* November 26, 1968. For similar examples concerning the South China Party leader, Tao Zhu, see Beijing *Jinggangshan,* February 27, 1967; Beijing *Pi Tao Zhanbao (Criticize Tao Combat Bulletin),* March 31 and June 12, 1967; *Renmin ribao,* September 11, 1967; and *Tao Zhu cuixing huibian* (A *Collection of Tao Zhu's Crimes),* ed. by the Capital Red Guard Congress Struggle Tao Zhu Preparatory Office (Beijing, March 1967), 1:15–22.

20. An invaluable guide to high-level politics in this period is Roderick MacFarquhar's imaginative *The Origins of the Cultural Revolution,* vol. 1, *Contradictions Among the People, 1956–1957* (New York: Columbia University Press, 1974).

21. Chou En-lai, "On the Question of Intellectuals," in *Communist China 1955–1959,* p. 130.

22. For examples of the criticisms, see the wall posters and speeches collected in Dennis J. Doolin, ed., *Communist China: The Politics of Student Opposition* (Stanford: Hoover Institution, 1964), and Roderick MacFarquhar, ed., *The Hundred Flowers Campaign and the Chinese Intellectuals* (New York: Praeger, 1960). See also Hualing Nieh, ed., *Literature of the Hundred Flowers,* 2 vols. (New York: Columbia University Press, 1981).

23. Doolin, *Communist China,* pp. 25–26.

24. Mao later admitted that he was "a bit worried" by the rightist activity in the spring of 1957. "Examples of Dialectics (Abstracted compilation)," in *Miscellany,* p. 209.

25. Mao, "On the Correct Handling of Contradictions Among the People," in *Selected Readings from the Works of Mao Tsetung* (Beijing: Foreign Languages Press, 1971), p. 464.

26. Ibid., p. 432.

27. Ibid., p. 443.

28. Ibid., p. 443.

29. Ibid., p. 434.

30. Ibid., p. 434.

31. Ibid., pp. 441–42.

32. Ibid., p. 432.

33. *Renmin ribao,* March 3, 1957; see also "Several Points of Understanding on Hearing Chairman Mao's Report," *Renmin ribao,* March 19, 1957.

34. An account by one person who heard the speech on tape is given in Robert Loh and Humphrey Evans, *Escape from Red China* (New York:

Coward and McCann, 1962) pp. 289–93. At least one recording of the speech made its way to Poland, where it was translated into Polish and again recorded. Sydney Gruson of the *New York Times* gained access to this tape, upon which he based an article (June 13, 1957). Gruson's excerpts are perhaps only one-sixth the length of the revised and official Chinese version, but they include such interesting points as Mao's proposal to publish the complete works of Jiang Jieshi (Chiang Kai-shek) and a volume of Voice of America broadcasts, so as to better understand the viewpoints of reactionaries. It is likely that the Central Intelligence Agency has a copy of the original version of the Contradictions speech, but if so, it has never been made public.

35. *Renmin ribao*, April 25, 1957.

36. MacFarguhar argues convincingly that the press was in fact closed to Mao during much of the period between the delivery and publication of the Contradictions speech. He suggests that this was the result of opposition within the Party to the Chairman's efforts to enlist non-Party critics in his drive for Party rectification. But MacFarquhar does not suggest that Mao's adversaries manipulated in any significant manner the theoretical portions of the speech; in fact, altering the message to emphasize the role of class conflict would have been in the interests of Mao's rivals (thereby tarnishing the bourgeois critics early on). The large numbers of persons with access to the unpublished speech, and the potential for political difficulties for anyone who might consciously misrepresent its content, reinforce the likelihood that the public discussion was in fact based upon what Mao really said in February. See MacFarquhar, *Origins*, 1:193–94, 217, and 371 *n*. 1. See also Mao's comments on the press in *Miscellany*, esp. pp. 67, 82, and 152.

37. As the following discussion indicates, I take exception to MacFarquhar's presumption of theoretical consistency between the two versions of the speech. A similar methodological criticism may be made of Richard H. Solomon's account in *Mao's Revolution and the Chinese Political Culture* (Berkeley: University of California Press, 1971), pp. 268–329.

38. Mao, "On the Correct Handling," p. 464; Lin Zhen, "Several Points of Understanding About Contradictions Among the People," *Xuexi* (April 3, 1957), 7:9.

39. *Renmin ribao* editorial, April 23, 1957; Mao, "On the Correct Handling," p. 463.

40. Li Honglin, "Discussing Contradictions Among the People," *Xuexi* (June 18, 1957), 12:15. See also *Renmin ribao*, April 25, 1957.

41. Mao, "On the Correct Handling," p. 434; *Renmin ribao*, April 13, 1957.

42. Xiao Yun, "Some Observations on Current Contradictions Among the People in the Countryside," *Xuexi* (May 18, 1957), 10:13; almost identical language is used by Lin Zhen, "Several Points of Understanding About the Problem of Contradictions Among the People," p. 10.

43. See *Renmin ribao*, February 21, March 19, and April 13, 1957.

44. For these two points, see "Several Points of Understanding on Hearing Chairman Mao's Report," *Renmin ribao*, March 19, 1957; Zheng

Siyuan, "Problems of Attitude in Handling Contradictions Among the People," *Xuexi* (May 18, 1957), 10:11–13; and Tao Zhu's speech in *Nanfang ribao,* May 4, 1957.

45. MacFarquhar points to, for example, evidence of resistance in Guangdong to Mao's treatment of the relationship between contradictions among the people and contradictions between the enemy and ourselves. *Origins,* 1:198. See also the April 23 *Renmin ribao* editorial, which criticizes "some cadres" who failed to grasp the significance of the basic completion of class struggle and the new role for contradictions among the people which this made possible.

46. This analysis of the Hundred Flowers follows some of the lines suggested by Edward Friedman, "Cultural Limits of the Cultural Revolution," *Asian Survey* (March 1969), 10(3):188–201.

47. "Concluding Speech at the Supreme State Conference," in *Mao Zedong sixiang wan sui! (Long Live Mao Zedong Thought!)* (n.p., 1969), p. 100. This is one of the two volumes of the same title containing dozens of previously unpublished speeches and notes by Mao, and apparently prepared for Post-Cultural Revolution political study. Although they were made available in the West by Taiwan sources, their authenticity is unquestioned. Much of this material has been translated in *Miscellancy* (note 4 above). This early hint by Mao of plans for revision and wider circulation of his speech weakens MacFarquhar's argument that it was revised and published in response to the appearance of extended excerpts in the *New York Times.* See MacFarquhar, *Origins,* 1:267.

48. *Miscellany,* p. 65. Mao also gave much greater attention to class conflict in his March 12 "Speech at the Chinese Communist Party's National Congress on Propaganda Work." But the most emphatic passages are the opening and the close (pp. 480 and 497 of the *Selected Readings*), inspiring suspicion that they may have been added much later, perhaps at the time of the first publication of this speech in 1965, by which time Mao's commitment to class struggle had been thoroughly renewed.

49. By these criteria, words and actions should help and not hinder: (1) national unity, (2) socialist transformation and socialist construction, (3) the consolidation of the people's democratic dictatorship, (4) democratic centralism, (5) Party leadership, (6) international socialist unity. "Of these six criteria, the most important are the socialist path and the leadership of the Party." Mao, "On the Correct Handling," pp. 467–68.

50. Quoted in *Renmin ribao,* August 20, 1967, trans. in *JPRS,* no. 43449 (November 24, 1967), p. 98.

51. This point has been recognized by others, such as MacFarquhar, *Origins,* 1:381; Friedman, "Cultural Limits"; Lowell Dittmer, *Liu Shaoch'i and the Chinese Cultural Revolution: The Politics of Mass Criticism* (Berkeley: University of California Press, 1974); and Jack Gray, "The Two Roads: Alternative Strategies of Social Change and Economic Growth in China," in Stuart R. Schram, ed., *Authority, Participation and Cultural Change in China* (Cambridge: Cambridge University Press, 1973), p. 131. Even Western observers without malicious intent have unfairly compared statements by Liu and Mao on class. See Schram's insightful introduction to *Authority, Participation and Cultural Change in*

NOTES: DISPLACEMENT OF CLASS

China, pp. 48–49; and Stanley Karnow, *Mao and China* (New York: Viking, 1972), p. 82.

52. Rich peasants in the old liberated areas (which had already completed land reform) were similarly eligible for a change of designation after a three-year period. The translation in Arthur P. Blaustein, ed., *Fundamental Legal Documents of Communist China* (South Hackensack, N.J.: Fred B. Rothman, 1962), p. 324 has been modified somewhat, on the basis of the text in *Tudi gaige xuexi ziliao (Land Reform Study Materials)* (Guangzhou, 1950), pp. 24–43.

53. Meng Xianzhang, "The Development and Mutual Relations of the Classes and Strata of Modern Society," *Xin zhonghua banyuekan (New China Semi-Monthly)* (August 1951), 14(15):11; Liu Xigeng, "Some Ideological Problems in Studying Land Reform Policy," *Xuexi* (December 16, 1950), 3(6):17.

54. On rural restratification after land reform, see John Wong, *Land Reform in the People's Republic of China* (New York: Praeger, 1973), pp. 158–95.

55. Hua Guofeng, "Fully Research the Development of Each Rural Stratum," p. 30, discusses the new and old lower-middle peasants. Edward Friedman's implication that this distinction was merely a conceit of Mao is far too sweeping a judgment, as it ignores efforts to deal with real economic differences in the countryside. "Cultural Limits," pp. 189–90.

56. Meng Xianzhang, "Development and Mutual Relations," p. 11. Still additional complexity was suggested, as Ke Qingshi hinted at the desirability of further differentiating among the lower-middle peasantry. Few cadres could cope with distinctions among new and old upper-lower-middle peasants and lower-lower-middle peasants, for such a detailed categorization never appeared. Ke Qingshi, "The High Tide of Agricultural Cooperativization and the Problem of Uniting with the Middle Peasants," *Xuexi* (November 1955), 11:26–28.

57. Walker, "Collectivisation in Retrospect," p. 15. See also Daniel H. Bays, "Agrarian Reform in Kwangtung, 1950–1953," in Ronald S. Suleski and Daniel H. Bays, *Early Communist China: Two Studies* (Ann Arbor: University of Michigan Center for Chinese Studies, 1969). A similar point is made in Thomas P. Bernstein, "Cadre and Peasant Behavior Under Conditions of Insecurity and Deprivation: The Grain Supply Crisis of the Spring of 1955," in A. Doak Barnett, ed., *Chinese Communist Politics in Action* (Seattle: University of Washington Press, 1969), p. 380.

58. Stephen Fitzgerald, *China and the Overseas Chinese* (London: Cambridge University Press, 1972), pp. 59–60.

59. Zhao Zhungxin, "Penetrating Investigation Clarified Muddled Thinking," *Xin hua banyuekan* (1957), 3:66–67.

60. "Reform Landlords and Rich Peasants to Become Self-Sufficient New People," *Renmin ribao,* September 26, 1956.

61. One person even denied that the land reform regulations had included provisions for change of class, arguing that such a notion had been falsely attributed to the central authorities by local cadres seeking ways of securing easy compliance to land reform: "If you leaf through the speeches of Mao Zedong and Liu Shaoqi, you will find no words of that

sort." But a 1959 report nonetheless claims that an unspecified portion of Guangdong's landlords and rich peasants had already changed their designations. See Guan Qingyan, "The Great Achievements of Political Legal Work in Kwangtung Over the Past Decade," *Shangyou (Upstream)* (1959), 17–18:48.

62. "Introductory Note to 'How the Dominant Position Passed from the Middle Peasants to the Poor Peasants in the Wutang Agricultural Producers' Co-operative of Kaoshan Township, Changsha County,' " *Selected Readings,* p. 427. This translation has been modified according to the text in *Mao Zedong xuandu (Selected Readings of Mao Zedong)* (Beijing: People's Publishers, 1969), pp. 322–324. See also Mao's September 1955 comments in *Miscellany,* p. 23.

63. Tao Zhu, "The Great Development of Agricultural Cooperativization in the New Area and the Problem of Guaranteeing Quality," *Xuexi* (December 1955), 12:8. See also Mao's comment on Jiangsu rural cadres in 1955, in "Second Speech at the Second Session of the Eighth Party Congress" (May 17, 1958), in *Miscellany,* p. 102.

64. Bernstein, "Cadre and Peasant Behavior," p. 389. See also Mao's observation that "a portion of the old cadres have become rich." "Interjection at Conference of Provincial and Municipal Committee Secretaries (Collected) (January 1957) in *Miscellany,* p. 50; and Jack Grey, "The High Tide of Socialism in the Chinese Countryside," in Jerome Ch'en and Nicholas Tarling, eds., *Studies in the Social History of China and Southeast Asia: Essays in Memory of Victor Purcell* (Cambridge: Cambridge University Press, 1970), p. 97.

65. Hua Guofeng, "Fully Research the Development of Each Rural Stratum," p. 30; and Zhang Jun, "A Criticism of Several Mistaken Viewpoints in Rural Class Struggle," *Xuexi* (November 1955), 11:38–40. See also Lin Ming, "The Ideology of Relying on the Poor Peasants Must be Firmly Established," *Xuexi* (November 1955), 11:28–29.

66. The strong resistance of Peng Zhen to Mao's demands for a Party rectification in 1957 indicates that many leaders were especially protective of lower-level cadres in this period. See MacFarquhar, *Origins.*

67. Jian Wei, "Oppose the Rich Peasant Tendency," *Xuexi* (March 1955), 3:29. See also Chen Boda, "An Explanation of the Draft Decision on the Problem of Agricultural Cooperativization," *Xuexi* (November 1955), 11:22; and Zhang Jun, "A Criticism of Several Mistaken Viewpoints in Rural Class Struggle," *Xuexi* (November 1955), 11:39. For policies governing admission to cooperatives, see Blaustein, *Fundamental Legal Documents,* pp. 369 and 414, and *Renmin ribao,* January 1, 1955.

68. Of four categories of applicants, three were defined by class: (1) workers, coolies, hired agricultural laborers, poor peasants, urban paupers, and revolutionary soldiers were given highest priority, followed by (2) middle peasants, office employees, intellectuals, and members of the liberal professions; (3) all other classes; and (4) persons who had left other political parties. These four categories were distinguished by the qualifications demanded of the applicant's two sponsors, the length of the probationary period prior to formal membership, and the level of the Party bureaucracy which had to approve the application. The justification for

these differences rested on a presumed association of ideological purity with membership in the oppressed classes. See *Zhongguo gongchandang dangzhang jiaocai (Instruction Materials on the Constitution of the Chinese Communist Party)* (Beijing: People's Publishers, 1951), pp. 53–55.

69. "The Constitution of the Communist Party of China," in *Eighth National Congress of the Communist Party of China* (Beijing: Foreign Languages Press, 1956), 1:144.

70. Teng Hsiao-p'ing, "Report on the Revision of the Constitution of the Communist Party of China," in *Eighth National Congress*, 1:213–14.

71. For one of many attacks, see *Guangzhou Zhonglin dongfanghong (Central-South College of Forestry East is Red)*, July 1, 1967.

72. That class designations were not to be abandoned overnight is evident from Mao's approving citation of a survey of class designations in Shaanxi. See *Miscellany*, pp. 48–49.

73. Deng qualified his remarks: "for a certain period of time" there would be differences of economic interest, and "for a considerable time" there would be "certain differences in outlook." "Speech by Comrade Teng Tzu-hui," in *Eighth National Congress*, 2:196.

74. See Doolin, *Communist China*, especially pp. 24, 43–44, 45–48, 57, and 61.

75. Kang Min, "Can Classes Naturally Be Transformed?" *Jilin ribao (Kirin Daily)*, November 16, 1957.

76. Li Guangyi, "How to Correctly Understand the Problem of Capitalists' 'Taking Off Hats,' " *Shishi shouce (Current Affairs Handbook)* (December 25, 1956), 24:17–19.

77. Fan Jingyuan, "How to Regard Capitalists After Joint State-Private Ownership," *Shishi shouce* (December 25, 1956), 24:14. See also Cui Pengyun, "Gradually Transform Capitalists into Laborers," *Zhengzhi xuexi (Political Study)* (April 13, 1956), 4:27–30.

78. "Resolutely Attack the Destructive Activities of Unlawful Landlords, Rich Peasants, and Counterrevolutionaries!" *Nongcun gongzuo tongxum (Rural Work Bulletin)* (August 8, 1957), 8:2.

79. Li Zhanwu, "Several Points of Understanding Concerning the Special Characteristics of the Petty Bourgeoisie," *Xuexi* (September 15, 1949), 1(1):37; *Renmin ribao*, May 26, 1957.

80. Deng Xiaoping, *Guanyu zhengfeng yundong di baogao (Report on the Rectification Movement)* (Beijing: People's Publishers, 1957), p. 20.

81. In some extreme cases persons have been paraded about, with real hats placed upon their heads, paper hats resembling the Western dunce cap, with the offense committed either inscribed upon the hat or written on a placard worn around the neck. Newspaper photographs from the early days of the Cultural Revolution showed that young Chinese still remember how to practice this striking and traditional form of humiliation which Mao had described forty years earlier in his "Report on an Investigation of the Peasant Movement in Hunan." *Selected Readings*, p. 29.

82. Labels are discussed in Gordon Bennett, "Political Labels and Popular Tensions." *Current Scene* (February 26, 1969), vol. 7.

83. For the workings of the Public Security Bureau in China, see Vic-

tor H. Li, "The Public Security Bureau and Political-Legal Work in Hui-yang, 1952–1964," in John Wilson Lewis, ed., *The City in Communist China* (Stanford: Stanford University Press, 1971), pp. 51–74. See also Jerome Alan Cohen, *The Criminal Process in the People's Republic of China, 1949–1963* (Cambridge: Harvard University Press, 1968).

84. But if not many people have labels, anyone is potentially eligible. One Cultural Revolution report from Guangdong referred to persons as old as seventy and as young as three being labeled counterrevolutionaries, surely an exceptional circumstance. "*Ying-te Hsien* Deserves the Nation's Attention," from Ying-te *Chiu-san chan-pao (Drag Out the Three Lines Combat News)* (May 1968), in *JPRS,* no. 46220 (August 19, 1968), p. 62.

Four: The Maoist Revival of Class

1. Mao Tse-tung, "The Situation in the Summer of 1957 (Excerpts)," *SCMP Supplement* (July 14, 1967), 191:21.

2. Wen Zhida, "Must We Still Use the Method of Class Analysis in Handling Contradictions Among the People?" *Xuexi (Study)* (June 18, 1958), 12:32. Even more telling may be the "Resolution Made by the Enlarged Meeting of the Military Affairs Commission of the Central Authorities of the CCP on Strengthening Political and Ideological Work in the Army" (October 20, 1960). This was a key document in establishing Lin Biao's reforms within the People's Liberation Army, a process often regarded as a critical initial step in the Maoist revival prior to the Cultural Revolution. This document, over forty pages in translation, contains one reference to "promoting class awareness" but no detailed exposition of the theory of class struggle. Thus even in the heart of what was later seen as the Maoist camp was there no evidence of a firm commitment to a class analysis. See *Documents of Chinese Communist Party Central Committee* (Hong Kong: Union Research Institute, 1968), 1:345–88. Stuart R. Schram points out that this document was revised by Mao. See Schram's "Introduction" to *Authority, Participation and Cultural Change in China* (London: Cambridge University Press, 1973), p. 66.

3. Bu Bai, "One Year After the Publication of 'On the Correct Handling of Contradictions Among the People,' " *Xuexi* (June 18, 1958), 12:6–7.

4. "The CCP Central Committee's Directive on Leading Personnel at All Levels Taking Part in Physical Labour" (May 14, 1957) in *Documents of Chinese Communist Party Central Committee* (Hong Kong: Union Research Institute, 1972), September 1956–April 1969, p. 262.

5. "Talks at the Chengtu Conference," in Stuart R. Schram, ed., *Chairman Mao Talks to the People: Talks and Letters, 1956–1971* (New York: Pantheon, 1974), p. 120.

6. *Current Background* (October 21, 1969), 892:6.

7. "Speech at the Hankow Conference" (April 6, 1958), *Miscellany of Mao Tse-tung Thought (1949–1968), JPRS,* nos. 61269-1 and 61269-2 (February 20, 1974), p. 85. Note also Mao's critical comments on a document which took a harsh approach toward class struggle, "Reply to

Article 'Tsinghua University Physics Teaching and Research Group Inclines Toward the 'Left' Rather than Right in Handling Teachers' " (December 22, 1958), *Miscellany*, pp. 149–50.

8. Documents concerning this incident have been collected in *The Case of Peng Teh-huai, 1959–1968* (Hong Kong: Union Research Institute, 1968).

9. Mao, "The Origin of Machine Guns and Mortars, etc." (August 16, 1959), in *Chairman Mao's Criticism of the P'eng-Huang-Chang-Chou Antiparty Clique* (n.d.), trans. in *Chinese Law and Government* (Winter 1968–1969), 1(4)74.

10. Mao, "Origin of Machine Guns and Mortars," pp. 73–76.

11. See Maurice Meisner, *Mao's China* (New York: Free Press, 1977), p. 303.

12. Byung-joon Ahn, *Chinese Politics and the Cultural Revolution* (Seattle: University of Washington Press, 1976), p. 155.

13. Ibid., pp. 56 and 77.

14. See John Gardner, "Educated Youth and Urban-Rural Inequalities, 1958–1966," in John Wilson Lewis, ed., *The City in Communist China* (Stanford: Stanford University Press, 1971), pp. 235–86. See also "Chronology of the Two-Road Struggle on the Educational Front in the Past Seventeen Years," in Peter J. Seybolt, ed., *Revolutionary Education in China* (White Plains, N.Y.: International Arts and Sciences Press, 1973), pp. 5–60.

15. See Merle Goldman, "The Chinese Communist Party's 'Cultural Revolution' of 1962–1964," in Chalmers Johnson, ed., *Ideology and Politics in Contemporary China* (Seattle: University of Washington Press, 1973), pp. 219–54.

16. Ahn, *Chinese Politics*, 37–38.

17. *Documents of Central Committee*, p. 121.

18. Two excellent accounts of Mao's intellectual reorientation since the Great Leap Forward are John Bryan Starr, "Conceptual Foundations of Mao Tse-tung's Theory of Continuous Revolution," *Asian Survey* (June 1971), 11(6):610–18; and Joseph W. Esherick, "On the 'Restoration of Capitalism': Mao and Marxist Theory," *Modern China* (January 1979), 5(1):41–78.

19. Mao, *Miscellany*, p. 91.

20. Mao in Schram, *Chairman Mao Talks to the People*, p. 175.

21. An overview of these commentaries is found in Richard Levy, "New Light on Mao: His Views on the Soviet Union's Political Economy," *China Quarterly* (March 1975), 61:95–117.

22. Trans. by Moss Roberts in Mao Tsetung, *A Critique of Soviet Economics* (New York: Monthly Review Press, 1977), p. 107.

23. "Critique of Stalin's *Economic Problems of Socialism in the USRR*," in Mao, *Critique of Soviet Economics*, p. 135.

24. "Concerning *Economic Problems of Socialism in the USSR*," in Mao, *Critique of Soviet Economics*, pp. 130–31.

25. Mao, *Critique of Soviet Economics*, p. 135.

26. Ibid., p. 79.

27. For documentation, see William E. Griffith, *The Sino-Soviet Rift*

(Cambridge: MIT Press, 1964); John Gittings, *Survey of the Sino-Soviet Dispute* (London: Oxford University Press, 1968).

28. *On Khrushchov's Phoney Communism and Its Historical Lessons for the World* (Beijing: Foreign Languages Press, 1964), p. 34 (This was also published in *Peking Review;* see note 3 to chap. 5).

29. In Schram, *Chairman Mao Talks to the People,* pp. 179–80.

30. James R. Townsend, "Intraparty Conflict in China: Disintegration in an Established One-Party System," in Samuel P. Huntington and Clement H. Moore, eds., *Authoritarian Politics in Modern Society* (New York: Basic Books, 1970), p. 303.

31. See James R. Townsend, "Political Institutions," in Joyce Kallgren, ed., *China After Thirty Years* (Berkeley: University of California Press, 1979), pp. 14–22.

32. "Chairman Mao Discusses Twenty Manifestations of Bureaucracy," in "Chairman Mao's Selected Writings" (n.d., n.p.), in *JPRS*, no. 49829 (February 12, 1970), pp. 40–43.

33. Mao, *Miscellany,* p. 282. See also pp. 131, 134, 190, 281–83, 293.

34. Ibid., p. 233.

35. "Talks at a Conference of Secretaries of Provincial, Municipal and Autonomous Region Party Committees. I. The Talk of January 18 (1957)," *Selected Works of Mao Tsetung* (Beijing: Foreign Languages Press, 1977), 5:350–51.

36. Mao, *Critique of Soviet Economics,* p. 117.

37. Ibid., p. 71.

38. Mao, *Miscellany,* p. 178.

39. Mao, "Strive to Learn from Each Other and Don't Stick to the Beaten Track and Be Complacent" (December 13, 1963), printed in *Peking Review* (September 13, 1977), vol. 20, nos. 37–38.

40. Mao's 1964 comment is quoted by Chih Hung, "Inner-Party Struggle and Party Development," *Peking Review* (August 20, 1976), 19(34):11. A very similar statement is dated January 29, 1965, in *Current Background* (October 8, 1969), 891:49.

41. André Malraux, *Anti-Memoirs* (New York: Holt, Rinehart and Winston, 1968), p. 369. Mao also raised this theme in the statement quoted by Chih Heng, "Inner-Party Struggle," p. 11: "Those leading cadres who are taking the capitalist road have turned, or are turning, into bourgeois elements sucking the blood of the workers; how can they possibly realize fully the imperative need for socialist revolution? These people are the target of the struggle, the target of the revolution, and we must never rely on them in the socialist education movement. We can rely only on those cadres who are not hostile to the workers and are imbued with revolutionary spirit."

42. Quoted in Roy Medvedev, *Let History Judge* (New York: Vintage Books, 1973), p. 425.

43. In discussing British political thought of the seventeenth century, C. B. Macpherson argues that a radical thinker may avoid clearly stating all assumptions from fear of offending the readers whom he wanted to convert to his conclusions, or "from fear of persecution . . . [A] cautious theorist who had reached an intellectual position which was a decisive

break with the received tradition might well think that some subterfuge was needed to carry his readers with him." C. B. Macpherson, *The Political Theory of Possessive Individualism* (London: Oxford University Press, 1962), p. 7.

44. *On Khrushchov's Phoney Communism*, p. 66.

45. Quoted in Richard Baum, *Prelude to Revolution: Mao, the Party, and the Peasant Question, 1962–1966* (New York: Columbia University Press, 1975), p. 17.

46. Mao, *Miscellany*, p. 321.

47. Mao complained to the Ninth Plenum (January 1961) that "last year the central leadership comrades devoted their main energy to international questions." *Miscellany*, p. 238.

48. Mao, "Democratic Centralism" (January 30, 1962), *Chairman Mao's Selected Writings* (n.d.), in *JPRS*, 50792 (June 23, 1970), pp. 45–46.

49. Mao, "Speech at the Tenth Plenary Session of the Eighth Central Committee," in *Chairman Mao's Criticism of the Antiparty Clique*, p. 86. The editorial note which identifies the reference to Peitaiho as the meeting of August 1958 is incorrect.

50. Mao, "Speech at the Tenth Plenary Session," pp. 86–87.

51. See Harold Kahn and Albert Feuerwerker, "The Ideology of Scholarship: China's New Historiography," in Feuerwerker, ed., *History in Communist China* (Cambridge: MIT Press, 1968), pp. 2–3.

52. For example, note the grumbling attributed to Wu Lengxi, head of the New China News Agency, in *Xinwen Zhanbao (News Combat Paper)*, May 6, 1967.

53. Such as, "How Did Landlords Sabotage Land Reform?" *Zhungguo Qingnian (Chinese Youth)* (November 1, 1964), 21:27.

54. By K'ung Hsi-chou, in Canton *Yang-ch'eng wan-pao (Ram City Evening News)*, July 2, 1963, in *SCMP Supplement* (May 5, 1964), 120:34. This article was called to my attention by Thomas Bernstein.

55. Ch'en Fu-lung, "Further Development of a Large-scale Socialist Education Movement for the Promotion of Production and Economy (February 9, 1963), in C. S. Chen, ed., *Rural People's Communes in Lien-chiang* (Stanford: Hoover Institution Press, 1969), p. 205.

56. Mao, *Miscellany*, pp. 319, 345.

57. Mao, "Speech at the Tenth Plenary Session," p. 92.

58. Anne F. Thurston, "The Revival of Classes in Rural Kwangtung: Production Team Politics in a Period of Crisis" (paper prepared for the Workshop in the Pursuit of Political Interests in the People's Republic of China, Ann Arbor, Michigan, August 10–17, 1977).

59. Guangzhou *Nanfang ribao (Southern Daily)*, June 5, 1965.

60. For example, see "A New Air in the Barbershops," *Nanfang ribao*, November 29, 1964.

61. Mao, *Miscellany*, pp. 337, 314.

62. Malraux, *Anti-Memoirs*, p. 466.

63. In Richard Baum and Frederick C. Teiwes, *Ssu-Ch'ing: The Socialist Education Movement of 1962–1966* (Berkeley: University of California Center for Chinese Studies, 1968), p. 120.

64. *Renmin ribao*, May 25, 1965.

65. Mao, *Miscellany*, p. 441.

66. Huang Hsueh-shih, "The Reactionary Theory of 'Combining Two into One' as Seen in Anhui Rural Class Struggle," *Hung-ch'i* (December 22, 1964), nos. 23–24 trans. in *JPRS*, 28359 (January 19, 1965), p. 44.

67. Adapted from Baum and Teiwes, *Ssu-Ch'ing*, p. 62.

68. Baum and Teiwes, *Ssu-Ch'ing*, p. 83.

69. I have been unable to identify these, but presumably they are documents which set up clearer criteria for the lower-middle peasant classification.

70. Baum and Teiwes, *Ssu-Ch'ing*, pp. 83–84.

71. Ibid., pp. 84, 90, 92.

72. Ibid., pp. 102, 110.

73. Ibid., p. 110.

74. Ibid., p. 116.

75. Ibid., p. 117.

76. Stuart R. Schram, "Introduction" to *Authority, Participation and Cultural Change in China* (London: Cambridge University Press, 1973), p. 77.

77. Mao, *Miscellany*, pp. 314, 316.

78. Mao, *Miscellany*, p. 349.

79. Mao, *Miscellany*, p. 351. These and other quotations in this section have been modified according to the text in *Mao Zedong sixiang wan sui! (Long Live Mao Zedong Thought!)* (1969), p. 495.

80. Mao, *Miscellany*, pp. 433–34. *Mao Zedong sixiang wan sui!* (1969), pp. 602–3.

81. I do not believe that language is being stretched too far by my translation of *biaoxian* as "behavior." It is perhaps more frequently rendered as "deeds" or "performance," choices which strike me as too circumscribed to convey the totality of conduct which is implied by the Chinese word. An alternative possibility is "manifestation," which best suggests the close relationship between a person's ideological condition and his or her consequent behavior, but this sounds a bit unnatural in English.

82. Indications of alteration of class designation are quite fragmentary, but the available evidence suggests a process of unsystematic, local decisions for modification. One case of such change was reported by a Hong Kong newspaper, the *Sing Tao Daily News,* which carried an account on July 5, 1965, of an area of Zhongshan County, Guangdong, in which many poor and middle peasants who had paid insufficient attention to collective production while enriching themselves through sideline efforts were reclassified as "new rich peasants." See *China News Summary,* July 8, 1965. Similarly, an allegation contained in "The Theory of Family Background," Beijing *Zhongxue wenge bao (Middle School Cultural Revolution News)* (February 1967), maintains that children of landlords and rich peasants were assigned a special designation during the socialist education movement. And Deng Xiaoping is said to have urged a change in class designation for well-behaved landlords and rich peasants on July 5, 1965, at a symposium on the Socialist Education Movement. See "Record of Teng Hsiao-p'ing's Reactionary Utterances," in *How Vicious*

They Are!, trans. in *SCMP Supplement* (October 26, 1967), 208:8. Additional discussions of changes in class designation during this period are to be found in A. Doak Barnett, *Cadres, Bureaucracy, and Political Power in Communist China* (New York: Columbia University Press, 1967), p. 407. See also Martin King Whyte, *Small Groups and Political Rituals in China* (Berkeley: University of California Press, 1974), pp. 150–51, and "Three Years of Blood and Tears," Canton *Chih-nung Hung-ch'i (Support the Peasantry Red Flag)* (January 1968), p. 3, trans. in *China Topics* (May 27, 1968), YB483:3. The last account charges that urban secondary school graduates who refused to go to the countryside were threatened with a change in class designation.

83. The following discussion is based on *Miscellany*, pp. 408–16, and on *Mao Zedong sixiang wan sui!* (1969), pp. 578–97. The use of "X X" to represent an anonymous official no doubt conceals the identity of a leading cadre disgraced in the Cultural Revolution.

Five: Class as Political Behavior

1. Liu Ya-pin, "Fully Recognize the Protracted Nature, the Complexity, and the Twists and Turns of Class Struggle," *Hung-ch'i* (September 19, 1970), no. 10, in *SCMM* (October 12, 1970), 691:6.

2. *Renmin ribao (People's Daily)*, April 23, 1968, p. 4; reprinted as "Never Forget Class Struggle, Take the Initiative and Persistently Attack the Class Enemy," in *Nanfang ribao (Southern Daily)*, April 24, 1968.

3. A powerful exposition of these themes is Mao's "On Khrushchov's Phoney Communism and Its Historical Lessons for the World," *Peking Review* (July 17, 1964), 7(29):7–28.

4. Li Tzu-yüan, "Adhere to the Party's Basic Line, Consolidate the Proletarian Dictatorship—Study 'The State and Revolution,' " *Hung-ch'i* (September 1, 1972), no. 9, in *SCMM* (September 25, 1972), 737:15. Among the most widespread Cultural Revolution labels, "ghosts and monsters" can in fact be traced to the Tang dynasty as an expression denoting persons holding heretical views.

5. Writing Group of Shantung Provincial Committee of the Chinese Communist Party, "Adhere to the Method of Class Analysis, Correctly Understand the Struggle Between the Two Lines," *Hung-ch'i* (December 1971), no. 13, in *SCMM* (December 23, 1971), 719:18.

6. "Speech at Enlarged Meeting of Central Committee Political Bureau," in *JPRS*, 49826 (February 12, 1970), p. 76.

7. "A Criticism of 'One Can Avoid Getting Involved,' " *Renmin ribao*, September 11, 1971, p. 4.

8. Li Tzu-hüan, "Adhere to the Party's Basic Line," p. 14.

9. "Arise to Arms in the Midst of Struggle," *Renmin ribao*, March 6, 1971.

10. Liu I-yung, "Make Efforts to Study Amid the Storm of Class Struggle," *Hung-ch'i* (October 1, 1970), no. 11, in *SCMM* (November 1, 1971), 715:17.

11. "Reform Landlord and Rich Peasant Elements to Become Self-sufficient New Persons," *Renmin ribao*, September 26, 1956, p. 5.

12. "Decisions on Agricultural Co-operation," in Albert P. Blaustein, ed., *Fundamental Legal Documents of Communist China* (South Hackensack, N.J.: Fred B. Rothman, 1962), p. 356.

13. Mao, "A Proposal Concerning the General Line of the International Communist Movement (June 14, 1963)," in William E. Griffith, the *Sino-Soviet Rift* (Cambridge: MIT Press, 1964), p. 277.

14. "Open Letter from the CPSU Central Committee to Party Organizations and All Communists of the Soviet Union (July 14, 1963)," in William E. Griffith, *Sino-Soviet Rift,* p. 130.

15. Meng Xianzhang, "The Development and Mutual Relations of the Classes and Strata of Modern Society," *Xin zhonghua banyuekan (New China Semi-Monthly)* (August 1951), 14(15):8.

16. In addition to the afore-mentioned "ghosts and monsters," other Cultural Revolution labels included "capitalist roader," "black-gang elements," "chameleon," and "little reptile"; the relationship of any of these names to the means of production is obviously indirect.

17. Political leaders have also manipulated a positive counterpart to the system of negative labels, through a set of such good social categories as "five-good commune member" or "five-good soldier." See the discussion in chapter 3 above.

18. Mao, "Introductory Note to the Third Lot of Material on the Hu Feng Counterrevolutionary Clique (Excerpts)," in *Current Background* (October 8, 1969), 891:21.

19. Liu Ya-pin, "Fully Recognize the Protracted Nature," p. 7.

20. Mao, "Talk Regarding 'Strategic Arrangements,' " in *JPRS,* 45281 (May 6, 1968), p. 12.

21. Writing Group of the Peking Municipal CCP Committee, "A Sharp Weapon for Criticizing and Repudiating Idealism," *Hung-ch'i* (April 1, 1971), no. 4, in *SCMM* (April 26, 1971), 703:17.

22. Mao Zedong, quoted in "Never Forget Class Struggle," Guangzhou *T'iao Chan (Challenge)* (July 1968), no. 3, in *Current Background* (September 3, 1968), 861:31.

23. Writing Group of the CCP Kirin Provincial Committee, "It is Necessary to Apply the Method of Class Analysis in Conducting Investigation and Study," *Hung-ch'i* (September 1, 1971), no. 10, in *SCMM* (September 27, 1971), 713:2.

24. Mao, Note to "Third Batch of Material on the Hu Feng Counterrevolutionary clique," *Renmin ribao,* June 10, 1955. Or as Liu Shaoqi said in 1964: "Now the class enemies have become clever. They know how to engage in clandestine work and in legal struggle. In this respect they are more capable than we. Our cadres have not yet learned this. This is the reason why, in struggling against bad cadres, we are cheated and do not win. . . . From the very first superiority is with them and not with us, because they are prepared." Quoted in "Liu Shao-ch'i's Reactionary Speeches," published by the Criticize Liu-Teng-T'ao Liaison Station, "Red Flag Commune," Peking Railway Institute, Red Guard Congress (April 1967), in *SCMM Supplement* (May 13, 1967), 25:30.

25. "Be a Pupil of the Masses Before Becoming Their Teacher," *Jen-min jih-pao* editorial, July 29, 1966, in *Current Background* (October 21, 1969), 892:40.

26. Yang Kao-chao and Chi Ch'eng, "Carry the Class Struggle in the Realm of the Economy Through to the End," *Jen-min jih-pao,* December 27, 1969, in *SCMP* (January 6, 1970), 4570:53.

27. "Use the Party's Basic Line to Guide All Kinds of Work," *Renmin ribao,* June 28, 1972, p. 2.

28. CCP Committee of No. 3 Peking Chemical Works, "Read Books Seriously and Persist in the Correct Political Direction," *Hung-ch'i* (July 1, 1971), nos. 7–8, in *SCMM* (August 9, 1971), 710:64, 61.

29. Liu I-yung, "Make Efforts to Study," p. 16.

30. "Link Ideology and Political Line, Read Books Seriously," *Renmin ribao,* March 18, 1972.

31. "In Branch Construction One Must Grasp Line Education," *Renmin ribao,* February 26, 1971, p. 3. See also "An Efficacious Formula for Raising Cadres' Awareness of the Line Struggle," *Renmin ribao,* February 4, 1971, p. 3; Zhong Zuowen, "Penetratingly Develop the Mighty Ideological Weapon of the Struggle Between Two Lines," *Renmin ribao,* March 9, 1972, p. 2.

32. Quoted in Michael Y. M. Kau, ed., *The Lin Piao Affair: Power Politics and Military Coup* (White Plains: International Arts and Sciences Press, 1975), p. 57.

33. Li Chien, "Attach Importance to the Revolution in the Superstructure," *Peking Review* (August 24, 1973), 16(32):5.

34. "Educate Cadres to Consciously Raise Awareness of Line Struggle," *Renmin ribao,* March 4, 1971, p. 1; "How Yangtou Commune Carried Out Education in the Struggle Between the Two Lines with Educated Youth," *Renmin ribao,* January 30, 1971, p. 4.

35. "In Branch Construction One Must Grasp Line Education"; Xiao Bin, "Seek Glory and Uprighteousness, Not Plots and Tricks," *Renmin ribao,* March 22, 1972, p. 2.

36. Zhong Zuowen, "Penetratingly Develop the Mighty Ideological Weapon."

37. Mao, "Democratic Centralism," *JPRS,* 50792 (June 23, 1970), p. 46.

38. *Mao Zedong sixiang wan sui! (Long Live Mao Zedong Thought!)* (1969), p. 136.

39. Mao, *Miscellany of Mao Tse-tung Thought, JPRS* 61269-1 and 61269-2 (February 20, 1974), p. 64.

40. For instance, see "Reference Material for Chairman Mao's 'On the Correct Handling of Contradictions Among the People,' " (Beijing) New China News Agency, (July 4, 1967), in *SCMP* (July 12, 1967), 3978:6.

41. As to the claim that the Contradictions speech was the source of the class theory of the 1960s, one merely need examine the articles which contain this assertion to discover that the most effective quotations in support of the new theory come not from 1957, but from 1962. Thus Mao's Beidaihe speech of August 1962 and his speech to the Tenth Plenum in September 1962 appear to be far more important in drawing

the parameters of the new theory, although it is said that "in these two speeches, Chairman Mao elaborated on the Marxist-Leninist thesis contained in 'On the Correct Handling of Contradictions Among the People.' " "A Theoretical Weapon for Making Revolution under the Dictatorship of the Proletariat," *Hung-ch'i* (June 21, 1967), no. 10, in *JPRS*, 41877 (July 18, 1967), p. 40.

42. Revolutionary Committee of the Cultural Work Regiment of the Political Department of the PLA Air Force, "Make a Strict Distinction Between the Two Different Types of Contradictions, Correctly Handle the Deceived Masses," *Hung-ch'i* (June 21, 1967), no. 10, in *JPRS*, 42140 (August 8, 1967), p. 9.

43. "Reference Material," pp. 6, 5, 8, 9.

44. Writing Group of the Revolutionary Committee of Liaoning Province, "A Radiant Beacon—Study 'On the Correct Handling of Contradictions Among the People,' " *Hung-ch'i* (September 30, 1969), no. 10, in *SCMM* (October 31, 1969), 666:5.

45. Liaoning Writing Group, "A Radiant Beacon," p. 5.

46. Benjamin I. Schwartz, *Chinese Communism and the Rise of Mao* (Cambridge: Harvard University Press, 1951), esp. pp. 191–99.

47. Schwartz, *Communism and China: Ideology in Flux* (Cambridge: Harvard University Press, 1968), pp. 19–21.

48. Schwartz, *Communism and China*, pp. 21, 175. Others have pursued this theme. The Italian novelist, Alberto Moravia, for instance, comments that "The moral category of goodness is the proletariat; of evil, the bourgeoisie. Consequently, the class struggle in China today is the struggle against evil. In other words, class is not something outside and around man, but inside him. Class is the eternal diabolical temptation against which an eternal struggle is necessary." *The Red Book and the Great Wall* (New York: Farrar, Straus and Giroux, 1968), p. 63. And Stuart Schram refers to "Mao's view according to which membership in the proletariat is defined above all by a state of mind, which anyone can acquire through study, or simply in a flash of illumination, and thus change his objective class essence." Stuart R. Schram, "The Party in Chinese Communist Ideology," *China Quarterly* (April–June 1969), 38:22.

49. Schwartz, *Communism and China*, p. 20.

50. A similar objection has been raised by Donald J. Munro, who asks, "Why should intellectuals have to work in factories if thought is 'independent?' " See Munro's review of James Hsiung's *Ideology and Practice: The Evolution of Chinese Communism in China Quarterly* (April–June 1972), 50:354. For a different critique of the simple ethical interpretation of class, see John Bryan Starr, "Conceptual Foundations of Mao Tse-tung's Theory of Continuous Revolution," *Asian Survey* (June 1971), 11:624.

51. "Reference Material," p. 7; "Factionalism Must Be Subject to Class Analysis," *Hung-ch'i* (July 1, 1968), no. 1, in *SCMM* (December 2, 1968), 635:35.

52. "Correctly Understand and Handle the Relationship Between Politics and Work," *Renmin ribao*, April 16, 1972; "Never Forget Class Struggle," *Hung-ch'i* (May 11, 1966), no. 7, in *JPRS*, 36587 (July 20, 1969), p. 5.

53. Writing Group of the Shantung Provincial Committee of the Chinese Communist Party, "Adhere to the Method of Class Analysis, Correctly Understand the Struggle Between the Two Lines," *Hung-ch'i* (December 4, 1971), no. 13, in *SCMM* (December 23, 1971), 719:18.

54. An Ch'ün, "Be Good at Making Comparison," *Hung-ch'i* (September 1, 1972), no. 9, in *SCMM* (September 25, 1972), 737:5–6.

55. Mao, "On the Correct Handling of Contradictions Among the People," *Selected Readings from the Works of Mao Tsetung* (Beijing: Foreign Languages Press, 1971), pp. 433–34; "Reference Material," p. 8.

56. "Decision of the Central Committee of the Chinese Communist Party Concerning the Great Proletarian Cultural Revolution (August 8, 1966—the '16-point Decision')," in *CCP Documents of the Great Proletarian Cultural Revolution, 1966–1967* (Hong Kong: Union Research Institute, 1968), p. 46.

57. Shantung Writing Group, "Adhere to the Method of Class Analysis," p. 20.

58. Wang Hsiao-yü, "Unite with the Greatest Number of People, Hit Hard at the Chief Enemy," *Jen-min jih-pao* (June 27, 1967), in *SCMP* (July 7, 1967), 3975:11, 10.

59. Mao, "On the Correct Handling," p. 447.

60. "Thoroughly Criticize and Repudiate the Reactionary Bourgeois 'Theory of Many Centers,' Fully Implement Chairman Mao's Policy Concerning Struggle Against the Enemy," *Kung-jen tsao-fan pao (Workers' Rebellion News)* (August 17, 1968), no. 157, in *SCMM Supplement* (November 18, 1968), 31:5.

61. "Thoroughly Criticize and Repudiate," p. 12. The theme of splitting the enemy is also evident in "A Radiant Beacon," by the Liaoning Writing Group, p. 10. The "four clean-ups" initially referred to rectification of rural administration of accounting, granaries, properties, and work-points. Maoists subsequently redefined the four subjects more abstractly, as politics, economics, ideology, and organization.

62. Liaoning Writing Group, "A Radiant Beacon," p. 10.

63. Mao, "A Four-Point Instruction Given at a Meeting of the Standing Committee of the Central Committee" (1967), in *Current Background* (October 21, 1969), 892:51.

64. See, for instance, the passage quoted in Chao Kuo-chun, *Agrarian Policy of the Chinese Communist Party, 1921–1959* (Bombay: Asia Publishing House, 1960), pp. 85–86.

65. "Comrade Teng Tzu-hui's Report to the Youth League Central Rural Work Conference," *Zhongguo qingnian (Chinese Youth)* (September 1954), 17:9.

66. Donald J. Munro, *The Concept of Man in Contemporary China* (Ann Arbor: University of Michigan Press, 1977), p. 19.

Contrast this with Chalmers Johnson's eagerness to classify Maoism as idealist: "It seems as though mind may actually be superior to social class, since 'naturally red' sons and daughters of workers or guerrilla veterans may go astray and 'naturally bourgeois' sons and daughters of Shanghai shopkeepers may become revolutionaries by working in the Sinkiang Production and Construction Corps of the PLA." Johnson, "Chinese

Communist Leadership and Mass Response," in Ping-ti Ho and Tang Tsou, eds., *China in Crisis* (Chicago: University of Chicago Press, 1968), 1:427.

67. "Critique of the Gotha Program," in Marx and Engels, *Selected Works* (Moscow: Foreign Languages Publishing House, 1955), 2:23.

68. Official claims for abrupt changes in policy were made during the Cultural Revolution, when the administration of Liu Shaoqi and his associates was repudiated, and following the death of Mao, when the influence of the Gang of Four was similarly rejected. Cautions against too ready an acceptance of such claims have been made by Andrew J. Nathan, "Policy Oscillations in the People's Republic of China: A Critique," *China Quarterly* (December 1976), 68:720–33; and Joel Glassman, "Incrementalism and 'Two-line Struggle': Continuity and Change in Chinese Communist Education Policy," *Contemporary China* (Summer 1978), 2(2):51–70.

69. This theme has been developed in the writings of Lowell Dittmer. See especially his " 'Line Struggle' in Theory and Practice: The Origins of the Cultural Revolution Reconsidered," *China Quarterly* (December 1977), 72:675–712; and "Thought Reform and Cultural Revolution: An Analysis of the Symbolism of Chinese Polemics," *American Political Science Review* (March 1977), 71(1):67–85.

70. See Ronald N. Montaperto, "From Revolutionary Successors to Revolutionaries: Chinese Students in the Early Stages of the Cultural Revolution," in Robert A. Scalapino, ed., *Elites in the People's Republic of China* (Seattle: University of Washington Press, 1972), pp. 592–93.

71. Adapted from *Current Background* (October 8, 1969), 891:67.

72. "Discredit the 'Guild' Mentality," Shanghai *Wen-hui pao,* March 14, 1967, in *SCMP* (March 20, 1967), 3902:19.

73. For discussions of Chinese factionalism, see Andrew Nathan, "A Factionalism Model for CCP Politics," *China Quarterly* (January–March 1973), 53:34–67; and Lowell Dittmer, "Bases of Power in Chinese Politics: A Theory and an Analysis of the Fall of the 'Gang of Four,' " *World Politics* (October 1978), 31(1):26–60.

74. For the former, see "Factionalism Must be Subjected to Class Analysis," *Hung-ch'i* (July 1, 1968), no. 1, in *SCMM* (December 2, 1968), 635:35–37; the latter tendency is exemplified by Yao Wen-yuan's *The Working Class Must Exercise Leadership in Everything* (Beijing: Foreign Languages Press, 1968).

75. In order to overcome the apparently irreconcilable hostility which had grown among Red Guard organizations competing to prove themselves the most revolutionary, Maoists organized workers into propaganda teams to bargain, soothe, cajole, and suppress fractious Red Guards into accepting more obviously proletarian leadership. See the account by William Hinton in *Hundred Day War: The Cultural Revolution at Tsinghua University* (New York: Monthly Review Press, 1972).

76. Quoted in *Hung-ch'i* (October 1968), no. 4, trans. in *SCMM* (October 28, 1968), 632:2.

77. Impressionistic evidence supports the idea that experience with the system of labels is widespread among cadres. Between one and a quarter

and two and a half million cadres, for instance, lost their positions during the Socialist Education Movement alone. See Stuart Schram's "Introduction" to *Authority, Participation and Cultural Change in China* (London: Cambridge University Press, 1973), p. 79. And a former provincial-level cadre suggested in an interview in 1972 that after twenty years, "nobody was pure," and that in organs with which he was familiar there almost no cadres completely unblemished by labels or historical problems.

78. Thus a "Rehabilitation Committee" was established to lobby for the rehabilitation of some targets of the 1955 campaign to suppress counterrevolutionaries. See Luo Ruiqing, "Our Nation's Achievements in the Struggle to Suppress Counter-Revolutionaries and Our Responsibilities for the Future," *Xuexi* (1958), 1:8. A wave of reversal of verdicts passed on supporters of Peng Dehuai took place in the early 1960s, and more recently, Liu Shaoqi and other cadres labeled during the Cultural Revolution have been rehabilitated since Mao's death in 1976. For an overview of rehabilitation politics in the Cultural Revolution, see Gordon A. Bennett, "Political Labels and Popular Tension," *Current Scene* (February 26, 1969), 7(4):1–16.

79. I do not wish to convey the impression that rehabilitation politics are a kind of exotic orientalism unlike anything in the industrial West. In the United States in recent years there have been organized efforts to "reverse the verdicts" on Vietnam war resisters, Alger Hiss, Ethel and Julius Rosenberg, and even Robert E. Lee (whose citizenship was rescinded during the Civil War).

80. See the articles on this case collected in *Current Background* (August 12, 1968), no. 860.

81. A collection of documents on this case is in *Current Background* (June 28, 1968), no. 856.

82. "Seeing That a Gust of Wind for Rehabilitation Has Been Stirred Up in Tsinghai, the Provincial Revolutionary Committee Asks the Central Committee to Make Some Rulings," in "A Collection of Materials on the Reversal of Verdicts," compiled by the Reversal of Verdicts and Criticize-the-Bourgeoisie Headquarters of the Revolutionary Masses of Kwangtung Province, Canton (January 1968), trans. in *Current Background* (April 29, 1968), 617:5.

83. For example, see "Report on an Investigation of Right-Deviation Reversal of Correct Decision in Some Middle Schools of Canton," Canton *Hung-se Tsao-fan-che (Red Rebels)* (late June 1968), new no. 2, trans. in *Current Background* (September 3, 1968), 861:1–18.

84. For an example of Mao's intervention, see Central Committee Document (67) 367 "On the Correct Treatment of the Old Rebel Factions Which Have Made Mistakes," *T'ien-shan feng-huo (T'ien-shan Beacon Fire)*, (January 15, 1968), nos. 4 and 5, trans. in *SCMP Supplement* (February 12, 1968), 217:5. Central cadres also attempted to retain the right to validate local decisions to label organizations as counterrevolutionary. See the Central Committee notice of April 1, 1967, in *CCP Documents of the Great Proletarian Cultural Revolution, 1966–1967* (Hong Kong: Union Research Institute, 1968), pp. 399–401.

85. The ten categories are given in the Guangdong Military Control

Commission's document no. 45 (67), in *Current Background* (April 29, 1968), 617:16; and in the Central Committee document of April 29, 1968, in *Current Background* (October 16, 1968), 864:9.

86. *Current Background* (April 29, 1968), 617:1–2, 30. See also *CCP Documents,* pp. 661–62.

87. For example, see "Collection of Materials on Cleaning Up the Class Ranks," jointly compiled by the Secondary Education Red Headquarters and the Primary Education Red Headquarters of Canton (July 1968), trans. in *Current Background* (October 16, 1968), no. 864; "*Chieh-fang Jih-pao* Answers Questions from Readers on Purging of Class Ranks," Guangzhou *Kuang-chou Hung-tai-hui* (June 22, 1968), no. 9, trans. in *SCMP* (July 23, 1968), 4223:4–6; "Questionnaire About Party's Policies on Reversal of Verdicts," Human *Shuang-ch'en Yüeh (Moonlight in Frosty Morning)* (January 10, 1968), no. 1, trans. in *SCMM* (June 3, 1968), 618:5–6; "The Wrongs Must be Redressed," Peking *Shou-tu Hung-wei-ping (Capital Red Guard),* November 13, 1966, trans. in *SCMP Supplement* (January 17, 1967), 161:3–11; and *Guanyu qingli jieji cailiao* (Compilation of Materials on Cleansing Class Ranks) (Yunnan, September 1968).

Six: Class as Caste

1. The 1968 regulations for conscription into the People's Liberation Army, for instance, stated that new soldiers should be "primarily the children of workers and poor and lower-middle peasants." Children of persons bearing class designations higher than middle peasant were not eligible. See "Decisions on Kwangtung's 1968 Conscription Work" (Canton: Provisional Conscription Work Committee of Kwangtung, November 1967), in *JPRS,* 46324 (August 29, 1968), p. 7.

2. Mao, *Miscellany of Mao Tse-tung Thought, JPRS,* 61269-2 (February 20, 1974), p. 357.

3. Cang Jianqiu, "We Should Correctly Differentiate and Consider the Family Backgrounds and Class Designations of Young People," *Zhongguo qingnian (Chinese Youth)* (July 1, 1962), 13:24. Note that this is the same issue which Mao, Zhou Enlai, Li Xuefeng, and "X X" were still unable to resolve late in 1964 (see the conclusion of chapter 4).

4. For a liberation-era discussion of the necessity of separating class designation from occupation, see Jun Lin, "The Principles and Standards of Class Differentiation," *Xuexi (Study)* (October 1, 1950), 3(1):24.

5. When class designations were determined in the early days of the People's Republic, family background was merely a supplementary concept, one primarily employed to discuss the class position of children. The "Decisions Concerning the Differentiation of Class Designations in the Countryside" referred to it almost as an afterthought: "Children and juveniles under 18 and young students at school should not, in general, have their class designations determined, but their family background should be determined. An exception is the head of a family at the time of Land Reform. In such cases class designations should be determined." In

Albert P. Blaustein, ed., *Fundamental Legal Documents of Communist China* (South Hackensack, N.J.: Fred B. Rothman, 1962), pp. 323–24. The translation has been modified slightly on the basis of the Chinese text in *Xuexi* (October 1, 1950), 3(1):35.

Family background was to be determined by examining the class designation of the family head. Thus a simple formula can be employed: family background equals father's designation. Some confusion arises from the existence of two different phrases to denote "family background." Although some Chinese emigrées offer complex distinctions between *jiating chushen* and *jiating chengfen* (lit.: family origin or background, and family designation), the two seem ultimately to be interchangeable. See, for instance, the use of both phrases in the discussions of "What To Do If Your Family Background Is Bad," in the Beijing *Gongren ribao (Workers' Daily)*, February 26 and April 7, 1965.

6. An early example of the latter may be seen in the "yes, but . . ." answer to the question, "Whether or Not Young Students of Landlord and Rich Peasant Family Background Can Participate in Mutual Aid Teams After Returning to the Villages," *Zhongguo qingnian* (September 16, 1954), 18:22. The former problem is especially evident in the mid-1960s—as in "Can One Carefully Draw an Ideological Boundary While Living Together with a Family of the Exploiting Classes?" *Zhongguo qingnian* (October 16, 1965), 20:18–19.

7. Richard Baum and Frederick C. Teiwes, *Ssu-Ch'ing: The Socialist Education Movement of 1962–1966* (Berkeley: University of California Center for Chinese Studies, 1968), p. 94.

8. A concise statement of this policy is the *Chinese Youth News* editorial of September 9, 1965—"The Party's Class Policy Lays Stress on Deeds," trans. in *JPRS*, 36453 (July 13, 1966), pp. 89–93.

9. Wang Fenglian, "Get Rid of the Mental Burden of Family Origin, Embark on the Revolutionary Road," *Zhongguo qingnian* (February 16, 1966), no. 4, trans. in *JPRS*, 37161 (August 22, 1966), p. 145. Wang was born into a landlord family, as was Cheng Tianmin, author of "An Ideological Revolution Carried Out Consciously," *Renmin ribao*, August 16, 1965, trans. in *JPRS*, 36453 (July 13, 1966), pp. 86–89. Special Attention was given to Sun Yunjie, daughter of a rich peasant, who wrote "Most Important Is One's Own Behavior," *Zhongguo qingnian* (February 16, 1966), 4:21–22. Her article was reprinted in *Nanfang ribao (Southern Daily)*, March 14, 1966. See also the *Zhongguo qingnian* editorial, "One Must Follow Sun Yunjie on the Revolutionary Road" (August 16, 1965), 16:18–21. Unlike these exemplary children of the former exploiting classes, many young people were reluctant to reveal information about their bad class origin. See the discussion of "What to Do if Your Family Background Is Bad" in *Gongren ribao (Workers' Daily)*, February 26, 1965, p. 4.

10. Sun Pao-ling, "Young People of Good Family Origin Must Pay Attention to Thought Reform Too" *Chung-kuo ch'ing-hien* (December 16, 1964), no. 24, trans. in *SCMM* (February 15, 1965), 456:6–7.

11. For an example involving the Pioneers, see "Let All Children of Eligible Age Wear Red Scarves," *Chung-kuo ch'ing-nien pao*, September

18, 1965, trans. in *JPRS*, 36453 (July 13, 1966), pp. 82–85. Also see "Place Membership Expansion in the First Position in Current CYL Organization Construction," *Chung-kuo ch'ing-nien pao*, October 9, 1965, in *SCMP* (October 25, 1965), 3564:9–14. These trends are discussed in James R. Townsend, *The Revolutionization of Chinese Youth: A Study of Chung-kuo Ch'ing-nien* (Berkeley: Center for Chinese Studies, University of California, 1967); and in Gordon White, *The Politics of Class and Class Origin: The Case of the Cultural Revolution* (Canberra: Australian National University, 1976), pp. 10–18.

12. These five red categories are to be distinguished from the five-category elements (landlord, rich peasant, counterrevolutionary, bad element, and rightist), who were also identified as the "five black categories."

13. An account of one Red Guard's experience in this controversy, presented in the context of other Cultural Revolution events, is in Gordon A. Bennett and Ronald N. Montaperto, *Red Guard: The Political Biography of Dai Hsiao-ai* (Garden City: Doubleday, 1971), pp. 66–146. For Red Guard politics, see esp. Hong Yung Lee, *The Politics of the Chinese Cultural Revolution* (Berkeley: University of California Press, 1978).

14. "Urgent Order," prepared by the Five Red Category Students of Hunchiang Municipal No. 2 Middle School, Kirin; printed in Beijing, September 5, 1966, trans. in *SCMP Supplement* (November 2, 1966), 157:30–31.

15. *"Lauzi yingxiung er haohan, laozi fandong er hundan."* The form of a couplet is drawn from its traditional appearance on two scrolls, one for each of the two balanced lines. This "reactionary couplet" is discussed in the following: "Can This Manner of 'Couplet' not be Criticized?," Beijing *Bingtuan zhanbao (Fighting Team Combat Bulletin)*, November 26, 1966; "Thoroughly Crush 'United Action' This Rightist Black Organization," Beijing *Jinggangshan*, January 21, 1967; "Was there a Pedigree Theory Before the Cultural Revolution?," Beijing *Zhongxue wenge bao (Middle School Cultural Revolution News)*, April 1, 1967; and "Thoroughly Crush Liu Shaoqi's Reactionary Pedigree Theory," *Bingtuan zhanbao*, April 27, 1967. A second slogan which propagated the pedigree theory was "Dragon Begets Dragon, Phoenix Begets Phoenix, the Son of a Rat Knows How to Burrow Underground."

16. This description is based on the following articles: "See What Kind of Goods is the 'Capital Red Guard United Action Committee' " and "Thoroughly Crush 'United Action,' This Rightist Black Organization," in Beijing *Jinggangshan*, January 21, 1967; "Refute 'United Action's' Reactionary Political Theory," Beijing *Xin sizhong (New Fourth Middle School)*, May 17, 1967; "We Must Thoroughly Criticize the 'United Action' Trend of Thought," Beijing *Shoudu fenglai (Capital Wind and Thunder)*, March 25, 1967; "Thoroughly Purify the United Action Trend of Thought," and "The Struggle Between Two Headquarters on the Question of Schools of the Children of Cadres," Guangzhou *Bayi fengbao (August First Storm)* (January 1968). Also see the accounts in David Milton and Nancy Dall Milton, *The Wind Will Not Subside: Years in Revolutionary China—1964–1969* (New York: Pantheon, 1976), pp. 159–62, Lowell Dittmer, *Liu Shao-ch'i and the Chinese Cultural Revolution: The Politics of*

Mass Criticism (Berkeley: University of California Press, 1974), pp. 136–41.

17. Representative attacks upon such schools are found in "The August 1st School System for Children of High-Ranking Cadres: The Ten Great Crimes of the 'August 1st' School" (Beijing, n.d.); and "The Reactionary Bloodline Theory and Boarding Schools for Cadre Children," Canton *August First Storm* (n.d.); both trans. in *Chinese Sociology and Anthropology* (Summer 1969), 1(4):3–36.

18. For a discussion of this variety of "royalist" Red Guard group, see Parris H. Chang, "Provincial Party Leaders' Strategies for Survival During the Cultural Revolution," in Robert A. Scalapino, ed., *Elites in the People's Republic of China* (Seattle: University of Washington Press, 1972), pp. 514–16.

19. "Canton Urgently Calls!!!," Canton *Hsin-nan-fang, ch'an-hsiu-ken (New South, Uprooting Revisionism)*, July 28, 1967, trans. in *SCMP Supplement* (August 24, 1967), 199:7; describes the high-level positions of the fathers of six leaders of the Doctrine Guards.

20. This section is based upon "Refute 'United Action's' Reactionary Political Theory"; "The Power-holders (Bourgeoisie) and the Theory of Family Background Alone," *Zhongxue wenge bao*, April 1, 1967; "Comrades Ch'en Po-ta and Wang Li Receive 25 Fighters of Hui-an Middle School, Fukien—Record of Discussion," compiled jointly by Red Guard Commune of the "Thought of Mao Tse-tung" and the Combat Group of the "Defense of Supreme Directives," Peking Film Studio (December 1966), trans. in *SCMM Supplement* (June 5, 1967), 16:15; Bennett and Montaperto, *Red Guard*, pp. 137–41, 243–44; "Have a Look at the True Face of Lushan," Beijing *Hongweibing (Red Guard)*, November 16, 1966; and "Overthrow Ho Lung—Ringleader Who Opposes the Party and Seeks to Seize Power in the Army," Peking *Tung-fang-hung (East is Red)*, January 27, 1967, trans. in *SCMP Supplement* (April 3, 1967), 172:18.

21. Through the autumn, opposition to the extreme views represented by the theory of blood relationships had grown. For example, see the self-criticism by a former five-red-category leader in Jiangmen *Hongse zaofanzhe (Red Rebel)*, November 12, 1967. The issue of the determinants of Red Guard politics is a very confusing one. I do not mean to imply that good and bad family background were always directly tied to conservatism and radicalism. One attempt to explain the family background connection is Ronald N. Montaperto, "From Revolutionary Successors to Revolutionaries: Chinese Students in the Early Stages of the Cultural Revolution," in Scalapino, *Elites*, pp. 575–605.

22. "Carry the Great Proletarian Cultural Revolution Through to the End," *Hung-ch'i* (January 1967), no. 1, in *SCMM* (January 9, 1967), 558:4.

23. Guangzhou *Bayi fengbao (August First Storm)*, January 1968.

24. "Chushen lun," translated as "Origin Theory," in Gordon White, *Politics of Class and Class Origin*, pp. 71–93. This article was written between July and September of 1966, revised in November, and published after the *Red Flag* New Year editorial's criticism of the pedigree theory as a special edition of *Zhongxue wenge bao* (February 1967).

25. The story of Yu's composition of "The Theory of Family Back-

ground" and of his subsequent arrest and exeecution was only revealed in the course of China's political struggles following Mao's death. See Zhou Lin, "A Promising Youth Who Was Executed," Xianggang *Zhengming (Contending)* (October 1979), 24:20–24; and Xue Ke, "Make Lin Biao and the 'Gang of Four' Repay This Debt of Blood!," Beijing *Siwu luntan (April 5th Forum)* (April 1, 1979), 8:15–17.

26. White, *Politics of Class and Class Origin,* p. 79.

27. Ibid., p. 89.

28. Ibid., pp. 90–93.

29. The following is based upon the three issues which were available to me of *Zhongxue wenge bao* (February, February 21, and April 1, 1967), the paper which most severely criticized family background; and "Sentence 'The Theory of Family Background' to Death," *Jiaogong zhanbao (Education Workers Combat News),* March 11, 1967.

30. See "Rebuke the Depraved Methods of Beijing Research Group on the Problem of Family Background," Beijing *Dongfeng bao (East Wind News)* (March 19, 1967), no. 7; " 'The Theory of Family Background Alone' and 'The Theory of Family Background' are Both Anti–Marxism-Leninism and Anti–Thought of Mao Zedong," *Dongfeng bao* (March 19, 1967), no. 7; as well as "Sentence 'The Theory of Family Background' to Death."

31. For example, see "On Family Background," by the Fifth Research Group, in Beijing *Zhi ba chunlai bao (Seize the Spring News)* (March 12, 1967), no. 2.

32. Beijing *Dongfang hong bao (East is Red News),* December 9, 1967, p. 4. This reference was brought to my attention by Stanley Rosen.

33. Among others, a June *Red Flag* article, "Creatively Study and Apply Chairman Mao's Writing, Correctly Handle Contradictions Among the People" (June 21, 1967), no. 10, attacked the "reactionary pedigree theory." See trans. in *JPRS,* 42140 (August 8, 1967), p. 6. An earlier article in Shanghai *Wen-hui pao* (February 28, 1967) attacked landlords, rich peasants, counterrevolutionaries, bad elements, and rightists, carefully adding in parentheses "referring not to their family background." See *SCMP Supplement* (March 23, 1967). 170:32.

34. Zhou Lin, "A Promising Youth."

35. Quoted in Chang, "Provincial Party Leaders' Strategies," p. 515.

36. "T'an Chen-lin's Ten Big Crimes," Peking *Ching-kang-shan* (March 15, 1967), in *SCMP Supplement* (May 29, 1967), 185:27. See also the use of family background by Tan's underling in the "liaison station of red rebels in the agricultural departments" in "How T'an Chen-lin Stirs Up the 'February Black Wind' in the Agricultural Departments," Peking *Chin-chuň pao (Marching Paper),* March 20, 1967, in *SCMP Supplement* (April 28, 1967), 178:35–36.

37. Even before the Cultural Revolution, *Zhongguo Qingnian* published a defensive letter from a Szechuanese reader entitled "Who Says the Children of Workers and Peasants are Stupid?" (August 16, 1964), 16:21.

38. See Stanley Rosen, "Background to Rebellion: Contradictions Dividing Middle School Students in Canton Prior to the Cultural Revolution" (paper prepared for the Workshop on the Pursuit of Political Inter-

est in the People's Republic, Ann Arbor, August 1977), esp. pp. 8–9, 13, and 17; Hong Yung Lee, "The Radical Students in Kwangtung During the Cultural Revolution," *China Quarterly* (December 1975), 64:674–78; John and Elsie Collier, *China's Socialist Revolution* (New York: Monthly Review Press, 1973), p. 130; Victor Nee, *The Cultural Revolution at Peking University* (New York: Monthly Review Press, 1969), p. 41.

39. See Ch'ü T'ung-tsu, *Law and Society in Traditional China* (Paris: Mouton, 1965), pp. 130–32, n. 4, where he links the *Yuehu* of Shansi and Shensi and the "fisherman of nine surnames in Chekiang" as groups stemming from defeated political elements in the Ming dynasty. Also, the legendary ancestors of the Guangdong boat people were traitors to a Sung emperor, who exiled them to live on the waters. See Hiroaki Kani, *A General Survey of the Boat People in Hong Kong* (Hong Kong: Chinese University of Hong Kong, 1967), p. 3.

40. Of filial respect, a letter to *Zhongguo Qingnian* (January 1, 1965), 1:21, demanded that "even toward the dead, we must carry out a class analysis."

41. This abbreviated version is quoted in "Combination of Old, Middle-Aged and Young Cadres in Leading Bodies," *Peking Review* (October 19, 1973), 16(42):11. A lengthier version, raising the negative example of Khrushchev in each point, is found in "On Khrushchov's Phoney Communism and Its Historical Lessons for the World," *Peking Review,* 7(29):26–27. A rambling discussion of the five requirements is in Mao, *Miscellany,* pp. 358–59.

42. Quoted in "Can this Manner of 'Couplet' not be Criticized?"

43. *Mao Zedong sixiang wan sui! (Long Live Mao Zedong Thought!)* (1969), pp. 602–603.

44. In 1930, a group of Mao's rivals in Jiangsi attempted precisely that: "Mao's class background was analyzed. His father was labeled a wealthy landlord, and it was argued that Mao possessed traits common to that class: self-interest, narrow-mindedness, and conservatism. To the rebels, this analysis explained many of the policy differences they had with Mao." Ronald Suleski, "The Fu-t'ien Incident, December 1930," in Suleski and Daniel H. Bays, *Early Communist China: Two Studies* (Ann Arbor: University of Michigan Center for Chinese Studies, 1969), p. 7.

45. Note Mao's demonstration to an audience of errant Red Guards of the good family backgrounds of Huang Yongsheng and Wen Yucheng. *Miscellany,* p. 477.

46. Canton *Ke-ming Ch'ing-nien (Revolutionary Youth),* November 10, 1967, trans. in *China Topics* (February 26, 1968), no. YB 465, appendix C. See also "The Reactionary 'Theory of Only Family Background' in the Villages," *Zhongxue wenge bao,* February 21, 1967. "Educated Youth" are discussed in Thomas P. Bernstein, *Up to the Mountains and Down to the Villages: The Transfer of Youth from Urban to Rural China* (New Haven: Yale University Press, 1977).

47. See Anne F. Thurston, "The Revival of Classes in Rural Kuangtung: Production Team Politics in a Period of Crisis" (paper prepared for the Workshop on the Pursuit of Political Interest in the People's Republic of China, Ann Arbor, Michigan, August 10–17, 1977).

48. For a discussion of sources of family income, see William L. Parish, "Socialism and the Chinese Peasant Family," *Journal of Asian Studies* (May 1975), 34(3):613–30. Parish and Martin King Whyte argue in *Village and Family in Contemporary China* (Chicago: University of Chicago Press, 1978), p. 105, that "As for those with 'bad class' labels, attempts to invert the old order had had the surprising effect of giving former landlords and rich peasants better than average incomes. Their difficulties in finding brides mean later marriage for sons and delayed childbirth, resulting in a higher than average labor-to-mouth ratio. For those who never marry, however, this prosperity is a temporary phenomenon. In their old age, with no sons to support them and possibly no 'five guarantee' support, they will suffer."

49. For instance, on the eve of the traditional Chinese New Year in 1965, peasants were encouraged to maintain their practice of exchanging family visits, but only with their kin who were not landlords and rich peasants. See "What Problems Should Be Heeded in Visiting Relatives?," *Nanfang ribao,* January 29, 1965.

50. Hans C. Gerth and C. Wright Mills, eds., *From Max Weber* (New York: Galaxy Books, 1958), pp. 186–87. Lung-chang Young argues that rural inequality during the Republican period (1911–1949) followed an opposite course to the one elaborated here for the People's Republic. Rather than a movement from class to status group, an earlier status stratification was increasingly supplanted by widespread concern for class inequalities. "Rural Stratification in Modern China: The Dialectic of Images and Social Reality," in "Modern China: The Dialectic of Images and Social Reality," *Social Research* (Winter 1970), 37(4):624–43.

51. Max Weber, *The Theory of Economic and Social Organization* (New York: Free Press, 1964), p. 428. The following discussion is based in part upon interviews conducted with former residents of rural China in Hong Kong, 1972.

52. *From Max Weber,* pp. 187–88.

53. *Nanfang ribao,* February 13, 1952, quoted in M. J. Meijer, *Marriage Law and Policy in the Chinese People's Republic* (Hong Kong: Hong Kong University Press, 1971), p. 164.

54. Lucy Jen Huang examined the national periodical *Zhongguo funu (Women of China)* for 1959 and 1960, and noted the emergence of increased numbers of interclass marriages. See "The Communist Chinese Attitude Towards Inter-Class Marriage," *China Quarterly* (October–December 1962), 12:183–90. And Jan Myrdal commented on the relaxed attitude toward the engagement of the Youth League secretary and the daughter of a counterrevolutionary in Liu Lin, Shaanxi, in 1962. See his *Report from a Chinese Village* (New York: Pantheon, 1965), pp. 195, 280–81.

55. See "Does One Lose One's Stand by Marrying a Person Born of a Family of the Exploiting Class?" *Kung-jen jih-pao,* May 6, 1965, in *SCMP* (June 2, 1965), 3469:14–15; and "How to Correctly Treat the Problem of Love and Marriage with Young People Whose Family Background is of the Exploiting Classes," *Zhongguo Quingnian* (May 1, 1965), 9:26.

56. Baum and Teiwes, *Ssu-Ch'ing*, p. 94; Parish and Whyte, *Village and Family*, p. 179.

57. "Kin or Not, the 'Line' Must be Drawn," *Nanfang ribao*, February 6, 1970.

58. Parish and Whyte found that 79 percent of rural marriages in the period 1968–1974 involved third-party introductions, but that only 21 percent of these marriages involved traditional matchmakers. *Village and Family*, pp. 172–73.

59. An example of this reasoning is found in "Can One Draw a Clear Ideological Line While Living Together With an Exploiting Class Family?" *Zhongguo Qingnian* (October 16, 1965), 20:18–19.

60. See Jack Chen, *A Year in Upper Felicity* (New York: Macmillan, 1973), pp. 74–104. One Hong Kong informant told of a landlord's daughter who was harassed during the Cultural Revolution for having judged a landlord's son to be good enough to take as her husband.

61. See Edwin E. Moise, "Downward Social Mobility in Pre-Revolutionary China," *Modern China* (January 1977), 3(1):3–31.

62. "Things Must be Easy to Understand and Memorize in Line Education," *Jen-min jih-pao* (September 21, 1971), trans. in *SCMP* (October 1, 2972), 4985:206.

63. A. Doak Barnett, *Cadres, Bureaucracy, and Political Power in Communist China* (New York: Columbia University Press, 1967), pp. 231–33.

64. Deborah Davis-Friedmann, "Welfare Practices in Rural China," *World Development* (1978), 6:614; Victor W. Sidel and Ruth Sidel, *Serve the People: Observations on Medicine in the People's Republic of China* (New York: Josiah Macy, Jr. Foundation, 1973), p. 91.

65. Martin King Whyte, *Small Groups and Political Rituals in China* (Berkeley: University of California Press, 1974), p. 152.

66. Chen, *A Year in Upper Felicity*, pp. 35, 101.

67. See the denunciation by Public Security Minister Xie Fuzhi of an incident in North China, where "In ten brigades, the landlords, rich peasants, counter-revolutionaries, bad elements and rightists and their children, including babies, were killed in one day." See "Summary of Proceedings of 13th Plenum of Peking Municipal Revolutionary Committee (May 15)," Canton *Wen-ko t'ung-hsün (Cultural Revolution Bulletin)* (July 1968), no. 16, in *SCMP* (July 25, 1968), 4225:12–13.

68. See "Organizational Rules of Poor and Lower-Middle Peasant Associations (Draft)," in Baum and Teiwes, *Ssu-Ch'ing*, pp. 95–101.

69. "Premier Chou's Speech to Representative of the Mass Organizations of Canton Area," Lhasa *Hung-se Tsao-fan Pao (Red Rebel Paper)*, October 12, 1967, trans. in *SCMP Supplement* (January 19, 1968), 215:9.

70. Marianne Bastid, "Levels of Economic Decision-making," in Stuart R. Schram, ed., *Authority, Participation and Cultural Change in China* (London: Cambridge University Press, 1973), p. 185.

71. Labor requirements imposed upon the members of the overthrown propertied classes sometimes imitate treatment given socially despised groups in imperial China. The yamen runners, who performed messenger duties for officials and who were held in contempt by "decent" members of society, were resurrected in the formation of a unit of former

landlords to take on these same tasks for the Communist government in a criticized incident in Fujian in 1955. See "One Cannot Allow Landlords and Controlled Elements to Transmit Documents," *Fujian ribao,* September 11, 1955. This article was drawn to my attention by Michel Oksenberg.

72. Bennett and Montaperto, *Red Guard,* p. 109. A similar account is found in A.Z.M. Obaidullah Khan, "Class Struggle in Yellow Sandhill Commune," *China Quarterly* (July–September 1972), 51:542. Such ·practices echo land reform–era treatment of class enemies described in Isabel and David Crook, *Revolution in a Chinese Village: Ten Mile Inn* (London: Routledge and Kegan Paul, 1959), p. 148.

73. There is little question that the five-category elements tend to dislike socialism, at least as defined by the results of Maoist social policy. My informants, none of whom shared the values of the high status category, discussed the widespread discontent among landlord and rich peasant families, even suggesting that they indeed may support restoration of the old regime. The story told of one landlord's son is illustrative: this child, born and raised since liberation, announced to educated young people newly sent down from the cities precisely which buildings, fields, and trees had belonged to his family prior to land reform. After repeated incidents, the poor and lower-middle peasant response was to beat the child severely—an approach which might well change his behavior, but which is not designed to increase his family's appreciation for the set of social arrangements which has followed liberation. Such accounts give credence to official warnings of landlord glee in 1962 in anticipation of a Jiang Jieshi (Chiang Kai-shek) invasion. See Hung Hsueh-shih, "The Reactionary Theory of 'Combining Two Into One' as Seen in Anhwei Rural Class Struggle," *Hung-ch'i* (December 1964), nos. 23–24, in *JPRS, 28359* (January 19, 1965), p. 45; C. S. Chen, ed., *Rural People's Communes in Lien-chiang* (Stanford: Hoover Institution Press, 1969), pp. 96–98; and Han Feng-chen, "How to Carry Out Class Education of Young Children," *Zhongguo Qingnian* (August 1, 1964), 15:26–27. A Guangxi account tells of a landlord who maintained a book recording his former property and its current owners. See Liu I-yung, "Make Efforts to Study Amid the Storm of Class Struggle," *Hung-ch'i* (October 1971), no. 11, in *SCMM* (November 1, 1971), 715:17–18.

74. The point that social categories become self-sustaining through use is made also in Erving Goffman's critique of the concept of "deviance" in social science: "It is remarkable that those who live around the social sciences have so quickly become comfortable with the term 'deviant,' as if those to whom the term is applied have enough in common so that significant things can be said about them as a whole. Just as there are iatrogenic disorders caused by the work of physicians (which then gives them more work to do), so there are categories of persons which are created by students of society, and then studied by them." Goffman, *Stigma: Notes on the Management of Spoiled Identity* (Englewood Cliffs, N.J.: Prentice-Hall, 1963), p. 140, n. 1.

75. Daniel Bell uses this phrase to discuss an American debate on family background prior to World War II, in *Marxian Socialism in the United States* (Princeton: Princeton University Press, 1967), pp. 82–85.

76. Feng Chao-ch'eng, "How I Learn the 'Dividing One Into Two' Viewpoint," *Red Flag* (March 31, 1970), no. 4, in *SCMM* (April 27, 1970), 680:94.

77. *From Max Weber,* p. 274.

78. Parish and Whyte, *Village and Family,* p. 39. According to Zhou Enlai in 1971, China's population included over 40 million former landlords and rich peasants, and over 10 million former capitalists. Jack Chen, *Inside the Cultural Revolution* (New York: Macmillan, 1975), p. 378.

79. Alexander Casella, "The Nanniwan May 7th Cadre School," *China Quarterly* (January–March 1973), 53:155.

80. Radio Canton, *Summary of World Broadcasts,* Part 3, FE/3700/BII/18. June 4, 1971.

81. "For the Red Flag to Wave Eternally, Emphasis Must Be Placed on Educating the Next Generation," *Renmin ribao,* May 4, 1972, p. 1. See also, "Only by Drawing a Class Line Can One Implement Policy," *Renmin ribao,* June 3, 1972; "Select Outstanding Young People to Send to College," *Renmin ribao,* March 4, 1972; "Strengthen Party Leadership; Seriously Do College Admission Work," *Renmin ribao,* March 22, 1972, p. 3; and "In Branch Construction, One Must Grasp Tightly Line Education," *Renmin ribao,* February 26, 1971, p. 3; and "Seriously Implement the Policy of Educable Children," *Renmin ribao,* April 21, 1972, p. 2.

82. "Do Well the Work of Uniting with and Educating Easily Educable Children," *Renmin ribao,* June 13, 1972, p. 2.

83. Kuo Chung-yeh, "Strive to Raise Consciousness in the Struggle Between the Two Lines," *Hung-ch'i* (November 17, 1970), no. 12, in *SCMM* (December 14, 1970), 695:17. Also see "Educate Cadres to Consciously Raise Awareness of Line Struggle," *Renmin ribao,* March 4, 1971, p. 1.

Seven: Class and the State

1. Quoted in "The Great Cultural Revolution Will Shine For Ever," *Peking Review* (May 21, 1976), 19(21):9.

2. See *Miscellany of Mao Tse-tung Thought (1949–1968), JPRS,* 61269-1 and 61269-2 (February 20, 1974), p. 70; and Mao Tsetung, *A Critique of Soviet Economics* (New York: Monthly Review Press, 1977), pp. 84, 132.

3. See the attack upon the cadre ranking system by Lin Xiling, a leader of the Hundred Flowers movement at Beijing University, in Dennis J. Doolin, *Communist China: The Politics of Student Opposition* (Stanford: Hoover Institution, 1964), p. 31.

4. Lowell Dittmer, *Liu Shao-ch'i and the Chinese Cultural Revolution* (Berkeley: University of California Press, 1974), pp. 190–91.

5. In Stuart Schram, ed., *Chairman Mao Talks to the People: Talks and Letters, 1956–1971* (New York: Pantheon, 1974), p. 96.

6. This episode is described in Dittmer, *Liu Shao-ch'i,* p. 186.

7. See Byung-joon Ahn, *Chinese Politics and Cultural Revolution* (Seattle: University of Washington Press, 1976), pp. 132–33.

8. For a representative critique, see Ding Da, "Oppose Absolute Egalitarianism," *Xuexi (Study)* (1958), 6:14–16.

9. Mao, *Miscellany*, p. 134: Mao, *Critique of Soviet Economics*, p. 84.

10. Mao, *Critique of Soviet Economics*, pp. 84–85.

11. Mao, *Miscellany*, p. 233.

12. Mao, *Critique of Soviet Economics*, p. 132. Elsewhere, Mao endorsed the correctness of the 1956 wage reform, saying that the problem was in its implementation, when the number of grades became too large. See *Miscellany*, p. 190.

13. See Mao's *On Khrushchov's Phoney Communism and Its Historical Lessons for the World* (Beijing: Foreign Languages Press, 1964), p. 69. Note also Mao's comments on China's wages for artists and intellectuals in *Miscellany*, p. 354.

14. Mao, *Miscellany*, p. 349. The reduction of high salaries between 1959 and 1963 is discussed in "Why Can't High Salaries Be Lowered?" *Shuang-ch'en Yue (Moonlight in Frosty Morning)*, January 10, 1968, in *SCMM* (March 25, 1968), 616:16–20.

15. See Victor Nee, "Revolution and Bureaucracy: Shanghai in the Cultural Revolution," in Nee and James Peck, eds., *China's Uninterrupted Revolution* (New York: Pantheon, 1975), pp. 342–47.

16. *Shuang-ch'en Yue*, January 10, 1968, in *SCMM* (March 25, 1968), 616:16–19. Other radical criticisms of the wage system include "Look at the Criminal Revisionist System of High Wages," Beijing *Feng Lei (Wind and Thunder)*, June 9, 1967; "The Special Rights of the Old Pearl River Film Studio's Noble Lords," Guangzhou *Xin zhuying (New Pearl River Film Studio)*, February 1968; "Once More Raising the Curtain on the Ping Pong Team," Guangzhou *Hungti bing (Red Athletic Warriors)*, October 14, 1967; "The Frightening High Salaried Stratum," Beijing *Dongfang hong (East is Red)*, June 13, 1967; and "Smash the Privileged Stratum in the Foreign Affairs Ministry," Peking *Wai-shih Hung-ch'i (Foreign Affairs Red Flag)*, June 14, 1967, in *JPRS*, 42977 (October 16, 1967), pp. 112–117.

17. Evidence of rather limited tinkering with wages and salaries is found in Peter Schran, "Institutional Continuity and Motivational Change: The Chinese Industrial Wages System, 1950–1973," *Asian Survey* (November 1974), 14(11):1014–32; Edgar Snow, *The Long Revolution* (New York: Vintage, 1973), pp. 129, 133, 168; Dittmer, *Liu Shao-ch'i*, pp. 266–67; and Jan S. Prybyla, "Notes on Chinese Higher Education: 1974," *China Quarterly* (June 1975), 62:281.

18. I have discussed these issues in "The Limits of Maoist Egalitarianism," *Asian Survey* (November 1976), 16(11):1081–96.

19. Shengwulian's "Program," "Resolutions," and polemical essay, "Whither China?" are collected in Klaus Mehnert, *Peking and the New Left* (Berkeley: University of California Center for Chinese Studies, 1969). This passage from the "Program" is on pp. 75–76.

20. "Whither China?" (January 6, 1968) in Mehnart, *Peking and the New Left*, p. 95.

21. Ibid., p. 99.

22. Minister of Public Security Kang Sheng, a close associate of Mao during the Cultural Revolution, denounced the organization bitterly in January 1968. His important speech is reprinted in Mehnert, *Peking and the New Left*. Articles condemning Shengwulian may be found in Guang-

zhou *Hongqi Bao (Red Flag Paper),* February 20, 1968; Xiangtan *Doupigai* (Xiangtan *Struggle-Criticism-Transformation*), March 3, 1968; and Guangzhou *Guangyin hongqi (Guangdong Printers Red Flag)* (March 1968).

23. On the ultraleft, see Barry Burton, "The Cultural Revolution's Ultraleft Conspiracy: The 'May 16 Group'," *Asian Survey* (November 1971), 11(11):1029–53.

24. "Certain so-called new ideas have recently gained currency in society. Their main content consists in twisting the principal contradictions of socialist society into contradictions between the masses of people and the so-called persons in authority who hold property and power in their hands, i.e., the privileged personages. These ideas demand that under the dictatorship of the proletariat social property and political power be continuously redistributed." "Comments on the So-called 'New Ideas'," Shanghai *Wen-hui Pao,* July 23, 1967, in *SCMP Supplement* (November 3, 1967), 209:39.

25. "Defend the Great Achievements of the Four Clean-Ups Movement," *Red Flag* (March 1967), no. 4, trans. in *JPRS* (March 31, 1967), p. 63.

26. The study by Andrew Walder, *Chang Ch'un-ch'iao and Shanghai's January Revolution* (Ann Arbor: Center for Chinese Studies, University of Michigan, 1978), describes the tough measures employed by one member of the Gang of Four to consolidate newly won political power.

27. In Schram, *Chairman Mao Talks to the People,* p. 277. See also *Miscellany,* pp. 466–67 for Mao's views on the need to allow mistaken cadres an opportunity to reform and join the Cultural Revolution.

28. Although Mao disassociated himself from the class analyses of the ultraleft in the Cultural Revolution, he continued his criticism of the work-grade hierarchy with no evident restraint. See the comment quoted in Dittmer, *Liu Shao-ch'i,* p. 193; as well as the passage from his speech to the Party's Ninth Congress (April 28, 1969) found in Schram, *Chairman Mao Talks to the People,* p. 288.

29. Although some may view this theme as evidence for Mao's revolutionary romanticism, it may also be interpreted as a proper suspicion of the claims for a generalized "efficiency" typically offered by the powerful in support of their efforts to enforce particular formulas for occupational specialization. See the analysis in Dietrich Rueschemeyer, "Structural Differentiation, Efficiency, and Power," *American Journal of Sociology* (July 1977), 83(1):1–25. Rueschemeyer argues that alleged efficiencies resulting from various divisions of labor are often untested, whereas their contributions to social control are rarely in doubt.

30. Quoted in *Peking Review* (May 14, 1976), 19(20):9. Of course, Mao's impatience with the division of labor echoes a similar theme less prosaically expressed by Marx: "For as soon as labour is distributed, each man has a particular exclusive sphere of activity, which is forced upon him and from which he cannot escape. He is a hunter, a fisherman, a shepherd, or a critical critic, and must remain so if he does not want to lose his means of livelihood; while in communist society, where nobody has an exclusive sphere of activity but each can become accomplished in any branch he wishes society regulates the general production and thus

makes it possible for me to do one thing today and another tomorrow, to hunt in the morning, fish in the afternoon, rear cattle in the evening, criticize after dinner, just as I have a mind, without ever becoming hunter, fisherman, shepherd or critic." Karl Marx and Friedrich Engels, *The German Ideology* (New York: International Publishers, 1947), p. 22.

31. Shanghai *Wen-hui Pao* editorial, September 5, 1968, *SCMP* (October 11, 1968), 4276:4–5.

32. According to Jack Chen, urban cadres, under pressure to limit their consumption while in the countryside, simply put more of their incomes into savings accounts, a step which did little to reduce urban-rural material inequalities. Not surprisingly, these cadres were instructed not to reveal their salaries to local peasants. *A Year in Upper Felicity* (New York: Macmillan, 1973), pp. 25–29, 46, 55. There were also ad hominem cases in which the salaries of individual cadres were illegally reduced, but this much-criticized practice in no way assumed the character of a structural reform of China's distribution system.

33. The phrase is Mao's, from a speech of 1967, but much quoted by radicals in the 1970s. See Chung Shih, "The Dictatorship of the Proletariat and the Great Cultural Revolution," *Peking Review* (February 13, 1976), 19(7):5; and Wang Hung-wen, "Report at the Central Study Class," in Raymond Lotta, ed., *And Mao Makes 5* (Chicago: Banner Press, 1978), p. 60.

34. Paul M. Sweezy, "Theory and Practice" in the *Monthly Review* (February 1977), 28(9):11. The matter is put somewhat differently by Joseph Esherick: "By the time Mao's theory of capitalist restoration is fully developed, these ambiguities have largely been resolved by defining the origins of classes substantially in terms of *power*." "On the 'Restoration of Capitalism,' Mao and Marxist Theory," *Modern China* (January 1979), 5(1):64.

35. Assessing the performance of rebel leaders in October, 1967, Yao Wenyuan complained of a "small number of comrades who began to grow intoxicated with dinner parties, applause, flattery and cars; some of them were hit by bourgeois sugar-coated bullets and they began to divorce themselves from the masses and were no longer so eager to go among the masses and become school-children of the masses." "Notification by CCP CC and Central Cultural Revolution Group Gathering Opinions on the Convening of the '9th Congress'," *SCMP Supplement* (March 3, 1969), 245:8.

36. Quoted in "A Basic Difference Between Marxism-Leninism and Revisionism," Peking *Kuang-ming jih-pao,* April 25, 1967, in *SCMP* (May 12, 1967), 3938:16.

37. Important guides to the political struggles of the period 1969–1976 are Michael Y.M. Kao's editorial introduction to *The Lin Piao Affair: Power Politics and Military Coup* (White Plains: International Arts and Science Press, 1975), pp. xix–lxxvii; John Bryan Starr, "From the 10th Party Congress to the Premiership of Hua Kuo-feng: the Significance of the Colour of the Cat," *China Quarterly* (September 1978), 67:457–88; Lowell Dittmer, "Bases of Power in Chinese Politics: A Theory and an Analysis of the Fall of the 'Gang of Four,' " *World Politics* (October 1978),

31(1):26–60; Roxane Witke, *Comrade Chiang Ching* (Boston: Little, Brown, 1977); Jurgen Domes, "The 'Gang of Four' and Hua Kuo-feng: Analysis of Political Events in 1975–76," *China Quarterly* (September 1977), 71:473–97; Jaap van Ginneken, *The Rise and Fall of Lin Piao* (New York: Avon, 1977); Chi Hsin, *The Case of the Gang of Four* (Hong Kong: Cosmos, 1977); and Tang Tsou, "Mao Tse-tung Thought, the Last Struggle for Succession, and the Post-Mao Era," *China Quarterly* (September 1977), 71:498–527.

38. Mass Criticism Group of Beijing and Qinghua Universities, "The Proletarian Dictatorship and the Renegade Lin Biao," *Hongqi* (May 1975), 5:25–26.

39. On this point, see Dittmer, "Bases of Power in Chinese Politics."

40. *Renmin ribao (People's Daily)* editorial, February 9, 1975.

41. *Marx, Engels and Lenin on the Dictatorship of the Proletariat* (Beijing Foreign Languages Press, 1975).

42. Zhang Chunqiao, "On Exercising All-Round Dictatorship over the Bourgeoisie, *Hongqi* (1975), 4:3–12, trans. in *Peking Review* (April 4, 1975), 14:5–11, Yao Wenyuan, "On the Social Basis of the Lin Piao Anti-Party Clique," *Hongqi* (1975), 3:20–29, trans. in *Peking Review* (March 7, 1975), 10:5–10.

43. *Marx, Engels and Lenin,* p. 38.

44. Ji Yen, "Ideological Weapon for Restricting Bourgeois Right," *Hongqi* (1975), 4:33, trans. in *Peking Review* (1975), 22:9.

45. *Marx, Engels and Lenin,* p. 2.

46. Zhang, "On Exercising All-Round Dictatorship," p. 10.

47. See Robert C. Tucker, *The Marxian Revolutionary Idea* (New York: Norton, 1969), pp. 54–91; and Henri Lefebvre, *The Sociology of Marx* (New York: Vintage, 1969), pp. 123–85.

48. "Report on the Investigation of the Counter-revolutionary Crimes of the Lin Piao Anti-Party Clique" (1973), in Michael Y. M. Kau, ed., *The Lin Piao Affair* (White Plains: International Arts and Sciences Press, 1975), p. 113. Note the different version of Lin's background in "Chairman Mao's Successor: Deputy Supreme Commander Lin Piao" (1969), in Kau, p. 6.

49. This and the following two quotations are all from Yao's article on Lin, cited above in note 42.

50. "Ideoglogical Weapon," p. 8.

51. Zhang, "On Exercising All-Round Dictatorship," p. 10.

52. "The Great Cultural Revolution Will Shine For Ever," *Peking Review* (May 21, 1976), 19(21):7.

53. Much of the discussion of class conflict which comprised the campaign to study the dictatorship of the proletariat focused not on production relationships but on the distribution system of the work-grade stratification. Although the radicals directed attention to this epiphenomenon of class, they also recognized the role of the state in organizing production—and thereby generating classes—in socialist society. "Socialist Political Economy," a book prepared under Zhang Chunqiao's supervision in Shanghai, maintained that "the question of ownership is actually a question of power." See Hu Naiwu and Wang Yungzhi, "An Out-and-

out Counterrevolutionary 'Political Economy,' " *Guangming ribao,* January 16, 1978, in *FBIS* (January 24, 1978), p. E13. For very different criticisms of the radicals for failing to pay sufficient attention to production relationships, see Benjamin I. Schwartz, "The Essence of Marxism Revisited," *Modern China* (October 1976), 2(4):464–65; and Charles Bettelheim, "The Great Leap Backward," *Monthly Review* (July–August 1978) 30(3):93–96.

54. For example, see the discussion of one cadre's son who was praised for withdrawing from Nanking University after his father utilized political connections to gain his admission. His request to withdraw is in *FBIS* (January 22, 1974), pp. B13–B15.)

55. See especially his remarks in his "Report at the Central Study Class," in Lotta, *And Mao Makes 5,* pp. 58, 62–66.

56. See the discussion of a book, "The Rise of Khrushchev to Power," allegedly prepared under the patronage of Yao Wenyuan. Beijing radio (February 13, 1977), in *FBIS* (February 14, 1977), p. E10.

57. Gong Zhun, "Expose the 'Gang of Four's' Plot to use the Labor Unions to Usurp Power," *Renmin ribao,* April 8, 1977.

58. Ji, "Ideological Weapon," p. 10.

59. The limited scope of the campaign in rural areas is analyzed in John P. Burns, "The Radicals and the Campaign to Limit Bourgeois Rights in the Countryside," *Contemporary China* (January 1977), 1(3):25–27.

60. Ji Yen, "Raise High the Socialist Revolution in the Countryside," *Hongqi* (August 1975), 8:8.

61. For examples, see the notes on p. 17 of *The Seeds and Other Stories* (Beijing: Foreign Languages Press, 1972) and on p. 15 of *Peking Review* (August 23, 1974), vol. 17, no. 34.

62. See Yang Rungguo, "Confucius—A Thinker Who Stubbornly Upheld the Slave System," *Peking Review* (October 12, 1973), 16(41):8:

"Confucius made up his mind to use the subjective concepts of the slave-owning class since the times of the Yin and Western Chou Dynasties to define and delimit the changing social realities. He hoped to restore by this method the original order—'The king is a king, the minister a minister, the father a father, and the son a son'—in a vain attempt to prop up the collapsing rule of the slave-owning aristocracy.

"Proceeding from the viewpoint of accurately defining concepts and rank, [*The Spring and Autumn Annals*] set out to reverse the realities in a changing society and restore the old order. Mencius extolled Confucius as a man who wrote *The Spring and Autumn Annals* to set right the confused concepts and rank and thereby exercised the supreme authority on behalf of the monarch of Chou, that is, consolidating the role of the slave system."

63. This is based upon interviews conducted in Hong Kong by Marc Blecher, who generously called this process to my attention.

64. In the campaign to discredit the radicals after Mao's death, members of the Ministry of Public Security alleged that the Gang of Four had discouraged spending time and effort on landlords and rich peasants, apparently feeling that such endeavors diverted resources from the more important issue of the "bourgeois class within the party." See the article

by the Theoretical Group of the Ministry of Public Security, "It is Impermissible to Point the Spearhead of Dictatorship at the Party," *Hongqi (Red Flag)* (June 1978), no. 6, in *FBIS* (June 27, 1978), p. E4.

65. Peter L. Berger and Thomas Luckmann, *The Social Construction of Reality* (Harmondsworth: Penguin, 1971), p. 145.

66. Li Jian, "Attach Importance to the Revolution in the Superstructure," *Peking Review* (August 24, 1973), 16(34):5.

67. Maurice Meisner, "The Maoist Legacy and Chinese Socialism," *Asian Survey* (November 1977), 17(11):1027.

68. "Mao Tse-tung's Private Letter to Chiang Ch'ing," *Issues and Studies* (January 1973), 9(4):96.

69. Quoted in Parris H. Chang, "The Passing of the Maoist Era," *Asian Survey* (November 1976), 16(11):1001.

70. See "A Desperate Move Before Destruction," *Peking Review* (December 24, 1976), 19(52):8–12, 32. Tang Tsou calls attention to the Gang's rearrangement of the paragraphs of a 1964 statement by Mao in "Mao Tse-tung Thought, the Struggle for Succession, and the Post-Mao Era," pp. 520–21.

Eight: China After Mao: More Inequality and Less Class Analysis

1. Quoted in "The Great Cultural Revolution Will Shine For Ever," *Peking Review* (May 21, 1976), p. 19(21):9.

2. It was alleged in 1978 that efforts within the Central Committee and State Council in 1974 and 1975 to implement similar pay increases to "a section of workers and staff members who earned low wages" was sabotaged by the Gang of Four. Beijing radio (January 1, 1978), in *FBIS* (January 3, 1978), pp. E16–E17.

3. Beijing radio (February 17, 1979), in *FBIS* (February 23, 1979), p. E11. See also "Resolutely Overcome Egalitarianism and Seriously Implement the Policy of Pay According to Work—Seminar on Pay According to Work in Agriculture Held in Peking," Beijing *Guangming ribao*, October 14, 1978, in *FBIS* (October 31, 1978), pp. E14–E19. Peasants have also been assured of higher incomes through more generous prices given by the state for agricultural commodities—which policy has in turn eliminated some of the industrial wage increases through inflation in urban food prices.

4. Beijing radio (April 26, 1978), in *FBIS* (May 12, 1978), p. K6; "Tianjin University and Nankai University Professors Continue to Move into New Housing; Baotou Teachers' Training Institute Gives Newly Constructed Dormitories Completely Over to Instructors," *Renmin ribao (People's Daily)*, November 29, 1979.

5. "Tianjin Prepares Special Club for High-level Intellectuals," Hong Kong *Wenhui bao*, November 28, 1979. This article was called to my attention by Suzanne Pepper. Summer vacations in scenic spots have also been restored for "outstanding" intellectuals. See *Beijing Review* (August 24, 1979), 22(34):7–8.

6. For example, see the regulations for prizes for inventions published in *Guangming ribao,* January 17, 1979, and for prizes in natural science in *Renmin ribao,* December 9, 1979. Of special interest is the prize system established for the faculty of Shanghai's Jiaotong University: 20 percent of its funds are drawn from the profits of factories run by the university, an unusually clear example of the extraction of surplus value by professors from their students. See the account in *Renmin ribao,* November 23, 1979.

7. See "Construction Company Founded in Shanghai," *Beijing Review* (August 24, 1979), 22(34):6; and "Renmin Ribao Advocates Building of Houses by Individuals," *FBIS* (August 1, 1979), pp. L12–L13.

8. See the speech by Ulanhu, head of the Party Central Committee's United Front Work Department, "On Policy Towards the National Bourgeoisie," *Beijing Review* (February 16, 1979), 22(7):11–16, 28. Also see Wang Chao, "To Pay Back Fixed Dividends to Capitalists Is to Implement the Party's Policy Toward Capitalists," Beijing *Gongren ribao,* July 31, 1979, in *FBIS* (August 14, 1979), pp. L1–L3.

9. Haikou radio (August 3, 1979), in *FBIS* (August 7, 1979), pp. P2–P3.

10. Changsha radio (March 21, 1979), in *FBIS* (March 23, 1979), p. P2.

11. "Don't Arbitrarily Divide Up the Production Teams," *Nanfang ribao,* March 1, 1979, in *FBIS* (March 2, 1979), pp. H1–H2; Guangzhou radio (March 21, 1979), in *FBIS* (March 23, 1979), pp. P3–P4; Changsha radio (March 21, 1979), in *FBIS* (March 23, 1979), p. P1; Guiyang radio (March 21, 1979), in *FBIS* (March 23, 1979), p. Q1. According to *Beijing Review* (September 15, 1980), 23(37):8, one quarter of China's production teams have been divided into smaller units.

12. Beijing radio (April 28, 1978), in *FBIS* (May 4, 1978), pp. E15–E16; Beijing radio (July 18, 1978), in *FBIS* (July 21, 1978), p. E15. It is not clear that the rural fairs necessarily put the poorest peasants at a disadvantage. Deborah Davis-Friedmann has argued that some of the poorest residents of rural China, such as elderly and disabled persons in families with little labor power, have benefited considerably from participation in market activities by selling handicraft articles, etc. "Welfare Practices in Rural China," *World Development* (May 1978), 6:609–19.

13. For example, see the articles under the headline "How Can the Peasants Enrich Themselves Quickly?," in *Renmin ribao,* January 1, 1980.

14. For example, a call to recruit social science research personnel classifies candidates not by level of talent and achievement but by age: candidates 35 and younger are eligible to become "research interns," those under 45 may become "assistant research personnel," those under 55 "associate research personnel," etc. *Renmin ribao,* December 4, 1979.

15. Hong Kong *Dagong bao,* November 8, 1977, in *FBIS* (November 16, 1977), p. N2; (Beijing) New China News Agency (March 18, 1978), in *FBIS* (March 21, 1978), pp. E20–E21.

16. *Renmin ribao,* April 10, 1978, in *FBIS* (April 14, 1978), p. E2.

17. Hong Kong *South China Morning Post,* May 5, 1978; (Hong Kong) French Press Agency (July 25, 1978), in *FBIS* (July 26, 1978), p. E2. Such

reports have been denied by the Chinese; see Tokyo *Kyodo,* May 22, 1978, in *FBIS* (May 22, 1978), p. E3.

18. Shenyang radio (May 15, 1978), in *FBIS* (May 22, 1978), p. L2; *Beijing Review* (January 28, 1980), 23(4):8.

19. French Press Agency (March 1, 1978), in *FBIS* (March 2, 1978), pp. D7–D8.

20. This section draws upon the detailed survey of changes in education policy offered by Suzanne Pepper, "Chinese Education After Mao: Two Steps Forward, Two Steps Back and Begin Again?," *China Quarterly* (March 1980), 81:1–65.

21. New China News Agency (August 23, 1979), in *Summary of World Broadcasts* (August 31, 1979), FE/6207/BII/7–8.

22. New China News Agency (June 27, 1979), in *Summary of World Broadcasts* (June 30, 1979), FE/6155/BII/5.

23. *Jilin ribao,* March 12, 1979, in *Summary of World Broadcasts* (March 30, 1979), FE/6080/BII/10–11.

24. Wang, "To Pay Back Fixed Dividends to Capitalists," p. L1.

25. New China News Agency (March 21, 1979), in *FBIS* (March 27, 1979), pp. 013–015.

26. See Charles Bettelheim's "The Great Leap Backward," *Monthly Review* (July–August 1978), 30(3):93–96.

27. See "False Leftists, True Rightists," *Renmin ribao,* February 6, 1977. Some discussions of the social basis of the "Gang" tried to discredit them by reviving the bloodline theory in linking them to bad family backgrounds. See "Yao Wenyuan is a Filial Progeny of the Landlord Class," *Renmin ribao,* April 27, 1977, in *SCMP,* no. 69340 (June 30, 1977), pp. 9–11; and "Renegade Jiang Qing's Sinful Family Background," *Guangming ribao,* April 28, 1977, in *FBIS* (May 11, 1977), pp. E1–E2.

28. For example, see Gu Shan, "The Trotskyites: A Mirror Reflecting 'Gang of Four,' " *Peking Review* (June 24, 1977), 20(26):19–24 (originally in *Renmin ribao,* March 19, 1977).

29. See "The Right-wing Face Beneath the 'Great Cloth,' " *Renmin ribao,* February 4, 1977; and "From Historical Counterrevolutionary to Practicing Counterrevolutionary," *Renmin ribao,* May 5, 1977.

30. Nor has the Chinese press ignored any opportunities to draw attention to the contrast between the radicals' theories and the luxurious privileges which characterized their life-style. Even before the death of Mao a celebrated 1974 wall-poster in Guangzhou described how the institutional reforms of the Cultural Revolution, despite their radical thrust, could still provide a basis for hypocritical "special privileges." The three authors of this essay were persecuted for their stance, to be liberated after the fall of the radicals. See "On Socialist Democracy and the Legal System," by "Li I-che," in *Chinese Law and Government* (Fall 1977), 10(3):55. The imprisonment of the Beijing electrician and political activist, Wei Jingsheng in 1979, however, suggests that the post-Mao leadership likes those dissidents best who criticized the previous administration.

31. For official overviews of the new approach to class, see two series in *Beijing Review:* "Fundamental Change in China's Class Situation"

(November 16, 1979), 22(46):9–13, and (November 23, 1979), 22(47):15–17; and "Theoretical Discussion: On Class and Class Struggle" (May 19, 1980), 23(20):24–26, (June 2, 1980), 23(22):24–26, (June 23, 1980), 23(25):13–16.

32. "Concoct" may seen a harsh word, but how else can one interpret the bond between theory and practice envisioned by Xue Muqiao, head of the Economic Research Institute of the State Planning Commission? Referring to the efforts of local officials in Beijing to resolve the unemployment problem by creating so-called "collective" enterprises (in fact a small-scale and profit-oriented form of organization), Xue said that "they hope that additional articles will be written in theoretical circles, to prove that to develop urban collective ownership is not to take the capitalist road." "Several Opinions on the Problem of Urban Employment," *Beijing ribao,* July 18, 1979. This article was called to my attention by Dorothy Solinger.

33. "Press On with the Three Great Revolutionary Movements Simultaneously," *Renmin ribao* editorial, April 22, 1978, in *Peking Review* (April 28, 1978), 21(17):4.

34. Wang Zhen, "Fake Left, Real Right," *Peking Review* (February 10, 1978), 21(6):6–7. Also see Jin Wen, "Is the 'Key Link' Class Struggle 'At Any Time'?" *Guangming ribao* (January 13, 1979).

35. "Carrying Out the Four Modernizations is the Biggest Politics," *Renmin ribao* editorial, April 11, 1979, in *Beijing Review* (April 27, 1979), 22(17):10. Also see Dong Huaizhong, "Class Struggle Must Not Be Expanded Anymore," *Renmin ribao,* February 29, 1979.

36. A long-projected volume 6 contains writings from Mao's most radical years, 1958–1976. A volume containing many of these articles was prepared in 1969 and circulated on a restricted basis among cadres. It was made available in the West after being secured by Taiwan intelligence sources, and forms an important basis for this book. No one anticipates that a final version of this now subversive set of documents will soon be published in China.

37. "Communique of the Third Plenary Session of the 11th Central Committee of the Communist Party of China (December 22, 1978)," *Peking Review* (December 29, 1978), 21(52):11.

38. "Tear Off 'Gang of Four's' 'Leftist' Masks," *Peking Review* (December 10, 1976), 19(50):16; and Peking Normal University Theory Group, "The 'Gang of Four's' Betrayal of Chairman Mao's Instructions on the Question of Theory," *Hongqi* (February 1977), 2:17; Zhang Zhaozun, Fang Sheng, and Hu Naiwu, "Commenting on the Book 'Political Economy,' " *Renmin ribao,* April 5, 1978, in *JPRS,* 71088 (May 10, 1978), pp. 6–8; Theoretical Group of the Party Committee of Ji County, "Heavy Snow Oppresses the Pines, but They Remain Upright," *Tianjin ribao (Tianjin Daily),* April 9, 1978, in *FBIS* (April 12, 1978), pp. K5–K7; Mass Criticism Group of the Shenyang PLA Units Military-Political Cadre School, "What Kind of Stuff is the 'Class Analysis' Advocated by Zhang Chunqiao?," Peking radio (April 27, 1977), in *FBIS* (May 2, 1977), pp. L3–L4.

39. For instance, see Su Shao-chih and Feng Lan-jui, "Refuting Yao

Wen-yuan's Fallacy that the Principle 'To Each According to His Work' Breeds Bourgeoisie," *Renmin ribao,* August 9, 1977, in *Peking Review* (February 10, 1978), 21(6):11–14; Li Honglin, "Is 'To Each According to His Work' a Socialist Principle or a Capitalist Principle?," *Renmin ribao,* September 27, 1977.

40. Zhang Decheng, "Stop Saying 'Grasp Revolution, Promote Production,' " *Renmin ribao,* March 9, 1979, in *FBIS* (March 19, 1979), pp. L5–L7; "Comrade Ye Jianying's Speech—At the Meeting in Celebration of the 30th Anniversary of the Founding of the People's Republic of China," *Beijing Review* (October 5, 1979), 22(40):17–18.

41. Li Xiulin and Zheng Hangsheng, "Class Struggle in the Absence of Exploiting Classes," *Renmin ribao,* October 31, 1979; Writing Group of the Military Academy, "Some Questions about Class and Class Struggle," *Guangming ribao,* August 22, 1979, in *Summary of World Broadcasts* (August 31, 1979), FE/6207/BII/1–7.

42. Han Ying, "Glorious Mission of the Chinese Youth," *Peking Review* (November 17, 1978), 21(46):9.

43. See *Renmin ribao* Special Commentator, "On Policy Towards Intellectuals," *Beijing Review* (February 2, 1979), 22(5):10–15.

44. Peking Radio (April 10, 1978), in *FBIS* (April 13, 1978), p. E13. Also see Sun Yuesheng, "Discussion of the Question of the Explosion of Knowledge and the Class Membership of Intellectuals," *Shehui kexue janxian (Social Science Front)* (1979), 2:111–16. This article was called to my attention by Deborah Davis-Friedmann.

45. Quoted in Luo Fu, "China's Intellectuals—Part of the Working Class," *Beijing Review* (March 31, 1980), 23(13):23.

46. *Peking Review* (November 24, 1978), 21(47):3.

47. See "Victory for the Policy of Remoulding the Exploiters," *Beijing Review* (February 16, 1979), 22(7):8.

48. This mass alteration of class designations was not accomplished without some grumbling by peasants with better designations. The army newspaper referred to "a few landlords and rich peasants" who "acted cocky after their designations were removed," and to the doubts this engendered among some peasants about the wisdom of the reform. And in Henan, the army (often seen as representing the interests of peasants because of its predominantly peasant composition) organized a special fact-finding group and forum to dispel doubts about the new policy. See Beijing radio (August 3, 1979) in *FBIS* (August 9, 1979), pp. L8–L9; and Beijing radio (August 22, 1979), in *FBIS* (August 24, 1979), pp. L5–L8.

49. "Resolve Well the Question of Removing the Labels of Four-Category Elements By Seeking Truth from Facts," *Renmin ribao,* January 30, 1979.

50. The mass reform of class designations was apparently initially implemented in selected key-point areas, standard Chinese administrative practice. See Xi'an radio (January 18, 1979), in *FBIS* (February 7, 1979), p. M2, for an account of a special work-team for Lintong County, Shaanxi Province. Procedures seem to have varied, however. In Liaoning the head of the provincial public security bureau insisted that there was no need for involving the masses in what he envisioned as simply an

administrative matter. A description of a production brigade on the out skirts of Beijing, however, reveals popular consultation about which for- mer landlords and rich peasants should have their designations removed, as well as mass meetings with public debate over individual cases. It is possible that officials in Liaoning, as well as in Shanghai, a former radical political base, simply seek to discourage mass mobilization over any is- sue, while Beijing cadres are less anxious. See Shenyang radio (February 7, 1979), in *FBIS* (February 9, 1979), pp. L2–L4; and "Class Status in the Countryside: Changes Over Three Decades," *Beijing Review* (January 21, 1980), 23(3):18–19.

51. For example, see "The Policy of Reforming Educational Admis- sions is Completely Correct," *Renmin ribao,* May 12, 1978.

52. "Sweep Away Feudal Ideology," *Renmin ribao,* July 18, 1980, in *Beijing Review* (September 8, 1980), 23(36):26.

53. An example of the former use of Soviet society as a negative ex- ample for China is "Sharp Class Polarization in Soviet Union," *Peking Review* (January 3, 1975), 18(1):27–29.

54. See Seymour Martin Lipset and Richard B. Dobson, "Social Strat- ification and Sociology in the Soviet Union," *Survey* (Summer 1973), 19(3):114–85.

55. Contrast the relative obscurity of class relationships in socialist China to Frank Parkin's claim that class is more "transparent" in the socialist societies of Eastern Europe than in Western capitalism. *Class In- equality and Political Order* (London: Paladin, 1972), pp. 160–65.

56. Charles Bettelheim, *Class Struggles in the USSR: First Period, 1917– 1923* (New York: Monthly Review Press, 1976), p. 21. For a spirited defense of the treatment of socialist bureaucrats in class terms, see the comment by Ross Gandy in *Monthly Review* (March 1976), 27(10):11–14.

57. Immanuel Wallerstein, "Class-Formation in the Capitalist World- Economy," *Politics and Society* (1975), 5(3):369.

58. Wlodzimierz Brus, *Socialist Ownership and Political Systems* (Lon- don: Routledge and Kegan Paul, 1975), pp. 10–11.

59. Stanislaw Ossowski, *Class Structure in the Social Consciousness* (New York: Free Press, 1963), pp. 186–87.

60. Hans H. Gerth and C. Wright Mills, eds., *From Max Weber* (New York: Galaxy Books, 1958), p. 190.

61. Stuart R. Schram, "Introduction" to *Authority, Participation and Cultural Change in China* (London: Cambridge University Press, 1973), p. 87.

62. Mao, "Talk Regarding 'Strategic Arrangements,' " Taibei *Feiqing yanjiu (Bandit Affairs Research),* in *JPRS,* 45281 (May 6, 1968), p. 15.

Index

Studies of the East Asian Institute

THE LADDER OF SUCCESS IN IMPERIAL CHINA, by Ping-ti Ho. New York: Columbia University Press, 1962.

THE CHINESE INFLATION, 1937–1949, by Shun-hsin Chou. New York: Columbia University Press, 1963.

REFORMER IN MODERN CHINA: CHANG CHIEN, 1853–1926, by Samuel Chu. New York: Columbia University Press, 1965.

RESEARCH IN JAPANESE SOURCES: A GUIDE, by Herschel Webb with the assistance of Marleigh Ryan. New York: Columbia University Press, 1965.

SOCIETY AND EDUCATION IN JAPAN, by Herbert Passin. New York: Teachers College Press, Columbia University, 1965.

AGRICULTURAL PRODUCTION AND ECONOMIC DEVELOPMENT IN JAPAN, 1873–1922, by James I. Nakamura. Princeton: Princeton University Press, 1966.

JAPAN'S FIRST MODERN NOVEL: UKIGUMO OF FUTABATEI SHIMEI, by Marleigh Ryan. New York: Columbia University Press, 1967. Also in paperback.

THE KOREAN COMMUNIST MOVEMENT, 1918–1948, by Dae-Sook Suh. Princeton: Princeton University Press, 1967.

THE FIRST VIETNAM CRISIS, by Melvin Gurtov. New York: Columbia University Press, 1967. Also in paperback.

CADRES, BUREAUCRACY, AND POLITICAL POWER IN COMMUNIST CHINA, by A. Doak Barnett. New York: Columbia University Press, 1967.

THE JAPANESE IMPERIAL INSTITUTION IN THE TOKUGAWA PERIOD, by Herschel Webb. New York, Columbia University Press, 1968.

HIGHER EDUCATION AND BUSINESS RECRUITMENT IN JA-PAN, by Koya Azumi. New York: Teachers College Press, Columbia University, 1969.

THE COMMUNISTS AND CHINESE PEASANT REBELLIONS: A STUDY IN THE REWRITING OF CHINESE HISTORY, by James P. Harrison, Jr. New York: Atheneum, 1969.

HOW THE CONSERVATIVES RULE JAPAN, by Nathaniel B. Thayer. Princeton: Princeton University Press, 1969.

ASPECTS OF CHINESE EDUCATION, edited by C. T. Hu. New York: Teachers College Press, Columbia University, 1969.

DOCUMENTS OF KOREAN COMMUNISM, 1918–1948, by Dae-Sook Suh. Princeton: Princeton University Press, 1970.

JAPANESE EDUCATION: A BIBLIOGRAPHY OF MATERIALS IN THE ENGLISH LANGUAGE, by Herbert Passin. New York: Teachers College Press, Columbia University, 1970.

ECONOMIC DEVELOPMENT AND THE LABOR MARKET IN JAPAN, by Kōji Taira. New York: Columbia University Press, 1970.

THE JAPANESE OLIGARCHY AND THE RUSSO-JAPANESE WAR, by Shumpei Okamoto. New York: Columbia University Press, 1970.

IMPERIAL RESTORATION IN MEDIEVAL JAPAN, by H. Paul Varley. New York: Columbia University Press, 1971.

JAPAN'S POSTWAR DEFENSE POLICY, 1947–1968, by Martin E. Weinstein. New York: Columbia University Press, 1971.

ELECTION CAMPAIGNING JAPANESE STYLE, by Gerald L. Curtis. New York: Columbia University Press, 1971.

CHINA AND RUSSIA: THE "GREAT GAME," by O. Edmund Clubb. New York: Columbia University Press, 1971. Also in paperback.

MONEY AND MONETARY POLICY IN COMMUNIST CHINA, by Katherine Huang Hsiao. New York: Columbia University Press, 1971.

THE DISTRICT MAGISTRATE IN LATE IMPERIAL CHINA, by John R. Watt. New York: Columbia University Press, 1972.

LAW AND POLICY IN CHINA'S FOREIGN RELATIONS: A STUDY OF ATTITUDES AND PRACTICE, by James C. Hsiung. New York: Columbia University Press, 1972.

PEARL HARBOR AS HISTORY: JAPANESE-AMERICAN RELA-TIONS: 1931–1941, edited by Dorothy Borg and Shumpei Okamoto, with the assistance of Dale K. A. Finlayson. New York: Columbia University Press, 1973.

JAPANESE CULTURE: A SHORT HISTORY, by H. Paul Varley. New York: Praeger, 1973.

DOCTORS IN POLITICS: THE POLITICAL LIFE OF THE JAPAN MEDICAL ASSOCIATION, by William E. Steslicke. New York: Praeger, 1973.

JAPAN'S FOREIGN POLICY, 1868–1941: A RESEARCH GUIDE, edited by James William Morley. New York: Columbia University Press, 1973.

THE JAPAN TEACHERS UNION: A RADICAL INTEREST GROUP IN JAPANESE POLITICS, by Donald Ray Thurston. Princeton University Press, 1973.

PALACE AND POLITICS IN PREWAR JAPAN, by David Anson Titus. New York: Columbia University Press, 1974.

THE IDEA OF CHINA: ESSAYS IN GEOGRAPHIC MYTH AND THEORY, by Andrew March. Devon, England: David and Charles, 1974.

ORIGINS OF THE CULTURE REVOLUTION, by Roderick MacFarquhar. New York: Columbia University Press, 1974.

SHIBA KŌKAN: ARTIST, INNOVATOR, AND PIONEER IN THE WESTERNIZATION OF JAPAN, by Calvin L. French. Tokyo: Weatherhill, 1974.

EMBASSY AT WAR, by Harold Joyce Noble. Edited with an introduction by Frank Baldwin, Jr. Seattle: University of Washington Press, 1975.

REBELS AND BUREAUCRATS: CHINA'S DECEMBER 9ERS, by John Israel and Donald W. Klein. Berkeley: University of California Press, 1975.

HOUSE UNITED, HOUSE DIVIDED: THE CHINESE FAMILY IN TAIWAN, by Myron L. Cohen. New York: Columbia University Press, 1976.

INSEI: ABDICATED SOVEREIGNS IN THE POLITICS OF LATE HEIAN JAPAN, by G. Cameron Hurst. New York: Columbia University Press, 1976.

DETERRENT DIPLOMACY, edited by James William Morley. New York: Columbia University Press, 1976.

CADRES, COMMANDERS AND COMMISSARS: THE TRAINING OF THE CHINESE COMMUNIST LEADERSHIP, 1920–45, by Jane L. Price. Boulder, Colo.: Westview Press, 1976.

SUN YAT-SEN: FRUSTRATED PATRIOT, by C. Martin Wilbur. New York: Columbia University Press, 1976.

CLASS CONFLICT IN CHINESE SOCIALISM, by Richard Kurt Kraus. New York: Columbia University Press, 1981.

JAPANESE INTERNATIONAL NEGOTIATING STYLE, by Michael Blaker. New York: Columbia University Press, 1977.

CONTEMPORARY JAPANESE BUDGET POLITICS, by John Creighton Campbell. Berkeley: University of California Press, 1977.

THE MEDIEVAL CHINESE OLIGARCHY, by David Johnson. Boulder, Colo.: Westview Press, 1977.

ESCAPE FROM PREDICAMENT: NEO-CONFUCIANISM AND CHINA'S EVOLVING POLITICAL CULTURE, by Thomas A. Metzger. New York: Columbia University Press, 1977.

THE ARMS OF KIANGNAN: MODERNIZATION IN THE CHINESE ORDNANCE INDUSTRY, 1860–1895, by Thomas L. Kennedy. Boulder, Colo.: Westview Press, 1978.

PATTERNS OF JAPANESE POLICYMAKING: EXPERIENCES FROM HIGHER EDUCATION, by T. J. Pempel. Boulder, Colo.: Westview Press, 1978.

THE CHINESE CONNECTION, by Warren Cohen. New York: Columbia University Press, 1978.

MILITARISM IN MODERN CHINA: THE CAREER OF WU P'EI-FU, 1916–1939, by Odoric Y. K. Wou. Folkestone, England: Wm. Dawson & Sons, 1978.

A CHINESE PIONEER FAMILY, by Johanna Meskill. Princeton: Princeton University Press, 1979.

PERSPECTIVES ON A CHANGING CHINA: ESSAYS IN HONOR OF PROFESSOR C. MARTIN WILBUR, edited by Joshua A. Fogel and William T. Rowe. Boulder, Colo.: Westview Press, 1979.

THE MEMOIRS OF LI TSUNG-JEN, by T. K. Tong and Li Tsung-jen. Boulder, Colo.: Westview Press, 1979.

UNWELCOME MUSE: CHINESE LITERATURE IN SHANGHAI AND PEKING, 1937–1945, by Edward Gunn. New York: Columbia University Press, 1979.

YENAN AND THE GREAT POWERS: THE ORIGINS OF CHINESE COMMUNIST FOREIGN POLICY, 1944–1946, by James Reardon-Anderson. New York: Columbia University Press, 1980.

UNCERTAIN YEARS: CHINESE-AMERICAN RELATIONS, 1947–1950, edited by Dorothy Borg and Waldo Heinrichs. New York: Columbia University Press, 1980.

THE FATEFUL CHOICE: JAPAN'S ADVANCE INTO SOUTHEAST ASIA, 1939–1941, edited by James W. Morley. New York: Columbia University Press, 1980.

DATE DUE

FEB 22			